The First World War moulded the global landscape and ━━━━━━━━
of the world. Where the majority of international researc
theatre, Antonio Garcia explores one of the peripheral ca   ... war.
South Africa's First World War campaign in German Soutł   ...ica was a daring
military undertaking epitomised by manoeuvre and rapidity.

The author takes a novel approach in comparing the campaign to manoeuvre warfare theory. Manoeuvre theory is based on the principles of mobility, rapidity and surprise which attempts to achieve victory with the least loss of resources and in the shortest time possible. In order to achieve a rapid victory against the German forces, the South African soldiers were pushed to the limits of exhaustion to achieve the Union of South Africa's strategic objectives.

The campaign in the deserts of German South West Africa became the setting for adventure and war, where Briton, Boer and People of Colour served together as a Dominion of the British Empire. Blacks, Coloureds and Indians fought for the hopes of better political franchise, an ambition which was not to be achieved until 80 years later. This account of the campaign highlights the contribution of People of Colour in providing the combat support needed to ensure victory. The book addresses the complex political dynamics in South Africa at the time of the Great War, the deep division between Afrikaners and British South Africans and the Afrikaner Rebellion.

With the backdrop of political difficulties and a lack of overwhelming support for the entry into the Great War, the Botha government needed a quick result so as to maintain the delicate balance of power. The author provides an analysis on the campaign through the lens of military theory so as to determine how the swift victory was achieved. The book answers the question of whether the campaign was won through numerical superiority or through the use of a superior operational strategy. The victory was the first campaign victory led by a British Dominion.

Antonio Garcia is a visiting scholar at New York University Centre on International Cooperation. Antonio has worked at the intersection of international peace and security training; research and development; and doctrine and policy. As a visiting lecturer he has taught at Durham University (UK) and New York University as well as at various military colleges and schools. He holds degrees in military science, geography and history; serves in an adjunct faculty position at the University of South Africa and is a PhD candidate at Stellenbosch University. Antonio has published in academic and professional journals, and has also published in poetry and literature anthologies. He is also a Fellow of the Royal Geographical Society, and certified Chartered Geographer (RGS-IBG). He has previously served in the South African National Defence Force as an officer and senior officer for 16 years. During his service he has been deployed in various internal, regional and international missions including, two peacekeeping missions, in the Democratic Republic of Congo (MONUSCO) and Sudan, Darfur (UNAMID), as well as internal missions in South Africa and operations on the border of South Africa, Zimbabwe and Botswana.

The First Campaign Victory of the Great War

South Africa, Manoeuvre Warfare, the Afrikaner Rebellion and the German South West African Campaign 1914-15

Dedication

I dedicate this book to my wife and love Tara Lyle who tirelessly reads and edits all my work.

The First Campaign Victory of the Great War

South Africa, Manoeuvre Warfare, the Afrikaner Rebellion and the German South West African Campaign 1914-15

Antonio Garcia

 Helion & Company Limited

Helion & Company Limited
Unit 8 Amherst Business Centre
Budbrooke Road
Warwick
CV34 5WE
England
Tel. 01926 499 619
Fax 0121 711 4075
Email: info@helion.co.uk
Website: www.helion.co.uk
Twitter: @helionbooks
Visit our blog http://blog.helion.co.uk/

Published by Helion & Company 2019
Designed and typeset by Mary Woolley, (www.battlefield-design.co.uk)
Cover designed by Paul Hewitt, Battlefield Design (www.battlefield-design.co.uk)
Printed by Hobbs the Printers, Totton, Hampshire

Text, tables, graphs, diagrams © Antonio Garcia 2019 antoniogarcia81@yahoo.com
Illustrations © as individually credited
Maps drawn by George Anderson © Helion & Company 2019

ISBN 978-1-911628-94-1

British Library Cataloguing-in-Publication Data.
A catalogue record for this book is available from the British Library.

For details of other military history titles published by Helion & Company Limited contact the above address, or visit our website: http://www.helion.co.uk.

We always welcome receiving book proposals from prospective authors.

Contents

List of Illustrations

List of Maps

List of Tables, Figures, Graphs

Acknowledgements

Thank you to my friends, family and colleagues for their guidance and inspiration in the writing of this book. I would like to thank my previous commander and now friend Colonel Andrew Dinwoodie for being a military role model and an upstanding human being. Lieutenant Colonel Barnard was my combat engineer teacher and I owe a great debt to his wisdom and insight. I would like to thank my colleagues, commanders, officers, non-commissioned officers and troops, for their time and for the opportunity to have shared our service together. To the South African National Defence Force, the SA Army and the SA Army Engineer Corps, I owe you a debt of gratitude as you are responsible for my formation.

I would like to thank Prof Ian Van Der Waag, who is arguably the best military historian in South Africa for his wonderful support, guidance and supervision. Thank you to Evert Kelynhans, David Katz and Will Gordon, a great team of military historians in South Africa, for your support and insight. My former professors, Nicholas Southey and Tilman Dedering are acknowledged and thanked for their teaching and guidance. I would like to thank Prof Abel Esterhuyse and Prof Vrey for their lectures in military strategy, and Professors Fankie Monama and Visser for their lessons in military history. A word of acknowledgement to the South African Department of Defence Archives and the South African National Archives. Thank you to Colonel Li, Colonel Neeraj and the North Kivu Brigade. A word of appreciation to Duncan, my editor, as well as the entire team that worked on this book: George, Mary and Paul.

Thank you to my dad, Jose for being my foundation, thanks to the boys, Raoul, Johnny, Maurice and Clyde for being my core. A word of appreciation to Maestro Gilmour for your support. Thanks to HEX – my partner in crime in studying military theory, history and strategy. The wisdom and positivity of Peter and Kaliani Lyle, my in-laws, who are an absolute blessing, is acknowledged and appreciated. Lastly to the most important person, I thank you Tara, my love, my friend and my wife.

Preface

This work is a contemporary history of the German South West African campaign and is aimed at reconciling a strategic approach to military history, while emphasising the primacy of the commander and soldier. The study of war has various dimensions and in the last century there has been a considerable widening of the field of military history. Where many new narratives and perspectives from the Great War are being analysed through a range of new and interesting lenses, my study remains primarily a work for the student of war and the profession of arms.

In making this statement I in no way diminish the importance of modern approaches to military history, which may include gender and social aspects as well as the histories of under represented demographic groupings – I celebrate the broadening of the discipline. While commending the expansion of the field, I also believe that the inclusion of new perspectives is not tantamount to the death of the 'great generals' of history. At times, I feel that modern academic scholarship on military history loses track of the fact that the greatest tribute should be paid to the sacrifice of the soldier, under the direction of political and military leaders. This is my lens.

The First World War to a large extent shaped the landscape of the modern world. The central focus of military analyses of the Great War has for the most part been concentrated on the European theatres of operations: the Western and Eastern Fronts which wrested the final decision of the conflict. Despite the mass destruction of the European mainland there is a growing interest in the peripheral theatres of the Great War. These were often characterised by lower intensity conflicts which in many ways contributed to the overall war effort and outcome. This book examines one such theatre, German South West Africa which saw a campaign of manoeuvre and rapidity.

This work explores South Africa's First World War campaign in German South West Africa[1] through a descriptive and analytical study. In terms of the justification of the study of a given topic, John Tosh states that a historian 'is completely justified in allowing current concerns to affect his or her choice'.[2] For me, current interests and justifications are twofold, firstly in terms of military theory, there is an international

---

1   Note that German South West Africa was a German colony from 1884 until 1915. German South West Africa refers to the area that is modern day Namibia.
2   J. Tosh and S. Lang, *The Pursuit of History* (London: Pearson Longman, 2006), pp. 214–218.

focus on manoeuvre warfare theory[3] and secondly the celebration of the centennial of the First World War has resulted in increased interest in the global conflict in all its dimensions. As E.H. Carr states, 'history is an unending dialogue between the past and the present'.[4] The present determines current interests and directions for new analyses of the past. With this in mind, the study of military history gives its readers, an understanding of past wars, campaigns and operations through a modern lens. B.H. Liddell Hart writes that for a soldier there is direct and indirect experience (through study); direct experience may be limited, whereas indirect experience may be broader and deeper and may assist with the mental preparation of soldiers.[5]

In this work, I have combined the study of military history with that of military theory to provide a novel and interesting approach to the history of the German South West African campaign. Much of the writing on the First World War is associated with the escalation of arms, the massing of military forces and attrition. This 'type' of warfare largely informs what is generally referred to as attrition warfare theory. However, the peripheral theatres each had their own unique context and in order to understand the South African experience I refer to the historiography of the campaign.

Where the first literature to appear on the campaign had a strong British historiographical tradition[6] there has also been a significant modern wave of publications which comprise varying historiographical perspectives.[7] Furthermore,

---

3   S. Gates and K. Roy, *Unconventional Warfare in South Asia: Shadow Warriors and Counterinsurgency* (New York: Routledge, 2016), pp. 24, 25; P. Kasarak, *A National Force: The Evolution of the Canadian Army 1950-2000* (Toronto: UBC Press, 2013), p. 265. See, R.D. Hooker, *Manoeuvre Warfare: An Anthology* (New York: Presidio, 1993); J.J.A. Wallace, 'Manoeuvre Theory in Operations other than War', Chapter in, B.H. Reid ed., *Military Power: Land Warfare in Theory and Practice* (New York: Routledge, 2013); H.T. Hayden, Warfighting: *Maneuver Warfare in the U.S. Marine Corps* (London: Greenhill Books, 1997).
4   Tosh and Lang, *History*, p. x.
5   B.H. Liddell Hart, *Strategy of the Indirect Approach* (London: Faber & Faber, 1941), p. 2.
6   See, DOD Archives, Secretary of Defence (hereafter SD), Box 252, 17138, Historical Record of the Campaign in German South West Africa, 4 November 1919. Anon., *Union of South Africa and the Great War, 1914-1918: Official History* (Pretoria: Government Printer, 1924); J.J. Collyer, *The Campaign in German South West Africa, 1914–1915* (Government Printer, Pretoria, 1937); H.F. Trew, *Botha Treks* (London: Blackie & Son, 1936); M.E. Ritchie, *With Botha in the Field* (London: Longmans, 1915); W. Whittal, *With Botha and Smuts in Africa* (London: Cassell, 1917); H.F.B. Walker, *A Doctor's Diary in Damaraland* (London: Edward Arnold, 1917); D.E. Reitz, *Trekking On* (London: Travel Book Club, 1947); P.K.J. Robinson, *With Botha's Army* (London: Allen & Unwin, 1916); Dane, *British Campaigns in Africa and the Pacific 1914-1918* (London: Hodder & Stoughton, 1919); W.W. O'Shaughnessy and W.S. Rayner, *How Botha and Smuts Conquered German South West* (London: Simpkin, 1916).
7   See, L'ange, *Urgent Imperial Service*; B. Nasson, *Springboks on the Somme* (Johannesburg: Penguin, 2007); T. Couzens, *The Great Silence* (Johannesburg: Sunday Times, 2014); A.M. Grundlingh, *Fighting Their Own War: South African Blacks and the First World War* (Johannesburg: Raven Press, 1988); J. Stejskal, *The Horns of the Beast: The Swakop River Campaign and World War I in South West Africa, 1914-1915* (Solihull: Helion, 2014); I.

there is a growing body of contemporary academic literature which re-evaluates various and specific themes of the campaign.[8]

The German South West African campaign, with its large expanses and use of mobile forces allowed for the use of sweeping envelopments. The character of the operations in the campaign had more in common with manoeuvre warfare theory than it did with attrition theory. The study of manoeuvre warfare theory received a great deal of international attention in the latter part of the 20th century and has thus influenced the study of military theory as a discipline. The book explores the nexus between military theory and history and uses manoeuvre warfare as a lens to bring out new and fresh perspectives on the campaign.

In using manoeuvre theory as an analytical overlay it is necessary to qualify the use of the framework as a modern construct. The commanders of the campaign were not necessarily consciously executing manoeuvre warfare in the modern sense, but rather warfare as per their custom, training, doctrine and commander's instruction. The force groupings and their commanders applied their existing knowledge of warfare in an attempt to win the campaign in the most efficient manner. It is with hindsight that I claim that the campaign makes for an ideal case study for manoeuvre warfare theory. The use of new primary evidence gives insight into the strategic plans and ideas of the commanders and adds a fresh dimension in the understanding of the campaign.

Gleeson, *The Unknown Force: Black, Indian and Coloured Soldiers through Two World Wars* (Rivonia: Ashanti, 1994); A. Cruise, *Louis Botha's War: The Campaign in German South West Africa 1914-1915* (Johannesburg: Zebra, 2015); H. Strachan, *The First World War, Vol 1: To Arms* (Oxford University Press, Oxford, 2001); T.R. Ungleich, 'The Defence of German South West Africa during World War I', MA thesis, University of Miami, 1974; B. Farwell, *The Great War in Africa 1914–1918* (New York: Norton, 1986); D. Williams, *Springboks, Troepies and Cadres: Stories of the South African Army 1912-2012* (Cape Town: Tafelberg, 2012; I. Van Der Waag, *A Military History of Modern South* Africa (Johannesburg: Jonathan Ball Publishers, 2015). A. Delport, 'Boks and Bullets, Coffins and Crutches': An Exploration of the Body, Mind and Places of 'Springbok' South African Soldiers in the First World War', Stellenbosch University, 2015; B. Nasson, *World War 1 and the People of South Africa* (Cape Town: Tafelberg, 2014); A. Samson, *World War I in Africa: The Forgotten Conflict among European Powers* (London: I.B. Taurus, 2013);

8   R.C. Warwick, 'The Battle of Sandfontein: The Role and Legacy of Major General Sir Henry Timson Lukin', *Scientia Militaria, South African Journal of Military Studies*, 34, 2, 2006; I. Van der Waag, 'The Battle of Sandfontein, 26 September 1914: South African Military Reform and the German South-West Africa Campaign, 1914–1915', *First World War Studies*, 4, 2, 2013; A. Garcia, 'Manoeuvre Warfare in the South African Campaign in German South West Africa during the First World War', MA thesis, University of South Africa, 2015. E. Kleynhans, 'A Critical Analysis of the Impact of Water on the South African Campaign in German South West Africa, 1914 1915', *Historia*, 61, 2, 2016; A. Garcia, 'A Manouevre Warfare Analysis of South Africa's 1914-1915 German South West African Campaign' *Scientia Militaria*. 45, 1, 2017.

In order to give perspective to the campaign I also discuss the period's political and socio-economic context and add a new viewpoint by analysing the 1914 Afrikaner Rebellion with the theory of relative deprivation. The politicising of grievances based on economic inequalities fomented the Afrikaner revolt. Furthermore, at the outbreak of hostilities South Africa was a Dominion of the British Empire, and was a fragmented society with fissions between, Briton and Boer and the oppressed African, Coloured and Indian populations. It was a time of change and competing interests: Afrikaner nationalism was on the rise, African nationalism and liberationist movements were in their nascent stages and British Imperialism was the driving force to South African inclusion in the War.

With the advent of the centennial, the world has recaptured the importance of the Great War as a central event in the 20th century. Underrepresented aspects of the conflict have been brought to life. The narratives of the previously oppressed have been given a voice and for the first time a centennial of a global conflict has been celebrated. What is perhaps most interesting is the moment in which the centennial is taking place. The world has never before been as interconnected with the technological innovations of the internet and social media. Thus the understanding of the Great War and the extent of its effect, destruction and influence can perhaps be understood in a new light.

While technology gives us access as never before, the colonial legacy of the Great War remains a difficult topic to deconstruct. Where many former colonies have received independence the centennial of the First World War remains a tricky subject, as it combines themes of oppression, serving and fighting for a colonial master with the hopes of greater post-conflict rights and franchise, and on many occasions post-colonial legacy conflicts. The topic of memory and the celebration of the First World War centennial may require further research.

The causes of the Great War are rooted in European competition for supremacy and the combination of a series of alliances which triggered a mass military escalation. There are few who hold the view that the motives for the First World War were 'fair or legitimate' where scholars often regard the war against Nazism as 'just and necessary'. History remains the study of unique events set in a specific place and time with period specific norms and thus history must be studied as such. Thus the German South West African campaign was an extension of British imperial interests. Within the imperial connection lies the story of Britain and South Africa, and the First World War campaign in German South West Africa. On a geo-strategic level, the German South West African campaign, is regarded as a side show however it was significant for the development of South Africa. It is within the imperial relationship that I look at the strategy and tactics which won the campaign - This book remains a military history of the general and soldier.

The study of the German South West African campaign and the military action during the Afrikaner Rebellion allows for the understanding of the first campaign conducted by the Union Defence Force, and the first campaign victory of the Great War. The analysis of the campaign as an example of manoeuvre warfare provides the opportunity to overlay contemporary theoretical concepts and frameworks to the study of the German South West African campaign. I give credit to the commanders, soldiers and support staff of the campaign regardless of race and ethnicity. The first honour goes to those who served.

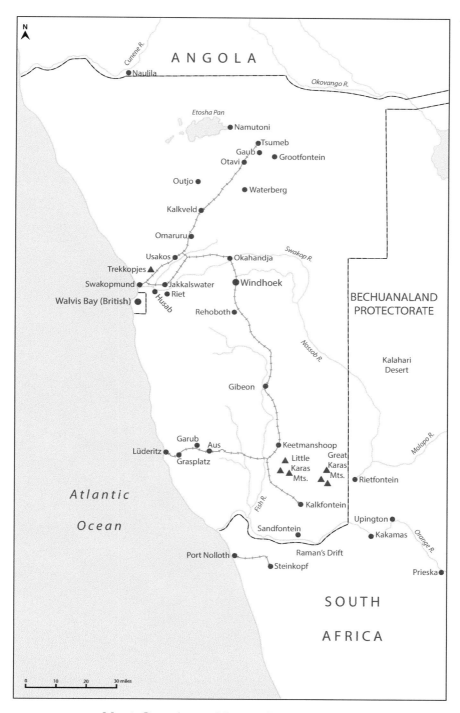

Map 1: General map of German South West Africa

1

The Union of South Africa's Entry into The First World War

The Union of South Africa was established in 1910 as a dominion of the British Empire and Louis Botha became its first prime minister. The Union was inextricably linked to the global British wartime effort and the German South West African (GSWA) campaign was South Africa's first 'boots on the ground' commitment to the global conflict. The GSWA campaign was an extension of Britain's geo-strategic interests and military strategy in the First World War.

The Boer republics, became British colonies after the Anglo-Boer War, 1899-1902. The Anglo-Boer war was caused by the clash of Afrikaner republican interests and British imperialist objectives. The Afrikaner republics, Transvaal and the Orange Free State, had large quantities of gold and diamonds which encouraged British expansionist ideas. The Anglo-Boer War brought in a new generation of Afrikaner generals-cum-politicians. Of these Louis Botha, Jan Smuts and J.B.M. Hertzog would dominate the political scene for much of the early 20th century.

Where the Anglo-Boer War represented the rise in Afrikaner nationalism, the post Anglo-Boer environment became an uneasy marriage of Boer and British political interests. Afrikaners achieved self-government during the first decade of the 20th century. At this time, African nationalism was nascent, and Afrikaner fears about Black encroachment, shaped the thinking of the day. Boer thought was essentially Eurocentric and became an ideology of white supremacy. Many of the precursors to Apartheid laws were drafted during this time, the 1913 Native Land Act being a case in point. The history of Black consciousness and African nationalism in South Africa, falls outside the scope of this book, however it should be acknowledged.

South Africa as a democratic state was initially formed as a composition of hunter-gatherer bands, disparate chiefdoms, Dutch and British colonies, Boer republics, British dominion, Apartheid state and then democratic republic. Within each respective period there were 'great men and women' of history which led their people, to name a few but which in no way constitutes a complete list includes Kings Shaka Zulu, Dingaan, Cetshwayo kaMpande, and Moshoeshoe, colonists Jan Van Riebeek and Simon van der Stel, Voortrekkers Hendrik Potgieter, Andries Pretorius, Piet

Retief, Boer republican presidents, Paul Kruger, M. Steyn and Boer generals Botha, Smuts, Hertzog, Christiaan De Wet, Koos De La Rey, Struggle leaders, Govan Mbeki, Oliver Tambo, Nelson Mandela, Ahmed Kathrada and Walter Sisulu.

The history of the formation of the Union of South Africa and the subsequent involvement in the German South West African campaign revolves around two central and towering figures, Louis Botha and Jan Christiaan Smuts. As the leaders of the campaign their military backgrounds, experience and abilities formed the basis of their approach towards the conduct of war.

Prior to the formation of the Union of South Africa, Botha was a proponent of a united white South Africa which he believed was only possible through cooperation with the British Empire.[1] During the South African War (1899–1902) Botha was initially a burgher[2], then commandant and he went on to became commandant general of the Transvaal commandos in 1900 after the death of Petrus Jacobus Joubert.

The Boer forces made a valiant effort during the first moments of the Anglo-Boer War where they won limited tactical victories and besieged Kimberley, Mafikeng and Ladysmith. Botha received much acclaim for successfully holding the defensive positions at the Tugela River on the Natal Front in the face of General Revers Buller's advance, and for stopping the British forces at the Battles of Colenso and Spioen Kop.[3] Botha's military ability came to the fore during the conventional phase of the South African War but also extended to the guerrilla phase (June 1900 to May 1902) after the fall of Bloemfontein and Pretoria.

After the war, Botha made large strides to reconcile the interests of English- and Afrikaans-speaking South Africans, however the Treaty of Vereeniging gave the Boer leaders little power and some hope for future self-governance. The interests and franchise of people of colour was proposed at the Middelburg peace talks of 1901, but was taken off the Vereeniging Treaty agenda as the British feared that the Boers would not agree. People of colour fought on the British and Afrikaner sides and provided an almost endless supply of labour, digging trenches, building railroads, driving waggon trains, limited security and policing roles and serving as guides and spies. Their efforts would win them little political capital in the post Anglo-Boer War peace.

Following the South African War, Botha and Smuts were included in the central committee of the Het Volk political party, which was formed in the Transvaal in 1904. The Het Volk promoted Afrikaner interests but also focused on the reconciliation of all white South Africans. The Transvaal differed from the Orange Free State in that it had a larger population of British settlers and the substantial economic power of the mining sector. Smuts put great effort into his proposal for the constitution of the

---

1   H.C. Armstrong, *Grey Steel, J.C. Smuts: A Study in Arrogance* (London: Arthur Barker, 1937), p 150.
2   The word means citizen but also refers to a soldier in the Boer military system.
3   T. Pakenham, *The Boer War* (London: Abacus, 1979), 174; Armstrong, *Grey Steel*, p. 97.

Transvaal after which he devoted all his energies into the Transvaal election campaign.[4] Their collaborative effort brought in positive results with Botha elected prime minister of the Transvaal and Smuts becoming the colonial secretary and minister of education in 1907.[5] The main objective of the Boer leaders was self-governance and all political efforts were dedicated to the attainment of political control in the aftermath of the disenfranchisement caused by the Treaty of Vereeniging.[6]

Botha formed the South African Party together with Smuts, his friend, colleague and confidant. The South African Party aimed to unite the different white political parties in the four provinces (Cape, Natal, Transvaal and Orange Free State) with the objective of creating a Union. Smuts and Botha formed a strong friendship and partnership in politics.

Botha had a charismatic personality; he was popular among his followers and inspired them with his magnanimity and optimism.[7] In contrast, Smuts was the quiet thinker, the intellectual of the partnership. A recipient of many academic awards, he graduated from Victoria College in Stellenbosch in 1891 and received a scholarship to attend Cambridge University where he graduated with top honours in 1893.[8] Smuts then returned to South Africa where he pursued a career in law and politics.[9] He was appointed as state attorney and aide-de-camp to President Stephanus Johannes Paulus Kruger of the Transvaal also known as the South African Republic in 1898, and headed a commando[10] during the guerrilla phase of the South African War in 1901. Smuts was renowned for his endless capacity for work and his boundless energy.[11]

Smuts worked vigorously towards a united South Africa and was responsible for compiling the framework for the Union of South Africa, which he put forward at the Intercolonial Conference in May 1908.[12] Lord Gladstone, the governor general of South Africa, and his contemporaries accepted the proposal of Union. The liberal British government under H. Campbell-Bannerman and then H. H. Asquith marked a break from previous conservative leaders, Lords Salisbury and Balfour, and facilitated the formation of Union. The Union of South Africa was formed in May 1910 and

---

4   W. K. Hancock and J. van der Poel (eds), *Selections from the Smuts Papers, Volume III* (London: Cambridge University Press, 1966), p. 205.
5   Armstrong, *Grey Steel*, p. 166.
6   The Treaty of Vereeniging ended hostilities in the Anglo-Boer War and discussions with the Boer leaders and Lord Kitchener alluded to future political independence.
7   South African National Archives (hereafter SANA), Smuts Papers, Box 112, Major General Thompson: Report on a visit to German South West Africa, 20-27 March 1915; A. Lentin, *Jan Smuts* (Johannesburg and Cape Town: Jonathan Ball, 2010), p. 19.
8   Armstrong, *Grey Steel*, p. 7.
9   Ibid., pp. 35, 36.
10 A grouping of voluntary Boer soldiers, organised and recruited on community lines: town, district and ward. Where a commandant was in command of a town a veldcornet was in charge of a ward.
11 Lentin, *Jan Smuts*, p. 23.
12 Hancock and Van der Poel (eds), *Selections from the Smuts Papers*, p. 331.

formal elections were held in September of the same year where Botha became the first prime minister.[13] Smuts held a triple appointment as minister of mines, interior and defence.[14]

There were many significant political figures that emerged in South Africa during this period. Some of them represented oppressed and or marginalised South African population groups and include Mohandas Gandhi, John Dube and Abdullah Abdurahman.[15] Many of the parties representing oppressed racial groupings, including the South African Native National Congress (SANNC) the predecessor of the African National Congress (ANC), and the African Political Organisation (APO) although strongly opposing discriminatory legislation[16] and the disenfranchisement of people of colour in the formation of Union, they supported South Africa's entry into the First World War in the hopes that their participation would secure under-represented groupings' further political rights and freedoms. Sol Plaatje, an author, intellectual and founding member of the SANNC, supported the recruiting of Black people for the war effort. Another prominent SANNC member John Dube also strongly supported the war effort. While some members of the SANNC such as J.T. Gumede spoke out against the pro-War stance[17], the overwhelming feeling was for the conflict.[18] A. Nzula, a member of the Communist Party would later criticise the SANNC for fighting on the side of white South Africans. The ANC should thus consider its stance on the First World War, and determine whether further research on this matter should be conducted.

Although understated in current literature, there was a considerable contribution from South African people of colour to the First World War.[19] There were a total

---

13   Botha beat J.X. Merriman in the 1910 elections and was Lord Gladstone's preferred choice for the first prime minister of the Union. Merriman was the former prime minister of the Cape Colony and stood in contention to be the first prime minister of the Union of South Africa. Lord Gladstone favoured Botha where much of the Cape political old guard supported Merriman who was devastated at the loss. See, V. Solomon., *Selections from the Correspondence of Percy Alport Molteno, 1892-1914* (Cape Town: National Book Printers, 1981), p. 321.

14   Armstrong, *Grey Steel*, p. 201.

15   With the advent of liberation in South Africa, there has been an increased focus on liberationist historiographies and the roles of leaders of oppressed groupings.

16   Franchise and Ballot Act (1892), the Natal Legislative Assembly Bill (1894), the General Pass Regulations Bill (1905), the Asiatic Registration Act (1906), the South African Act (1910).

17   A. Grundlingh, *War and Society: Participation and Remembrance, South African Black and Coloured Troops in the First World War, 1914-1918* (Stellenbosch, Sun Press, 2014), p. 11.

18   Nasson, *World War 1*, p. 42.

19   See, A. Grundlingh, *Participation and Remembrance: South African Black and Coloured Troops in the First World War, 1914 – 1918* (Stellenbosch: Sun Press, 2014); B. Nasson, 'Delville Wood and South African Great War Commemoration', *English Historical Review*, 119, 480, 2004; I. Gleeson, *The Unknown Force: Black, Coloured and Indian Soldiers through the Two World Wars* (Rivonia: Ahanti, 1994); W.M. Bisset, 'Unexplored Aspects of South Africa's

of 33,000 auxiliaries deployed in the German South West African campaign.[20] The auxiliaries provided an essential support function to the expeditionary force. Commissioned ranks were given batmen and horse handlers from the auxiliaries. Warrant officers and non-commissioned officers also requested this privilege but were turned down by Defence headquarters.[21] This was a tradition of the commando system.

The importance of the role of people of colour during the German South West African campaign, is demonstrated in the strength returns of the final phase of operations, which comprised 3,032 Black, Coloured and Indian support forces of the total 13,037 troops and officers. People of Colour became the engine of ox and waggon based logistics and artillery enabling the mobile forces to operate. [22] Where the service of Blacks, Coloureds and Indians were not well documented in the German South West African campaign, this was not the case of the South African Native Labour Contingent (SANLC), which was formed in 1916, and financed from British coffers. The contingent provided non-combat manual tasks in support of the war effort in German East Africa and on the Western Front.[23] The strength of the SANLC in 1919 was just over 25,000 People of Colour, and the total deaths during the First World War were 1,167.[24] The exploits of the Cape Coloured Corps, which served in German East Africa, Palestine and France is well recorded, but perhaps also due for a review.[25]

Black support forces were deployed as part of the British and Belgian forces which mobilised on the north eastern Rhodesian (modern Zimbabwe) border.[26] Furthermore, the Rehoboth Basters mounted a limited offensive against the German forces in the South West African campaign despite Botha's attempts at keeping it a 'white man's war'.[27] The original German South West African inhabitants, had suffered extensively at the hands of their German colonial masters, with the genocide of the Herero and the

First World War History', *Scientia Militaria*, 6, 3, 1976. A.I. Venter, *Coloured: A Profile of Two Million South Africans* (Cape Town: Human & Rouseau, 1974); A. Grundlingh, *Fighting their own war. South African Blacks and the First World War* (Johannesburg: Ravan Press, 1987).

20 B. Nasson, *Springboks on the Somme* (Johannesburg: Penguin, 2007), p. 65.
21 Department of Defence Archives (hereafter DOD Archives), Adjutant General 1914 – 192 (hereafter AG 14-21), G/42/25, Correspondence with Defence Headquarters regarding Batmen, 1914.
22 DOD Archives, Secretary of Defence (hereafter SD), Box 252, Strength of Units, July 1915.
23 See, DOD Archives, South African Native Labour Contingent, Box 2517, List of Deaths in East Africa, 1919.
24 DOD Archives, South African Native Labour Contingent, Box 2517, Commemoration of the 'missing' SANLC, 1926.
25 South African National Archives (hereafter SANA), Governor General, Report on German East Africa, 1916; I.D Difford, *The Story of the 1st Battalion Cape Corps, 1915-1919*, (Cape Town: Hortons, 1920).
26 DOD Archives, SD, Box 278, German East Information, July 1915.
27 DOD Archives, SD, Box 1129, Correspondence between Louis Botha and Van Wyk, April 1915; DOD Archives, SD, Box 252, Brigadier General McKenzie's Despatch, 27 August

Nama. The brutal attempts at exterminating a nation, had far reaching consequences, which included a complete lack of local support for the German colonial forces. This can be contrasted to the combined effort of General Von Lettow-Vorbeck and the Askaris in German East Africa. The War was never to be a white man's war despite history's attempts at silencing the role of People of Colour.

The Anglo-Boer War at the turn of the 20th century had smashed the concept of a white war, where Boer and British made extensive use of People of Colour. The Boers made use of an unspecified number of black labourers, *agterryers*[28] and assistants. Kitchener admitted to have used approximately 7,000 Black soldiers and 3,000 Cape Coloured soldiers and policemen in his war effort.[29]

The impact and destruction of the German genocide and the role of South African Blacks, Coloureds and Indians in the Great War is increasingly being focussed and unearthed as the unending dialogue with the past takes new forms. The abuses of the Germans and the genocide of the Nama and Herrero were investigated by a South African British commission and published as a Blue Book[30], and has received considerable contemporary interest.[31]   The manoeuvre warfare which I ultimately propose led to the first 'campaign' victory of the Great War, was equally enabled by People of Colour and white forces who powered the transport, logistics and supply of the Union war machine. This is demonstrated through primary evidence which shows the force composition of the brigades responsible for the final envelopment and subsequent surrender of the German forces.[32] A new wave of histories are coming to the fore which brings forward new narratives and voices.

There is certainly a limited historiography of the role of Africans, Coloureds and Indians in the German South West African campaign. Starting from the first attempts at capturing the campaign history, the Defence Headquarters never mentioned the contribution of People of Colour save for the inclusion of statistics

1915; G.J.J. Oosthuizen, 'The Military Role of the Rehoboth Basters during the South African Invasion of German South West Africa, 1914-1915', *Scientia Militaria*, 28, 1 , 1998.

28   Non-white assistant to burghers. The term has a negative connotation.

29   Pakenham, *Boer War*, p. 547. These included scouts and spies: The United Kingdom National Archives (hereafter TNA), War Office (hereafter WO), 132/ 9, Intelligence Reports, 1899.

30   Cd 9146, Report on the Natives of South West Africa and their Treatment by the Germans, Blue Book, 1918; J. Silvester and Jan-Bart Gewald, *Words Cannot Be Found: German Colonial Rule in Namibia: An Annotated Reprint of the 1918 Blue Book* (Boston: Brill, 2003).

31   New York Times, Germany Grapples with its African Genocide, https://www.nytimes.com/2016/12/29/world/africa/germany-genocide-namibia-holocaust.html?mcubz=3. Accessed 24 September 2017; J. Sarkin, *Germany's Genocide of the Herero: Kaiser Wilhelm II, His General, His Settlers, His Soldiers* (Cape Town: UCT Press, 2010); E.R. Baer, *The Genocidal Gaze: From German Southwest Africa to the Third Reich* (Detroit: Wayne State Press, 2017).

32   DOD Archives, SD, Box 252, Strength of Units, July 1915; DOD Archives, SD, Box 252, Strength of Commanders Brigades, July 1915; DOD Archives, SD, Box 252, Strength of Headquarters Brigade, July 1915.

where a 'native' column indicated the strength of People of Colour attached to the various force groupings.[33] There are also limited accounts, where Black, Coloured and Indian casualties are indicated in Battle reports and despatches, such as the Battles of Sandfontein and Gibeon,[34] and other service and medal lists can be found at the British National Archives.[35] Thompson's report on the German South West African campaign makes reference to the role of People of Colour in maintaining the mobility of the train systems. He states that 'the railway runs through shifting sand dunes, which necessitate the employment of 200 natives continuously shovelling to keep the railway clear.'[36] In his explanation of the construction of one part of the railway line, Thompson explains that, '500 coloured boys, supervised by two officers and six N.C.O's performed the work.'[37]

In Collyer's account of the campaign as well as the Official History both books refer to the two white races with no mention of People of Colour.[38] Where many of the earlier accounts of the conflict give little to no mention of Africans in the campaign, O'Shaughnessy and Rayner give a limited account of Africans working on clearing dunes from the railway and German South West African local scouts assisting South African intelligence sections, of which some after capture, were hung by the Germans.[39] In mentioning the use of Black, Coloured and Indian scouts during the later stages of the campaign Botha states that 'native reports indicated considerable withdrawal of the enemy forces northwards.'[40] L'ange dedicates a brief chapter in his book on the campaign to People of Colour, and states that approximately 30,000 Black and Coloured men served in a largely support role in the campaign.[41] Nasson gives the figure of Black, Indian and Coloured auxiliaries who were tasked with transport, railway and road work as well general labour and support at 33,000.[42] Bisset, in his 1976 article, perhaps best opened up the discussion on the role of People of Colour in

33   DOD Archives, SD, Box 252, 17138, Historical Record of the Campaign in German South West Africa, 4 November 1919.
34   DOD Archives, SD, Box 252, 17138, Reports of Force Commanders in German South West Africa, Operations of the Central Force from 15 to 27 April 1915 including the action at Gibeon station, 15 May 1915; DOD Archives, SD, Box 252, 17138, Reports of Force Commanders in German South West Africa, Operations in and around Sandfontein 25, 26 and 27 September 1914, 19 August 1915.
35   See, TNA, WO 372, War Office: Service Medal and Award Rolls Index, First World War.
36   SANA, Smuts Papers, Box 112, Major General Thompson: Report on a visit to German South West Africa, 20-27 March 1915.
37   SANA, Smuts Papers, Box 112, Major General Thompson: Report on a visit to German South West Africa, 20-27 March 1915.
38   J.J. Collyer, *The Campaign in German South West Africa, 1914–1915* (Pretoria: Government Printer, 1937), p. 173.
39   O'Shaughnessy and Rayner, *How Botha and Smuts conquered German South West*, 67, 97.
40   DOD Archives, SD, Box 252, Despatch number 4 by General Botha covering the period 15 May to 18 July 1915.
41   G. L'ange, *Urgent Imperial Service* (Rivonia: Ashanti, 1991), p. 227.
42   Nasson, *Springboks on the Somme*, p. 65.

the German South West African campaign, mentioning that 30 Herero scouts were employed by the Union Defence Force intelligence section.[43] The German South West African population were disaffected and where some scouts were directly employed by the Union's intelligence sections, it was also common for the local population to supply the South African forces with up to date information on German movements. Botha claims that 'this information... given by runaway natives, (was) a constant almost invariably reliable, source of intelligence.'[44] In terms of the role of Coloureds in the campaign in German South West, Difford states that their contribution was significant. Furthermore, the extent of Indian stretcher bearers in the campaign requires further study. Bisset states that Cpl E. Mkosi, an African soldier, received the 1914 Star and Victory medal, for his service as part of the South African Mounted Rifles, Field Artillery Battery; and Michael van der Poel, a Coloured serviceman, served with the South African Mounted Rifles, Field Artillery as a driver and received the 1914-1915 Star.[45]

During the first decade of the 20th century, the Union of South Africa went through a period of political transformation and competition as well as economic growth. The Union of South Africa faced growing resentment between English- and Afrikaans- speaking South Africans despite attempts by Botha and Smuts to unify them.[46] English speaking South Africans and British colonials were largely associated with leading mining conglomerates, organised labour and large scale business whilst Afrikaners were generally more involved in farming.[47] Where English South Africans hung on to British notions of empire for self-identification, Afrikaners, increasingly saw themselves as independent or republicans. Afrikaner nationalism became a powerful force in South African politics. The Anglo-Boer War 1899-1902, had been devastating to the Afrikaner population, where concentration camps were utilised to hold women and children, in attempts to force the surrender of Boer forces - these camps led to the death of over 40,000 of its inhabitants, of which 26,000 were White women and children and over 14,000 were Black men and women.[48] In the face of British jingoism, the republics of the Orange Free State and the Transvaal, found a common cause in the defence and the solidification of ideas of Afrikaner nationalism.

43   Bisset, 'Unexplored Aspects', pp. 55, 56.
44   DOD Archives, SD, Box 252, Despatch number 4 by General Botha covering the period 15 May to 18 July 1915.
45   Bisset, 'Unexplored Aspects', pp. 55, 56.
46   Armstrong, *Grey Steel*, p. 201.
47   Following the mineral revolution of the 1800s, there was increased Afrikaner and African participation in mining. Furthermore, much of the labour for these operations were supplied by poor Afrikaners and Blacks.
48   V. B. Parkhouse, *Memorializing the Anglo-Boer War of 1899-1902: Militarization of the Landscape: Monuments and Memorials in Britain* (Leicestershire: Matador, 2015), 390. See, B. Nasson and A. M. Grundlingh (eds), *The War at Home: Women and Families in the Anglo-Boer War* (Cape Town: NB Publishers, 2013).

As a dominion of the British Empire, South Africa's Botha government tried to establish a balance between Imperial and Afrikaner nationalist interests. This set up an intense rivalry between J.B.M Hertzog, a former Anglo-Boer War general, and Botha. Hertzog, who had the support of most of the Orange Free State became the champion of republicanism in a politically evolving White South Africa. While Hertzog famously promoted a two-stream policy, for Afrikaans and English South Africans, Botha and Smuts fought for a united White South Africa, completely forgoing any Black, Coloured or Indian franchise. The Botha government in fact pushed forward the initial prototype of Apartheid legislation, in forwarding the idea of Black self-government under control of a paternalistic white overseer.[49]

The constant challenge of Hertzog and his mostly Afrikaans supporters as well as the demands of labour and big business took its toll on Botha who tried to find a middle ground for White South Africans through a policy of conciliation. Important issues which were debated and contested in parliament, included farming, mining, policy on People of Colour and matters of defence. The Defence Act of 1912 was the source of much discussion and debate in the parliament of the newly formed Union of South Africa.[50] The turbulent past of the Union and the legacies of the Anglo-Boer War made matters of defence a bitter yet prominent talking point. Following the formation of the Union of South Africa, the Defence Act was promulgated on 14 June 1912, which commissioned the formation of the Union Defence Force.[51]

Smuts was the minister of defence and was largely the architect of the Defence Act with the support of J.J. Collyer and H.R.M. Bourne, who was appointed undersecretary of defence.[52] Collyer was a captain when the Defence Act was drawn up, 1910 until mid- 1912. He subsequently became chief staff officer in October 1914, carrying the temporary rank of colonel.[53]. He eventually retired as a brigadier general and chief of the general staff.

The Botha government wanted a defence force that could defend the interests of the Union in any type or size of conflict.[54] At its inception in 1910 the Union did not have a permanent national defence force because historically, each of the four provinces in the Union modelled its own particular style of defence as an independent outgrowth of its individual type of government. The Cape had a small permanent force, Natal had a

49   J.C. Smuts, *War-Time Speeches: A Compilation of Public Utterances in Great Britain* (New York: Doran, 1917), 80-83; Hancock and Van der Poel (eds), *Selections from the Smuts Papers*, p. 53.
50   W.A. Dorning, 'A Concise History of the South African Defence Force 1912–1987', *Militaria, South African Journal for Military Studies*, 17, 2, 1987, p. 2.
51   A.C. Lillie, 'The Origin and Development of the South African Army', *Militaria, South African Journal for Military Studies*, 12, 2, 1982, p. 7.
52   Dorning, 'A Concise History', p. 2.
53   DOD Archives, AG 14-21, Box 8. Commander and Chief. Letter to Collyer from HQ, October 1914.
54   H. Strachan, *The First World War, Vol 1: To Arms* (Oxford: Oxford University Press, 2001), 547.

militia-style force, while the Transvaal had a volunteer system, as did the Orange Free State. The Union Defence Force was formed in 1912 and incorporated the military forces of the four provinces.[55]

The Union Defence Force comprised the Permanent Force; Active Citizen Force; Coast Garrison Force; Royal Naval Volunteers Reserve; and provision was also made in the Defence Act of 1912 for Special Reserve Units. The Union Defence Force established the Permanent Force on 1 April 1914, which was known as the South African Mounted Riflemen.[56]

The largest component of the Union Defence Force was the Active Citizen Force which comprised many of the old commando units from the previous military establishments of the four provinces of the Union South Africa. The commandos were comprised of mounted infantry who were renowned for their mobility and guerrilla tactics. The former prime minister of Britain and once war correspondent Winston Churchill, who was captured by the commandos during the Anglo-Boer War, had high praise for the skill of the commandos. Boer commandos were commanded by elected officers and they had a strong sense of kinship.[57] A point regarding the commando system that should also be brought forward, is that it was not exclusively white in composition. Commandos also comprised Black people who generally provided a support role and were given the title *agterryers* - they effectively served as batmen.[58] Except for the paternalistic superiority of the Boers there was often little difference in appearance between commando and *agterryer* as they dressed similarly, spoke Dutch and provided specialised support functions including, weapon maintenance, herbal medical treatment and other tasks.[59]

The commandos applied their military skills to war which were especially well suited for guerrilla warfare requiring high mobility, the capability to converge on one's opponent, inflict damage and withdraw without engaging in a pitched battle. The commandos were reinvented as the Active Citizen Force. The strength of the Active Citizen Force on 31 December 1913 was 23,462[60] and the Union Defence Force had a total strength of 30,000 in early 1914.[61] The German South West African campaign made extensive use of Active Citizen Force mounted troops.

---

55   J. Collyer, *The Campaign in German South West Africa, 1914–1915*, pp. 13, 14.
56   Lillie, 'The Origin and Development of the South African Army', pp. 8–10.
57   See, DOD Archives, SD, Box 252, 17138, Historical Record of the Campaign in German South West Africa, 4 November 1919.
58   See, N. Nkuna, 'Black involvement in the Anglo-Boer War, 1899-1902', *Military History Journal*, 11, 3, 1999; B. Nasson, 'Africans at War', Chapter in, J. Gooch (ed.), *The Boer War: Direction, Experience and Image* (New York: Routledge, 2013).
59   B. Nasson, *Abraham Esau's War: A Black South African War in the Cape, 1899-1902* (Cambridge: Cambridge University Press, 1991), p. 99.
60   Lillie, 'The Origin', p. 10.
61   Collyer, *The Campaign in German South West Africa, 1914–1915*, p. 16.

The Great War in many ways represented the end the cavalry tradition with the advent of mechanisation. The First World War also represented the last hoorah for the commando tradition. At the start of the Great War the commando system was incorporated within a more conventional Defence Force system. This reflected the modernisation of South Africa and resulted in a clash of civilisations and traditions which was mirrored in broader South African society as well as in the Union Defence Force.

The Union found itself in a precarious position at the outbreak of the First World War. The Union Defence Force was still in its developmental stage and was untested as a cohesive fighting force. The military was comprised of two divergent groupings with different doctrinal traditions which operated using different systems. On the strategic and operational levels, the conflict between British and commando traditions was managed by the strength of personality of Botha and the administrative and intellectual power of Smuts.

Botha's commitment to the British Empire necessitated a game of brinkmanship, as he requested Afrikaners to fight on the side of their former enemy, the British. South Africa was a dominion of Britain and when the British Empire declared war on Germany on 4 August 1914, the Union of South Africa was in effect also at war with Germany.[62] Lewis Vernon Harcourt, the secretary for the colonies requested the Union to invade German South West Africa, capture its seaports and destroy its wireless communication stations, describing it as 'a great and urgent imperial service'.[63] Botha confirmed the request and then set upon convincing the members of parliament about the importance of the invasion.

Botha and Smuts strongly supported the British war effort but Hertzog contested the assumption that the association with the British Empire constituted an automatic involvement in the war.[64] In parliament, as was the case with the population at large, there was support for and against the proposed invasion of German South West Africa. The Defence Act of 1912 stipulated that members of the Union Defence Force could only render defence in protection of the Union of South Africa.[65] Accordingly, Botha motivated the invasion of GSWA as necessary for the defence of the Union. There was a number of minor events on the German South African border which was used to further motivate the Union's invasion. A section of German troops were found reconnoitring the Union's northern border, at Nakob, which was initially purported as an invasion but was later confirmed as a non-offensive operation.[66] On another occasion on the Union's border, a minor engagement between German soldiers and South African farmers took place, in which the Germans came off worse with

62   R.J. Bouch, *Infantry in South Africa* (Pretoria: Documentation Service SADF, 1977).
63   Collyer, *The Campaign in German South West Africa, 1914–1915*, p. 6.
64   Strachan, *The First World War*, p. 545.
65   Dorning, 'A Concise History', p. 4.
66   DOD Archives, SD, Box 601, 95C, Reported fortifying of Kopje at Nakob by the Germans, 24 August 1914.

two soldiers killed. This incident was also used in support of the Union's offensive posture.[67] Botha's motion for the invasion was passed in parliament on 10 September 1914 by 91 votes to ten[68] and the Union officially entered the First World War on 14 September 1914.[69] The motion was a mere formality as invasion plans were well underway by August 1915.[70]

By this time Britain was already engaged in warfare with the Germans on the Western Front in France and mobilised its colonies and dominions in support of its geostrategic objectives which required a considerable amount of troops and resources. Botha freed up the British troops stationed in South Africa for deployment elsewhere and stated that South Africa would rely on its own military for defence. Furthermore, Britain required international trade and supply to continue and its sea routes to be safeguarded. In this regard the Union of South Africa would play a key role in securing the sea routes to the east.

Great Britain wanted the Union Defence Force to take control of the German South West African ports of Lüderitzbucht and Swakopmund, thus preventing Germany from using them to refuel, re-supply and repair German warships. In addition, the British required the destruction of the wireless stations in Windhoek, Lüderitzbucht and Swakopmund, which were able to provide and maintain communications between Berlin and German warships at sea.[71] The German South West African campaign was thus part of the global context of the First World War, with international objectives; however the conflict was also situated within specific localised conflicts in the forms of domestic rebellions and revolt.

The 1914 Afrikaner Rebellion took place in a context where English and Afrikaans-speaking South Africans had varying and layered feelings about the war. There were many impoverished, barely literate Afrikaners who lived in rural areas who certainly did not identify with the British cause.[72] Apart from political differences, the Afrikaner Rebellion was also linked to the grave economic situation in the decades following the Anglo-Boer War.[73] The combination of poverty, deprivation, republicanism, anti-

---

67   Hancock and Van der Poel (eds), *Selections from the Smuts Papers*, p. 53.

68   Strachan, *The First World War,* 546; L'ange gives the final votes as 92 to 12 in favour of Botha: L'ange, *Urgent Imperial Service*, p. 17.

69   I. Van der Waag, 'The Battle of Sandfontein, 26 September 1914: South African Military Reform and the German South-West Africa Campaign, 1914–1915', *First World War Studies*, 4, 2, 2013, p. 3.

70   DOD Archives, SD, Box 252, 17138, Reports of Force Commanders in German South West Africa, Operations in and around Sandfontein 25, 26 and 27 September 1914, 19 August 1915; DOD Archives, Diverse Group 1 (hereafter DG 1), Box 2, Rebellion Commission of Enquiry Volume 1, Testimony by General Louis Botha, 29 June 1916. DOD Archives, DG 1, Box 2, Rebellion Commission of Enquiry Volume 1, Testimony by General Coenraad Jacobus Brits, 15 March 1916.

71   L'ange, *Urgent Imperial Service*, p. 7.

72   Nasson, *Springboks on the Somme*, p. 10.

73   Van der Waag, 'The Battle of Sandfontein, 26 September 1914', p. 7.

British sentiment, bitterness about the Anglo-Boer War and the Union's entry into the First World War resulted in the rebellion. Over 70 years later, the Afrikaner Rebellion would remain in South African consciousness, and was a central part of the first meeting and discussion between giant and former president Nelson Mandela and stalwart of Apartheid government *Die Groot Krokodil* (The Great Crocodile) P.W. Botha. Mandela drew parallels between the growth of Afrikaner nationalism at the turn of the 20th century and that of African nationalism at the turn of the 21st century. Both the 1914 Afrikaner Rebellion and the Struggle were forms of resistance to the status quo.

At the beginning of the campaign the Union faced an existential internal threat in the form of the 1914 Afrikaner Rebellion. This uprising was a manifestation of the dissatisfaction felt by many Afrikaners about the Union's involvement in a "British" war at a time when anti-British sentiments were still very much in evidence in the aftermath of the Anglo-Boer War. Seeing this as an opportunity they could exploit, the Germans fomented rebellion by meeting with prominent republican-inclined Afrikaner military leaders who were heading the rebellion, such as Commandant S.G. Maritz and General C.F. Beyers.[74] The Afrikaner Rebellion impacted the German South West African campaign in that it delayed the invasion. The consequence of German complicity in the rebellion was that Maritz did not support Colonel H. Lukin (later Sir, Major General Lukin) at the Battle of Sandfontein, which contributed directly and indirectly to the South African defeat. The rebellion became inextricably intertwined with the GSWA campaign, in that it became the trigger cause of the revolt and because the Union Defence Force had to suppress the rebellion before commencing with the reinvasion of GSWA. From September until December 1914, the Union halted its invasion of German South West Africa.

The German South West African campaign was unique in that it employed the Union Defence Force for the first time in conventional warfare as an expeditionary force. At the beginning of the campaign the South African forces numbered approximately 50,000 compared to the modest German force numbering about 7,000.[75] The German forces (the *Schutztruppe*)[76] adopted a defensive strategy from the outset. Their commander, Colonel J. von Heydebreck hoped to make maximum use of the geography of the colony as well as the German internal lines of communication to delay the Union Defence Force for as long as possible. In this way he hoped to prevent their redeployment to other theatres of the Great War.[77]

In order to understand the reasons behind the South African victory in the German South West African campaign, the book examines whether the Union won because

---

74   Collyer, *The Campaign in German South West Africa, 1914–1915*, p. 5; B. Farwell, *The Great War in Africa 1914–1918* (New York: Norton, 1986), p.75.
75   L'ange, *Urgent Imperial Service*, p. 158.
76   The *Schutztruppe* were the colonial forces of imperial Germany.
77   Van der Waag, 'The Battle of Sandfontein, 26 September 1914', p. 3.

of superior numbers or because of its superior strategy and tactics. T.R. Ungleich, in the most recent pro-German secondary account of the campaign, holds the opinion that the South African victory was a result of superior military numbers which resulted in the defeat of the Germans in a campaign which is often regarded as of little consequence in the broader picture of the First World War.[78] Ungleich argues that the South African numerical superiority forced the Germans to retreat time and again, after which they made their last stand in the northeast of the colony.[79] Whereas the South African force had the numerical superiority, Collyer indicates some of the military advantages which the Germans had over the South Africans, including an undivided command; a conventionally trained, homogeneous force; superior artillery; and good logistics, which included a well-structured rail system.[80] On the issue of numerical superiority, David Killingray states that it was a central factor in the defeat of the Germans.[81] J.C. Smuts junior, the son of General Smuts, claims 'the victory was due to superior tactics as well as overwhelming strength'.[82] This study questions whether the victory over the German forces was a result of numerical superiority or rather superior tactics and operational strategy and is central to the analysis of the German South West African campaign.

The book proposes that the application of manoeuvre warfare theory resulted in the success of the campaign and that the numerical superiority of the Union Defence Force was not the most overwhelming factor in the victory. Essentially, it argues that the German South West African campaign is a text book example of manoeuvre warfare theory. The next chapter provides a conceptual framework for manoeuvre warfare which is applied throughout the book.

78   T.R. Ungleich, The Defence of German South West Africa during World War I' (MA thesis, University of Miami, Miami, 1974), p. 205.
79   Ibid., p. 52.
80   Collyer, The Campaign in German South West Africa, 1914–1915, p. 21.
81   D. Killingray, 'The War in Africa', Chapter 7 in H. Strachan, (ed.), The Oxford Illustrated History of the First World War (Oxford: Oxford University Press, 1998), p. 93.
82   J.C. Smuts, Jan Christian Smuts (London: Cassell, 1952), p. 259.

2

Manoeuvre Warfare Theory

This chapter outlines manoeuvre warfare theory, which is the central premise for this analysis of the German South West African campaign. In this chapter, I discuss manoeuvre warfare theory as a type of military theory, the differences between manoeuvre and attrition, the levels of war; the central tenets of manoeuvre warfare, the ways of achieving victory, decision making cycles, morale and psychological factors associated with warfare.

The objective of this chapter is to provide a framework to understand and analyse the German South West African campaign. Where many of the book chapters describe the campaign through a historical study and narrative, the use of manoeuvre theory is used to provide a military analysis.

Manoeuvre Warfare in Broad

In general, the study of warfare theory encompasses the competing theories of manoeuvre and attrition. These are not mutually exclusive and wars are a combination to differing extents of these two approaches.[1] The interrelation of manoeuvre and attrition theory provides an abstract framework to further study and understand military operations.[2] This book argues that manoeuvre warfare theory is an effective and efficient means of analysing and conducting war and accordingly underpins the North Atlantic Treaty Organisation's (NATO) philosophy on war.

Manoeuvre theory is derived from military history and military strategies which have been employed in past campaigns. This theory of warfare resurfaced as a field of study in the late 1970s after initially receiving much attention during the period from the 1920s until the 1940s. At that time, Colonel John Boyd proposed that a

---

1   J.A. Springman, 'The Rapier or the Club: The Relationship between Attrition and Manoeuvre Warfare' (MSS thesis, United States Army War College, Carlisle, 2006), p. 1.
2   J. Angstrom and J.J. Widen, *Contemporary Military Theory: The Dynamics of War* (New York: Routledge, 2015), p. 115.

study of warfare should follow what he called the OODA cycle, namely: observation, orientation, decision, and action (also called the OODA loop). Boyd's theories influenced manoeuvre warfare theory in that a rapid decision-making cycle was deemed essential for victory. Boyd based his theories on his experience as a fighter pilot and by conducting interviews with veteran commanders about their war experiences. Boyd also read widely on military history and drew on the experiences and lessons of past campaigns.[3]

Boyd wrote his essay 'Destruction and Creation' in 1976, and gave a slide presentation to US military senior staff, which he named 'New Conception for Air-to-Air Combat' in which he first outlined some of the aspects which would become fundamental in the conceptualisation of the OODA cycle. He proposed that confusion or entropy affects the ability of commanders to take decisions and thus take action.[4] The inability to make the correct decision in time, results in the incorrect action being taken which is central to losing a battle or an operation. Boyd gave further presentations from 1986 until 1996, by which time the OODA cycle theory was fully developed. These presentations promoted his OODA loop theory and concepts on command which further influenced manoeuvre warfare theory.[5] W. Lind, was a modern military theorist, who drawing on previous theorists, further developed a substantial part of the components of manoeuvre warfare theory. The culmination of Boyd and Lind's work was that the United States Army Training and Doctrine Command (TRADOC) embraced manoeuvre theory which was encapsulated in their field manual 'FM 100–5' and the Marines followed suit with 'FMFM-1'.[6] The United States and Allied victory in the First Gulf War was in part attributed to manoeuvre theory and vindicated manoeuvre theorists.[7]

The framework which will be applied in this book is derived largely from the works of Lind, R. Simpkin and R. Leonhard which have much in common.[8] Leonhard encapsulates the theory by explaining that 'the highest and purest form of manoeuvre warfare is to pre-empt the enemy that is to disarm or neutralise him before the fight'.[9]

3   W.S. Lind, *Manoeuvre Warfare Handbook* (London: Westview Press, 1985), pp. 4-6.
4   J.R. Boyd, 'Destruction and Creation', Unpublished essay, September 1976.
5   W.S. Angerman, 'Coming Full Circle with Boyd's OODA Loop Ideas: An Analysis of Innovation Diffusion and Evolution' (MSMIS thesis, United States Air Force Institute of Technology, Dayton, 2004), p. 16; S.C. Tucker, *The Almanac of American Military History* (Santa Barbara: ABC Clio, 2013), p. 2061.
6   S. Naveh, *In Pursuit of Military Excellence: The Evolution of Operational Theory* (London: Frank Cass, 1997), pp. 261, 262.
7   A. Cedergren, 'Doctrine, Expertise and Arms in Combination: A Reflection of the Iraq War', Chapter in, J. Hallenberg and H. Karlsson (eds), *The Iraq War: European Perspectives on Politics, Strategy and Operations* (New York: Routledge, 2005).
8   R. Leonhard, *The Art of Maneuver* (New York: Ballantine, 1994); Lind, *Manoeuvre Warfare Handbook*; R.E. Simpkin, *Race to the Swift* (London: Brassey's Defence Publishers,1986).
9   Leonhard, *The Art of Maneuver*, p. 19.

Within the framework of manoeuvre warfare theory Simpkin identifies dislocation and pre-emption as possible methods of attaining victory, where dislocation refers to the application of manoeuvre once conflict has broken out; and where pre-emption refers to the use of manoeuvre to prevent the outbreak of combat.[10] Manoeuvre warfare is linked to a rapid decision-making cycle, lower level command initiative and a decentralised command system. Lind discusses the aspect of decentralisation of military forces and comments that the decision making cycle of a given military force must be executed at a pace that is faster than that of the enemy so as to gain the advantage.[11] A rapid decision-making cycle relates to achieving victory by pre-emption or dislocation.

Leonhard builds on the theory as set out by Lind and Simpkin taking into account the study of warfare on the continuum between attrition and manoeuvre theory. Leonhard describes attrition as the way of defeating an enemy force in war, campaign or battle through destruction of the enemy's mass.[12] A victory based on attrition theory necessitates materiel superiority.[13]

Conversely, attrition theory emphasises destroying the enemy in a pitched battle in the hope that the damage done by one's own force on the enemy outweighs the relative destruction of the enemy. Attrition theory is analogous to positional theory and strives to inflict casualties and material losses.[14] Leonhard describes 'an immovable focus on attrition theory … aimed at destroying rather than defeating, at fighting fairly rather than stealing every advantage over the enemy, and at pursuing perfection in method rather than obtaining decisive results'.[15]

The central concept behind attrition theory is the breaking of the opponents will by destruction through direct attack. Manoeuvre warfare on the other hand emphasises avoiding the 'enemy's strength in favour of attacking his weakness'.[16] Firepower over movement is the focus of attrition theory, which emphasises the material loss of the enemy. Attrition aims to hold ground by inflicting more damage on the enemy than can be delivered in return. Attrition warfare is essentially static and linear in its approach to warfare.[17]

Attrition differs from manoeuvre theory in terms of its focus on destruction as opposed to the defeat of the enemy through pre-emption, disruption or dislocation. Manoeuvre warfare theory emphasises the importance of movement, envelopment and placement of forces over firepower and destruction which is epitomised in attrition

10   Simpkin, *Race to the Swift*, p. 140.
11   Lind, *Manoeuvre Warfare Handbook*, p. 6.
12   Leonhard, *The Art of Maneuver*, p. 19.
13   Angstrom and Widen, *Military Theory*, p. 114.
14   South African Army College, *Operational Concepts: Staff Officer's Operational Manual, Part VII* (Pretoria: 1 Military Printing Regiment, 1996), p. 7/3-1.
15   Leonhard, *The Art of Maneuver*, p. 4.
16   Ibid., p. 14.
17   South African Army College, *Operational Concepts*, p. 7/3-1.

warfare theory. Manoeuvre theory is thus focused on the dislocation or pre-emption of forces as opposed to an overwhelming focus on firepower in pitched battle. Thus the use of superior firepower and technology is directly related to the employment of attrition theory,[18] where large forces are used to fight consecutive battles.[19]

Attrition theory focuses on the tactical level and the main purpose is to bring the belligerents to a decisive battle through the massing of forces. Essentially this is warfare in the classic Clausewitzian mould where the ultimate aim is to involve large forces in fierce high intensity fixed battles.[20] The Western Front of the First World War provided a prime example of attrition warfare.[21] Strachan claims that attrition theory prevails in the event of failed manoeuvre warfare which was the case on the Western Front during the First World War.[22]

On the Western Front the option of envelopment was exhausted due to the mass concentration of forces. The belligerents had to traverse the opposing force's extensive defensive positions which in turn allowed for no outflanking to take place. The result was an attrition-based operation on the Western Front which resulted in a high mortality rate.[23]

The difference between manoeuvre and attrition theory can be divided into a focus on the human element of war and a focus on the technological aspect of war respectively. The debate on whether the most influential element in warfare is firepower or manoeuvre remains undecided. This book takes the point of view that manoeuvre warfare theory is of central importance in the conduct of war. It is undisputed that a certain amount of firepower and attrition is required in military operations despite the significance of manoeuvre. Some of the critique levelled against manoeuvre warfare theory relates to claims that conflict can be free of hard fighting.[24]

There is a definite and continuous relation between attrition and manoeuvre warfare theory in the conduct of war. Manoeuvre theory is an ideal in military theoretical

18   A. Esterhuyse, 'The Theories of Attrition versus Manoeuvre and the Levels of War', *Strategic Review for Southern Africa*, 23, 2 (2001), p. 86.
19   M.N. Vego, *Joint Operational Warfare: Theory and Practice* (Newport: Naval War College, 2007), p. XIII-3.
20   B.H. Liddell Hart, *Strategy* (London: Faber & Faber, 1967), p. 190.
21   Static warfare with an emphasis on firepower.
22   Angstrom and Widen, *Contemporary Military Theory*, p. 115.
23   C.S. Gray, *War, Peace and International Relations* (London: Routledge, 2007), pp. 80, 81.
24   See, P. Johnston, 'The Myth of Manoeuvre Warfare: Attrition in Military History', Chapter in, A.D. English, (ed.), *The Changing Face of War: Learning from History* (Kingston: McGill-Queen's University Press, 1998); W.F. Owen, 'The Manoeuvre Warfare Fraud', *The Small Wars Journal*, http://webcache.googleusercontent.com/search?q=cache:OOzaJk7LWUwJ:smallwarsjournal.com/blog/journal/docs-temp/95-owen.pdf%3Fq%3Dmag/docs-temp/95-owen.pdf+&cd=3&hl=en&ct=clnk&gl=za; C.A. Tucker, *False Prophets: The Myth of Maneuver Warfare and the Inadequacies of FMFM-1 Warfighting* (Fort Leavenworth: US Army Command and General Staff College, 1995).

terms which aims at victory in the shortest possible time with minimal loss of life and materiel.

Abel Esterhuyse has analysed the relationship between manoeuvre and attrition theory on the various levels of war (refer to Figure 2.1)[25] and highlights the point that despite the difference in theoretical underpinnings, all wars include some level of attrition.[26] The levels of war include the strategic, operational and tactical levels and the respective level of war dictates the type of military planning and action that is required. The strategic level concerns itself with objectives on a national level authorised by the national command; the operational level pertains to campaigns and is organised around armies and corps; and the tactical level refers to battles and engagements usually with divisions, brigades and battalions.[27] Manoeuvre warfare is conducted on the different levels of war and is aimed at achieving a rapid victory at a low cost to resources and human life.

The concept of an operational level and operational art was first expounded by Russian military theorist General A.A. Sveckin in the 1920s who proposed that there is an intermediary level between strategy and tactics. These ideas became central to Russian military theory in the 1930s.[28] It is widely held that manoeuvre warfare

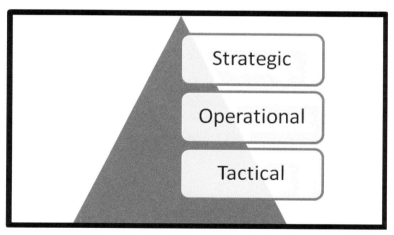

Figure 2.1: Hierarchy of the levels of war[29]

25   The levels of war include the strategic, operational and tactical.
26   Esterhuyse, 'The Theories of Attrition versus Manoeuvre', p. 87.
27   Leonhard, *The Art of Maneuver*, p. 6.
28   Vego, *Joint Operational Warfare*, p. I-23.
29   A. Garcia, "Manoeuvre Warfare in the South African Campaign in German South West Africa during the First World War", MA thesis, University of South Africa, 2015, p. 13.

extends over the three levels of war,[30] although some theorists maintain that manoeuvre theory is confined to the operational level.[31] If indeed manoeuvre theory exists on the different levels of war then the relation between attrition and manoeuvre warfare would vary accordingly. Regardless of manoeuvre or attrition, the strategic level decides on the objectives of policy, where the core aspects of strategy and the means to attain the required ends are identified. If military means are selected to achieve the ends of policy then leaders on the strategic and operational levels are responsible for formulating plans and carrying out military operations to achieve the required objectives.

Clausewitz and Liddell Hart define strategy in the same vein, referring to the military force of a state as a means to be used to fulfil its political ends.[32] The operational level is the realm where strategic aims are met and where many theorists opine that manoeuvre warfare is executed.[33] 'Grand tactics' is an antiquated term that refers to the planning and movement of large forces between battles which is currently referred to as the operational level of war.[34]

The operational level takes shape in campaigns and is always faced with the decision of when or whether to accept battle which is based on a range of considerations. Should battle be accepted or chosen then military operations are shifted into the realm of tactics. On the tactical level manoeuvre and attrition theories are interwoven where manoeuvre is translated into mobility and attrition into firepower.[35] The slower moving attrition element, with reference to its firepower, provides the stability which manoeuvre cannot provide on the tactical level.[36]

Leonhard defines manoeuvre as focusing on the operational level without including tactical battles, 'it [manoeuvre] can be defined as the movement towards an objective with the ultimate purpose to gain an advantage over the enemy whether positionally or psychologically'.[37] Manoeuvre theory deals with the dual spheres of the psychological and the physical, where the effect of a rapidly advancing force can demoralise an enemy.

30   B.T. Solberg, 'Maneuver Warfare: Consequences for Tactics and Organisation of the Norwegian Infantry' (MMAS thesis, United States Army Command and Staff College, Kansas, 2000), p. 5.

31   Angstrom and Widen, *Contemporary Military Theory*, p. 115.

32   R. Holmes, *The Oxford Companion to Military History* (Oxford: Oxford University Press, 2001), p. 879.

33   Leonhard, *The Art of Maneuver*, p. 8.

34   Holmes, *The Oxford Companion to Military History*, p. 895.

35   Esterhuyse, 'The Theories of Attrition versus Manoeuvre', p. 91.

36   Simpkin, *Race to the Swift*, p. 23.

37   Leonhard, *The Art of Maneuver*, p. 18.

Military Theory: An Overview

In order for military history to have a practical purpose, its study should result in the formation of principles and theories. Principles are classified as laws which are based on what has been observed, while theories involve the analysis of history in order to determine how a system should function.[38] Manoeuvre can be interpreted as a theory of warfare and a principle of war. Manoeuvre is defined as, 'a fundamental truth regarding the prosecution of war ... the object is to deploy a force in such a manner so as to place the enemy at a relative disadvantage and achieve results that would otherwise be costly in men and materiel'.[39]

Theories of war are essentially an abstract supposition based on the different principles, philosophical ideologies and doctrine relative to different military forces and their respective commanders. Manoeuvre warfare theory delves into the philosophy of war and focuses on the achievement of victory in the fastest and most efficient way.[40]

Prominent scholars influenced military theory from the West and the East of which one such writer was Liddell Hart who served on the Western Front during the First World War. He wrote extensively on mechanisation and the use of armoured warfare. Liddell Hart formulated what he referred to as the indirect approach which emphasises the importance of avoiding direct attack on enemy defensive positions in favour of an enveloping or surprise attack.[41] Many of the military theorists of the 1920s and 1930s including Liddell Hart and J.F.C. Fuller aimed to bring manoeuvre back to warfare following the static warfare and attrition of the First World War.[42] During the 1950s Liddell Hart went even further and incorporated concepts similar to that of *Blitzkrieg*[43] in his theories and was in correspondence with senior German officers after the Second World War.[44]

Liddell Hart, although certainly not the first theorist, formalised certain concepts relating military theory to the psychology of combat. Military theorists throughout history have to varying extents noted the importance of the human condition in combat. The importance of morale was echoed by strategists across the world and throughout the ages. Tzu was the first strategist who recorded the importance of the

38 Ibid., pp. 78, 79.
39 South African National Defence Force, 'The Principles of War', *South African Military History Reader* (Stellenbosch: University of Stellenbosch, 2004), p. 40.
40 Leonhard, *The Art of Maneuver*, p. 61.
41 Liddell Hart, *Strategy*.
42 Johnston, 'The Myth of Manoeuvre', Chapter in, English, *Changing Face of War*, p. 29.
43 The term literally means lightening warfare, and was the tactics and doctrine utilised by the German military in the Second World War, which incorporated rapid mobile armour attacks, with coordinated air support.
44 Naveh, *Military Excellence*, p. 109.

psychological and human dimension of warfare.[45]; Napoleon Bonaparte famously claimed that 'morale is to material as three is to one'[46]; the Roman army's leadership understood that a military community fostered morale[47]; M. Musashi's 16th century exposition on combat in Japan highlighted the importance of confidence and morale[48] and western enlightenment military theorists such as C. von Clausewitz, A. Du Picq and A. Jomini understood the fundamental importance of cohesion and morale in warfare.[49] Clausewitz claimed that the loss of morale is linked to the loss of ground[50]; Jomini maintained that 'the superiority in armament may increase the chances of success in war, however it does not in itself win battles'[51] and further claimed that 'weapons are effective only insofar as they influence the morale of the enemy'.[52]

Morale is defined by the United States Army as 'the mental, emotional and spiritual state of the individual. It is how he feels, [be it] happy, hopeful, confident, appreciated, worthless, sad, unrecognised or depressed.'[53] Morale is recognised as the most important aspect of a fighting force where discipline and training are also regarded as necessities.[54]

Morale is one of the intangibles of war and is a concept and phenomenon that has been studied in depth by military psychologists and historians. The fundamental function of morale is to provide the soldier with the will to win. Studies in the psychological motivation of individuals and groups towards commitment to battle are intrinsically linked to the different levels of morale within the group and whether the individual and/ or group identifies with the need to commit to battle.[55] The strong ties between soldiers, based on shared hardship and common purpose, leads to a will to fight on.[56]

45 S. Tzu, tr., L Giles, *The Art of War*, http://www.gutenberg.org/files/132/132.txt, ebook, Accessed 23 January 2012, p. 15.
46 D. Evans, *War: A Matter of Principles* (London: MacMillan Press, 1998), pp. 21, 22.
47 B. Campbell, *War and Society in Imperial Rome, 31 BC–AD 284* (New York: Routledge, 2002), pp. 34-36.
48 M. Musashi, tr. T. Cleary, *The Book of Five Rings* (London: Shambala, 2005). The original work was produced in Japan in the 1640s.
49 J.M. Malik, 'The Evolution of Strategic Thought', Chapter in, C.A. Snyder (ed.), *Contemporary Security and Strategy* (New York: Routledge, 1999), p. 18.
50 C. von Clausewitz, tr., J.J. Graham, *On War*, http://www.gutenberg.org/files/1946/1946-h/1946-h.htm, ebook, Accessed 23 January 2012, p. 120.
51 G. Parker (ed)., *The Illustrated History of Warfare: The Triumph of the West* (Cambridge: Cambridge University Press, 1995), p. 2.
52 Leonhard, *The Art of Maneuver*, p. 44.
53 R. Gal and D.A. Mangelsdorff (eds), *Handbook of Military Psychology* (New York: John Wiley & Sons, 1991), p. 454.
54 Gray, *War, Peace and International Relations*, p. 5.
55 B. Shalit, *The Psychology of Conflict and Combat* (New York: Praeger, 1988), p. 35.
56 A. King, *Combat Solder: Infantry Tactics and Cohesion in the Twentieth and Twenty-First Centuries* (Oxford: Oxford University Press, 2013), p. 25

Furthermore, Clausewitz contributed the term 'friction' to the theory of warfare referring to the human aspects of fear, anxiety, frustration and tiredness and how these factors influence the course of warfare. In adding the term friction, Clausewitz explains that warfare is intrinsically related to chance.[57] Manoeuvre warfare incorporates psychology into its framework including concepts such as such as morale, frustration and fear and how these factors influence the outcome of battles and operations.[58]

The focus of manoeuvre theory is on the human condition. Liddell Hart deliberates on the primary, yet incalculable element of war: the human will and how aspects of movement and surprise can dislocate the physical and psychological dimensions of the enemy, elements that are fundamental to combat cohesion.[59] An attack on the enemy should ideally have two psychological effects: firstly, to destroy the enemy's will to resist and secondly, to destroy the enemy's cohesion.[60]

B. Solberg applies the indirect approach as elucidated by Liddell Hart, in his study on the importance of manoeuvre warfare and its application to the Norwegian infantry. Solberg maintains that divergent lines of operation and deep enveloping movements that create a feeling of being trapped, lead to paralysis and psychological dislocation.[61] The indirect approach aims to dislocate the psychological and physical dimensions of the enemy on a continuous basis. Manoeuvre warfare thus attempts to pre-empt or defeat the enemy by disrupting its psychological and physical capabilities.[62]

Manoeuvre warfare theory focuses on the psychological impact of causing a loss of morale in the enemy force, resulting in their retreat. This loss of morale and flight is intrinsically coupled with the pursuit of the enemy.[63] Manoeuvre warfare theory draws a causal relationship between the loss of morale and the defeat of the enemy, which is not always related to troop numbers, capabilities and military equipment. Don Starry, a four-star general in the United States Army, commented that the outcome of battles is often decided by factors other than numerical superiority.[64]

Du Picq promulgated theories on the study of morale and unit cohesion in combat. He linked the impact of weapons to the morale of the enemy as opposed to purely the destruction of the enemy's military hardware. Du Picq states, 'in studying ancient combats, it can be seen that it was almost always an attack from the flank or rear, a surprise action that won battles, especially against the Romans'.[65] Martin van

---

57   Von Clausewitz, tr. Graham, *On War*, p. 43.
58   Shalit, *The Psychology of Conflict and Combat*; Gal and Mangelsdorff (eds), *Handbook of Military Psychology*; B. Glad (ed.), *Psychological Dimensions of War* (London: Sage, 1990).
59   Liddell Hart, *Strategy*.
60   South African Army College, *Operational Concepts*, p. 7/5-5.
61   Solberg, 'Maneuver Warfare', p. 30, 31.
62   South African Army College, *Operational Concepts*, p. 7/5-4.
63   Leonhard, *The Art of Maneuver*, p. 112.
64   Simpkin, *Race to the Swift*, p. x.
65   A. du Picq, trs., J.N. Greenly and R.C. Cotton, *Battle Studies*,http://www.gutenberg.org/files-h.htm, ebook (Accessed 23 Janaury 2012), p. 55. Leonhard draws on Du Picq in framing the context of manoeuvre warfare.

Creveld reinforces the previous point by commenting that from the time of Napoleon in the late 18th century to Helmuth von Moltke, Alfred von Schlieffen and Liddell Hart in the early 20th century, the object of battle has been to outflank the opponent so as to envelop and encircle the enemy force and ensure that it is cut off from its logistical supplies resulting in victory in the battle and potentially also the campaign; this method is tacitly or explicitly understood as the means of gaining victory in a confrontation between conventional military forces – as was the case in Ulm in 1805[66] and is accepted as a convention of war whereby the encircled army accepts defeat when cut off.[67]

The study of 20th century Russian and German operational theory indicates a difference in the understanding of the limits of envelopment. Where the German forces that used *Blitzkrieg* saw envelopment as an end in itself which extended to the operational level, Russian theory restricted envelopments for the most part to the tactical realm.[68] The extended lines of communication and supply challenges which resulted from extensive German envelopments in the Second World War, was testament to the extent of *Blitzkrieg* styled operations.

Manoeuvre warfare theory and military theory as a whole, were influenced by the works of the eminent theorists of war, Clausewitz and Jomini. Clausewitz coined the term centre of gravity as the hub of all power[69] and he also commented on the friction of warfare which affects the psychology of combatants and commanders alike.[70] Jomini spoke of lines of advance and attack on key points with the placement of an overwhelming force so as to achieve an objective.[71] The strategic thinking brought forward by the Napoleonic era was built on by Alfred Von Schlieffen in his treatise 'Cannae' and encouraged flanking attacks even by numerically inferior forces, on larger opponents.[72] Lettow-Vorbeck in the German East African and Von Heydebreck in German South West Africa attempted limited forms of offensive manoeuvre with limited forces, with partial success.

Manoeuvre theory adapted the term 'centre of gravity' and describes it as the critical vulnerability where Clausewitz defines the centre of gravity as 'the hub of all power and movement on which everything depends'.[73] Clausewitz was a product of

---

66   Napoleon and the French army effectively surrounded and cut off the Austrian army forcing it to surrender.

67   M. van Creveld, *The Transformation of War* (New York: The Free Press, 1991), p. 91.

68   Naveh, *Military Excellence*, p. 213.

69   The 'centre of gravity' is a philosophical abstract in military theory which must be analysed and identified by real time commanders in the execution of operational planning. The centre of gravity is the objective of an attack, advance or the positioning of forces.

70   Von Clausewitz, tr. Graham, *On War*, p. 119.

71   A.H. Jomini, tr., G.H. Mendell and W.P. Craighill, *The Art of War* (Rockville: Art Manor, 2007).

72   See, F. Jon Nesselhuf, 'General Paul Von Lettow-Vorbeck's East African Campaign: Maneuver Warfare on the Serengeti', MA thesis, University of North Texas, 2012.

73   Jomini, tr., Mendell and Craighill, *The Art*, p. 26.

the *grand armee* era[74] and as such was a proponent of massed and focussed battles. The centre of gravity, according to Clausewitz should always be the belligerent's forces where the central purpose is achieving a decisive victory.[75] Manoeuvre warfare theory adapts the concept of the centre of gravity to refer to the critical vulnerability, which if compromised leads to the paralysis of the enemy and not just a reduction of the enemy's military capabilities.[76]

The theoretical underpinnings of the indirect approach as postulated by Liddell Hart are hypothetically superimposed on the divergent advances of a military force on a central objective or through divergent advances on successive decisive points en route to the centre of gravity. Liddell Hart focused on attacking along the line of least expectation and the line of least resistance,[77] where this idea can be achieved through the consideration of the lines of advance in operations and the decisive points of the opposing force.[78]

Central Tenets of Manoeuvre Warfare

Manoeuvre warfare theory aims to dislocate or pre-empt the enemy by enveloping or cutting him off. The principles of manoeuvre warfare are largely congruent with the principles expressed by Sun Tzu.[79] Tzu claims that supreme excellence lies not in winning every battle but rather in defeating the enemy without resistance.[80] Manoeuvre warfare theory and Tzu's theory hold the same central tenet.[81] Tzu's theory on warfare is elaborated on by Liddell Hart in his indirect approach, which has similar elements to manoeuvre warfare.[82] Many military theorists hold precepts which have some commonality and which have for the most part been learned from the direct or indirect study of war.

Manoeuvre warfare theory, as a way of conducting warfare, aims to defeat the enemy with the least amount of effort while suffering minimal operational losses. Manoeuvre is regarded as an important means of achieving victory in warfare,[83] based

---

74 This underpins Napoleonic warfare where large armies were concentrated for a decisive pitched battle.
75 Von Clausewitz, tr. Graham, *On War*, p. 119.
76 Leonhard, *The Art of Maneuver*, p. 44.
77 Liddell Hart, *Strategy*, p. 335.
78 Solberg, 'Maneuver Warfare', p. 29.
79 Sun Tzu was a Chinese general and military theorist in ancient times, who introduced prominent concepts such as deception, surprise and the importance of morale to military theory over 2,000 years ago. His treatise on military theory has been translated into English among other languages and is accepted in the Western military tradition.
80 S. Tzu, tr. A.L. Sadler, *The Art of War* (Tokyo: Tuttle, 2009), p. 4.
81 Leonhard, *The Art of Maneuver*, p. 28.
82 South African Army College, *Operational Concepts*, p. 7/3-1.
83 Solberg, 'Maneuver Warfare', p. 21.

on capitalising on the vulnerabilities of human nature.[84] As a means of achieving victory manoeuvre warfare identifies three possible methods, namely: pre-emption, dislocation and disruption. Pre-emption refers to the use of manoeuvre to prevent the outbreak of combat, while dislocation refers to the application of manoeuvre once conflict has broken out.[85] Similarly, disruption is relevant after the commencement of hostilities.

Pre-emption is a decisive approach which prioritises speed and is characterised by lower levels of destruction and human loss. Pre-emption relies on movement and the element of surprise over firepower and calls for a rapid decision making cycle.[86] Pre-emption denies the opposing force freedom of action which removes the initiative from the enemy.[87] This means of achieving victory is based on intuition more than intelligence.[88]

Dislocation involves the removal of the enemy's combat strength from the decisive point. It includes avoiding combat where the enemy is stronger and choosing how to position one's forces to ensure the best results. An example of this is the surprise attack by the German forces on Sedan during the Second World War. The Germans opted to advance through the Ardennes forest which the Allies did not expect. The forest, which was a natural obstacle, was believed to be impregnable.[89] Dislocation is based on a good intelligence network and makes use of surprise, deep penetrating drives and envelopment to dislocate the physical and psychological spheres of the enemy.[90]

Disruption involves the attack and destruction of the enemy's fighting capability with the aim of paralysing the enemy force.[91] Disruption is the third means of achieving victory through manoeuvre warfare and involves defeating the enemy by attacking the enemy's centre of gravity/critical vulnerability.[92]

The levels of war are intrinsically related to the centre of gravity and by attacking and neutralising the enemy's centre of gravity/critical vulnerability one should theoretically defeat the enemy. The centre of gravity can be on the strategic, operational or tactical levels of war.

In terms of the operational level of war, where manoeuvre warfare is employed the centre of gravity is often a headquarters, a central place where senior personnel govern,

---

84   British Army, *Operations, British Army Doctrine* (Andover: Army Publications, 2010), p. 5-2.
85   Simpkin, *Race to the Swift*, p. 140.
86   Leonhard, *The Art of Maneuver*, p. 63, 64.
87   British Army, *Operations, British Army Doctrine*, p. 5-16.
88   South African Army College, *Operational Concepts*, p. 7/5-6.
89   Leonhard, *The Art of Maneuver*, pp. 67, 68; South African Army College, *Operational Concepts*, p. 7/5-10.
90   British Army, *Operations, British Army Doctrine*, 5-16; South African Army College, *Operational Concepts*, p. 7/5-6.
91   South African Army College, *Operational Concepts*, 7/5-6; British Army, *Operations, British Army Doctrine*, p. 5-17.
92   Leonhard, *The Art of Maneuver*, p. 73.

command and direct their forces.[93] The centres of gravity at each level of war are related to the objective of that respective level (refer to Figure 2.2).[94] Lawrence speaks of the confusion between the strategic and tactical levels in which some commanders believe it to be an end of strategy to commit to battle.[95]

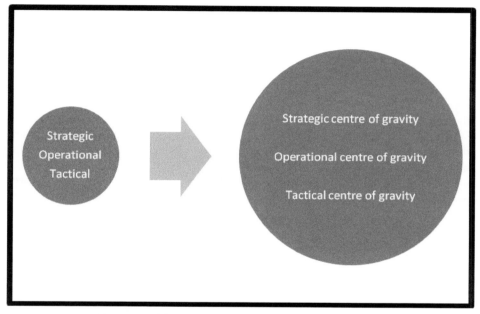

Figure 2.2: The levels of war and their centres of gravity[96]

The confusion alluded to by Lawrence is magnified by the reality that certain strategic objectives do not always have a tactical solution. Von Moltke stated that in the case where tactics dictate the objects of strategy there is a reversal in the traditional role of strategy.[97]

The strategic level must determine the strategic objectives whereas the operational level must determine how to achieve the strategic ends. The strategic level must formulate and develop security policy and military strategic and operational plans. The operational and tactical levels must formulate the operational and battle concept

93   Ibid., pp. 20–23.
94   South African Army College, *Operational Concepts*, p. 7/11-2.
95   T.E. Lawrence, *Seven Pillars of Wisdom* (London: Jonathan Cape, 1935), p. 197.
96   Garcia, 'Manoeuvre Warfare', p. 32.
97   Gray, *War, Peace and International Relations*, p. 20.

and then fight the war.[98] Military operations and statecraft pursue a collective aim and are parts of the same whole.[99]

Military commanders often have the daunting task of identifying operational and strategic objectives and centres of gravity. The commander must direct resources allocated to the focus of the main effort which is directed against the enemy's centre of gravity/critical vulnerability.[100] Leonhard states: 'Operational planners must determine how to use the available combat power to achieve the goals of a campaign.'[101]

The notion of achieving results and attacking the centre of gravity with minimal loss is central to the conceptualisation of manoeuvre theory. This idea is also a fundamental part of Chinese strategic thought which states that the objective should not be the physical and military centre of gravity but rather the enemy's moral and psychological centre of gravity.[102] The military scientific path to the attainment of the centre of gravity involves the realisation of decisive points on the respective lines of operations. Decisive points are defined as positions in time and space which can threaten the centre of gravity. Lines of operations link decisive points and centres of gravity.[103]

This theoretical application is not always as clear cut as it may appear. A decisive point may for example be the command and communication centres of a military force which allows for a further objective to be taken. Liddell Hart states that a dispersed advance could have a single objective or a number of successive objectives or alternatively a dispersed advance could have simultaneous objectives.[104]

Tzu famously commented that 'supreme excellence is not to fight and conquer in all your battles but rather in breaking the enemy's resistance without fighting'.[105] This statement on the aim of strategy is reinforced by Liddell Hart who writes 'the perfection of strategy ... [is] to achieve a decision without any serious fighting.'[106] Manoeuvre warfare thus aims at the enemy's critical vulnerability, the centre of gravity, and not necessarily at the enemy's strong point. Leonhard further describes these terms by stating: 'pre-emption involves ... relying more on speed than on firepower; speed of advance must rob the enemy into retreat ... movement fulfils the purest form of manoeuvre warfare in defeating the enemy without risk of direct-fire engagements.'[107]

According to Leonhard, 'one of the operational commander's primary functions during a campaign is to decide whether to accept battle or whether to decline

98   South African Army College, *Operational Concepts*, p. 7/1-3.
99   Tzu, tr. Sadler, *The Art of War*, p. 25.
100 South African Army College, *Operational Concepts*, p. 7/11-7.
101 Leonhard, *The Art of Maneuver*, p. 10.
102 Tzu, tr. Sadler, *The Art of War*, p. 28.
103 Solberg, 'Maneuver Warfare', p. 27.
104 Liddell Hart, *Strategy*, p. 201.
105 Tzu, tr. Sadler, *The Art of War*, p. 5.
106 Liddell Hart, *Strategy*, p. 190.
107 Leonhard, *The Art of Maneuver*, p. 64.

through manoeuvre'.[108] Tzu alludes to what he terms the essentials of victory, which include 'knowing when to fight; knowing how to handle superior and inferior forces [and] high morale in all ranks.'[109] While, the philosophy of war considers, morale, numerical differences and strategic, operational and tactical choices, the evaluation of the practical difficulties in operations is also crucial.

Friction, according to the British Army doctrine, is the force which makes the execution of certain actions difficult.[110] The factors that are fundamentally linked to friction are physical exertion, danger, intelligence and uncertainty.[111] Friction implies that things generally go wrong and soldiers and people make mistakes which are amplified due to stress and exhaustion.[112] These factors dwell as much in the physical as in the psychological realm and can be perceived or real. The difference between a real and perceived threat in the mind of the soldier is minimal because the psychological effect is almost identical.[113] Defeating an opposing force has a large psychological dimension which includes morale and courage which in turn is affected by surprise and mobility as key aspects of manoeuvre theory.[114]

These and other factors such as determination are also intertwined with soldiers' faith and confidence in their leadership. When social unity collapses and soldiers' faith in their commanders dwindles then the level and impact of combat stress reactions increase.[115] The fear that is felt on the battlefield is magnified by isolation.[116]

The movements that comprise manoeuvre as a concept should at all times pose a threat to the enemy. Du Picq added that if the enemy felt threatened in its position by a large envelopment then it would instinctively retreat.[117] When a military force threatens the communication lines of an enemy force, the closer that the cut is made to the enemy force, the greater the psychological impact.[118] This type of envelopment is fundamentally linked to surprise. Surprise often results in panic where the individual or group feels entrapped. The uncertainty and fear which stems from feeling trapped is often accompanied with the immediate search for escape.[119]

The psychological consequence of entrapment occurs as a result of the physical movements and placement of forces. If the line of least resistance is followed in the physical sphere, the line of least expectation (surprise) must be followed in the

108 Leonhard, *The Art of Maneuver*, p. 11.
109 Tzu, tr. Sadler, *The Art of War*, p. 6.
110 British Army, *Operations, British Army Doctrine*, p. 3-2.
111 Solberg, 'Maneuver Warfare', p. 22.
112 Gray, *War, Peace and International Relations*, p. 25.
113 Gal and Mangelsdorff (eds), *Handbook of Military Psychology*, p. 511.
114 Leonhard, *The Art of Maneuver*, p. 29, 30.
115 Gal and Mangelsdorff (eds), *Handbook of Military Psychology*, p. 513.
116 Glad (ed.), *Psychological Dimensions of War*, p. 229.
117 Leonhard, *The Art of Maneuver*, p. 45.
118 Liddell Hart, *Strategy*, p. 199.
119 Glad (ed.), *Psychological Dimensions of War*, p. 229.

psychological sphere.[120] The use of the element of surprise, whether in the operational or strategic context, should penetrate to great depths within the enemy area of operations without offering battle. This will dislocate the enemy forces and psychologically impair their commanders.[121] In order to execute effective manoeuvre warfare, one must attack the psychological dimension of the adversary by attacking the physical enemy in such a way that surprise and dislocation is achieved. The effect of a lost battle is more psychological than physical and the retreating force will withdraw until they reach a strong defensive position that can be held or reinforced with reserves.[122]

Theoretically the efforts of a military force should be directed against the vulnerable points of the opposing force. Should a military force be directed to fight strong and defensible positions of the opposing force in a direct confrontation, the likely result would be substantial loss and destruction. In conceptual terms, the efforts of a military force should rather be directed against the will and cohesion of the opposing force.[123] These psychological aspects are central to the morale of any force and are eroded by friction and uncertainty, which negatively influences the mind of the commander.[124]

The effects of retreating and being surrounded may lead to combat stress reactions. Combat stress reactions compromise the effective functioning of the leadership of a military unit which is often caused by a drop in morale with the primary causal factor being the fear of death in combat.[125]

Two fundamental considerations which are critical to the defeat of a given enemy are its will to resist and its cohesion.[126] Manoeuvre should be carried out in such a way that the enemy feels overwhelmed by the attack or advance (or the *threat* of the attack or advance). In psychological terms this is related to stress casualties which become more likely where there is low morale. Under severe conditions of stress, soldiers feel incapable of fighting even if they are not physically wounded.[127] Enemy morale is often unrelated to its physical wellbeing and even if a military force experiences no losses it may become panic-stricken and be useless as a fighting force.[128] In order to attack the psychological wellbeing of the enemy, its will to resist and cohesion should be attacked. By attacking the will of the enemy one destroys the enemy's belief that it can win.[129]

120 Liddell Hart, *Strategy*, p. 194.
121 Simpkin, *Race to the Swift*, p. 30.
122 Von Clausewitz, tr. Graham, *On War*, p. 133.
123 Solberg, 'Maneuver Warfare', p. 26.
124 C. Fouche, 'Military Strategy and its Use in Competitive Strategy with Reference to the Nelson Mandela Metropole Automotive Industry' (MBA thesis, Nelson Mandela Metropolitan University, Port Elizabeth, 2005), p. 27.
125 Gal and Mangelsdorff (eds), *Handbook of Military Psychology*, pp. 507–511.
126 South African Army College, *Operational Concepts*, p. 7/5-5.
127 Gal and Mangelsdorff (eds), *Handbook of Military Psychology*, pp. 483, 484.
128 Leonhard, *The Art of Maneuver*, p. 75.
129 South African Army College, *Operational Concepts*, pp. 7/5-5, 7/5-6.

Movement and surprise are two of the elements which are available to destroy the enemy's will to resist. Movement lies in the physical realm and surprise exists in the psychological dimension. The two elements are proportional and interrelated because movement creates surprise and surprise gives rise to movement.[130] The effect of movement and surprise affects the enemy's morale and will to resist.[131]

Within the psychological sphere there are factors that lower morale and there are also factors that boost morale. A competent and motivational commander inspires their forces and boosts morale. Field Marshal B.L. Montgomery commented, 'if the approach to the human factor is cold and impersonal, then you achieve nothing'.[132] Napoleon's charisma had a magnetic effect on his soldiers and an equally intimidating impact on his opponents. Similarly, General Erwin Rommel held great sway over his soldiers and equally over his enemies.[133] The charisma of great commanders such as Napoleon and Rommel acts as a force multiplier.[134]

The greater the psychological impact on an opposing force, the fewer the resources that will be required to defeat it. This psychological effect is achieved by deception and surprise and by the positioning of own forces in the rear of the opposing force.[135] The indirect approach personifies the dislocation of the enemy's mental and physical spheres using minimal resources.[136] The dislocation takes place on the advance or attack and thus manoeuvre theory is essentially offensive in nature, however there may be occasions when a defensive position has to be taken which serves as a launching pad for the advance and attack.[137]

Simpkin states that ground should only be held if it is a fixed enemy resource such as a bridge or an important base.[138] Fixed resources such as bridges and landing strips facilitate the movement and management of logistics. Logistics are fundamental to modern warfare and determine the size and type of force that can be deployed and sustained. Furthermore, logistics also determine how these forces are to be maintained in terms of rations, ammunition, fuel and other requirements and the flow and rhythm of operations.[139]

An operational pause must be taken at a time when combat is no longer sustainable. The operational pause along one line of operations should theoretically be met with the hastening of the tempo on an alternative line of operations.[140] Liddell Hart states

130 Liddell Hart, *Strategy*, pp. 189, 190.
131 Leonhard, *The Art of Maneuver*, p. 75.
132 Glad (ed.), *Psychological Dimensions of War*, p. 232.
133 Gray, *War, Peace and International Relations*, p. 44.
134 Simpkin, *Race to the Swift*, p. 142.
135 South African Army College, *Operational Concepts*, p. 7/3-2; Solberg, 'Maneuver Warfare', pp. 79–82.
136 Solberg, 'Maneuver Warfare', p. 34.
137 Ibid., 21.
138 Simpkin, *Race to the Swift*, p. 22.
139 Holmes, *The Oxford Companion to Military History*, p. 513.
140 South African Army College, *Operational Concepts*, p. 7/12-1.

that dislocation can be produced by forcing an enemy to change front by separating its forces, endangering its supplies and/or cutting off possible routes of retreat.[141]

Tzu speaks of the military components necessary to execute a decisive attack and they include, 'an "ordinary" force that would pin down the enemy and an "extraordinary" force that would perform a manoeuvre so as to outflank the enemy'.[142] Jomini supports this model and maintains that the chances of victory are far greater when there is a direct attack and a flanking manoeuvre.[143] Flanking tactics have been used throughout the ages by militaries all over the word including, Chinese[144] and Mongol Empires[145] to the German Army's ambitious 'Schlieffen Plan'[146] which extended to the operational level. The development of flanking and envelopment have occurred organically throughout the history of combat, as a practical recourse where a given military force fixes and another force envelops enemy.[147]

Lawrence claims that the only tactic which he found worked effectively were rapid mounted charges at the enemy's rear.[148] The methods of direct and indirect attack have been used by different commanders in different historical periods across the world to achieve their military objectives. Direct and indirect strategies can result in a multitude of different operational plans.[149] When transitioning from planning to the execution phase, the decision making cycle is of fundamental importance. The execution of operational plans involves a series of decisions which is vital to the success of a given plan of action.

Boyd's decision cycle or loop is a continuous process of 'observation, orientation, decision and action (OODA)'.[150] By completing this cycle before the enemy can do so and thus disrupting the enemy's OODA cycle, one gains the initiative. Boyd's theory is largely psychological and addresses the will and morale of fighting forces.[151] The OODA loop forms a building block of manoeuvre warfare, as the theory aims to disrupt the thought processes of the opposing commanders.[152] A rapid OODA

141 Liddell Hart, *Strategy*, p. 193.
142 Solberg, 'Maneuver Warfare', p. 32.
143 Jomini, tr., Mendell and Craighill, *The Art of War*, p. 149.
144 See, M.C. Whiting, *Imperial Chinese Military History 8000BC-1912AD* (New York: Writers Club Press, 2012), p. 59.
145 See, M. Burgan, *Great Empires of the Past: Empire of the Mongols* (New York: Facts on File, 2005), p. 19.
146 See, G.E. Rothenberg, 'Moltke, Schlieffen, and the Doctrine of Strategic Envelopment', Chapter in, P. Paret (ed.), *Makers of Modern Strategy: From Machiavelli to the Modern Age* (Princeton: Princeton University Press, 1986), p. 318.
147 Gooch, 'The Use of History in the Development of Contemporary Doctrine', p. 13.
148 Lawrence, *Seven Pillars of Wisdom*, p. 96.
149 Tzu, tr. Sadler, *The Art of War*, p. 9.
150 Leonhard, *The Art of Maneuver*, p. 51.
151 Solberg, 'Maneuver Warfare', p. 38.
152 Esterhuyse, 'The Theories of Attrition versus Manoeuvre', p. 91.

cycle creates confusion and a sensory overload on the enemy, and thus generates opportunities which can be exploited.

In order to achieve surprise and retain the initiative the OODA cycle of the enemy must be compromised.[153] On the operational level an example of taking the initiative is cutting the enemy's logistical lines through an enveloping advance or attack. Figure 2.3 is a representation of a direct and enveloping attack on the enemy and shows the link between the psychological and physical dimensions.

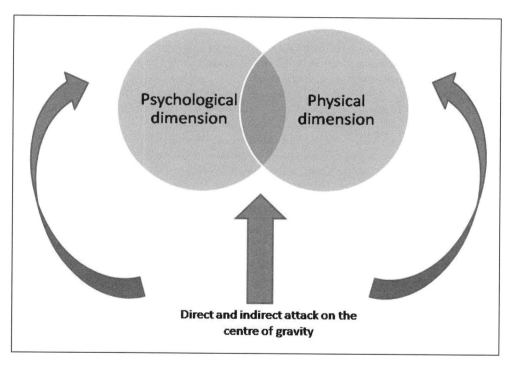

Figure 2.3: Direct and indirect attack[154]

The side that seizes and maintains the initiative is often the side that wins the battle as opposed to winning by numerical superiority alone.[155] Liddell Hart states that whereas the enemy's outward appearance of numbers and resources indicate strength these factors are dependent on morale, control and supply.[156] In order to attack the cohesion

153 Simpkin, *Race to the Swift*, p. 182.
154 Garcia, 'Manoeuvre Warfare', p. 42.
155 Simpkin, *Race to the Swift*, p. x.
156 Liddell Hart, *Strategy*, p. 4.

of the enemy one could use tempo, simultaneity or surprise. Tempo is attacking the enemy at a varying rate; one to which the enemy is unable to respond effectively. Simultaneity is related to tempo and aims to attack the enemy from many different routes and angles which overloads the decision making ability (OODA cycle) of the enemy commanders. Surprise creates shock and is based on doing the unexpected where the enemy is not given time to respond.[157]

The aim of manoeuvre warfare is to attempt to gain victory through methods other than pitched battle. The theory of manoeuvre warfare occurs at a high cognitive level and is often misunderstood by those focused on the tactical level. The ultimate role of the commander is to defeat the enemy as opposed to destroying the enemy.[158] The true aim of strategy, according to Liddell Hart, 'is not to seek battle but rather to seek a strategic situation so advantageous that if it does not in itself produce the decision, its continuation by a battle is sure to achieve this'.[159]

Application of Manoeuvre Theory to the German South West African Campaign

Manoeuvre warfare theory is studied as part of military strategy as a framework for understanding operations.[160] The strategic framework is the link between politics, the military and the different levels of war. The levels of war provide the construct that enable an understanding of the conceptual and physical requirements of military activities and theory.[161]

Thomas Edward Lawrence, or Lawrence of Arabia as he was known, wrote that the purpose of tactics is to achieve strategic ends.[162] Strategy aims to achieve political and national objectives through military means. Between the strategic level of war and the tactical level of war there is the operational level of war. The operational level consists of the overall conduct of campaigns whereas the tactical level is specifically concerned with battles.[163] S. Naveh expounds on the complexities of the operational level of war in his significant study, 'In Pursuit of Military Excellence: The Evolution of Operational Theory'.[164]

---

157 South African Army College, *Operational Concepts*, pp. 7/5-7, 7/5-8.
158 Leonhard, *The Art of Maneuver*, pp. 24–29.
159 Liddell Hart, *Strategy*, p. 192.
160 J. Gooch, 'The Use of History in the Development of Contemporary Doctrine', Conference paper at a conference sponsored by the director of development and doctrine at Larkhill, Larkhill, 1996; J. Baylis *et al.*, *Contemporary Strategy* (London: Croom Helm, 1987); Van Creveld, *The Transformation of War*; M.I. Handel, *Masters of War* (London: Frank Cass, 1992); J.A. Olsen and C.S. Gray (eds), *The Practice of Strategy* (Oxford: Oxford University Press, 2011); Gray, *War, Peace and International Relations*.
161 South African Army College, *Operational Concepts*, p. 7/2-1.
162 See, Lawrence, *Seven Pillars of Wisdom*.
163 Leonhard, *The Art of Maneuver*, p. 9.
164 Naveh, *Military Excellence*, p. 2.

Campaigns are fought at the operational level of war which links the strategic objectives to military actions at the tactical level. Paul Montanus links the study of manoeuvre warfare to the Saratoga campaign during the American War of Independence. The Saratoga campaign was analysed in terms of the manoeuvre concepts of movement, placement of forces and seeking of gaps in defensive lines.[165] Some further examples of historical case studies which relates operations to manoeuvre warfare include Operation Desert Storm,[166] General Sherman's Atlanta campaign,[167] and General Lettow-Vorbeck's campaign in German East Africa.[168] This book follows a similar pattern in the study of the German South West African campaign.[169]

The study of manoeuvre warfare theory as a military theory and military strategy are fundamentally interlinked because they aim to explain the nature and application of military forces in war. The study of theory and strategy in history allows for the re-analysis of historical military campaigns which sheds new light on them. Ken Booth comments that there is much to be gained from strategic history.[170] In this vein the re-evaluation of the German South West African campaign within the framework of manoeuvre theory allows for the determination of the causes of victory and defeat.

The reasons behind the victory of the Union Defence Force are inextricably linked to the reasons for the German defeat in German South West Africa. The causes of victory and defeat are by their nature complex and are often oversimplified for varying reasons – often these stem from an inaccurately applied methodology. The German defeat is analysed by using the relevant parts of the theories expounded by E.A. Cohen and J' Gooch[171] as well as that put forward by M.I. Handel.[172] These authors explore the causes of defeat relative to organisational factors as well as tangible and intangible aspects which influence the outcome of battles and campaigns.

Gooch and Cohen have devised a methodology for analysing defeat which requires the determination of the cause of the military failure (in this case from the German perspective) followed by determining the critical lapses or tasks which were not completed and thus led to the defeat. The third step is to do a layered analysis which

165 P.D. Montanus, 'The Saratoga Campaign: Maneuver Warfare, the Continental Army, and the Birth of the American Way of War' (MMS thesis, United States Marine Command and Staff College, Quantico, 2001), p. iii.
166 Cedergren, 'Doctrine, Expertise and Arms', Chapter in, Hallenberg and Karlsson (eds), *The Iraq War*, p. 155.
167 M.L. Hoyt, *Maneuver Warfare and General W.T. Sherman's Atlanta Campaign* (Newport: Naval College, 1997).
168 Nesselhuf, 'General Paul'.
169 A. Garcia, 'A Manoeuvre Warfare Analysis of South Africa's 1914-1915 German South West African Campaign' *Scientia Militaria*. 45, 1, 2017.
170 Baylis *et al.*, *Contemporary Strategy*, p. 55.
171 E.A. Cohen and J. Gooch, *Military Misfortunes: The Anatomy of Failure in War* (New York: The Free Press, 1990).
172 M.I. Handel, *War Strategy and Intelligence* (London: Frank Cass, 1989).

includes investigating some of the organisational aspects which led to defeat.[173] Handel identifies a formula to determine military power. This he states as total military power is equal to quantity multiplied by materiel quality multiplied by non-materiel quality.[174] This equation is used in the analysis of the GSWA campaign when comparing the Union Defence Force and the German force.

The quantitative elements are the numbers of soldiers and military equipment. Materiel quality refers to whether the equipment used by a given military is of a good standard and non-materiel quality refers to the intangibles of military forces such as morale, motivation, level of training, doctrine, staff work and organisation.[175] This equation works well in the case of conventional warfare.

The discussion on the course of events of the campaign will show how the German South West African campaign provided a text-book case of manoeuvre warfare theory. The following sections describe the cause and course of operations and provides an analysis of the campaign.

173 Cohen and Gooch, *Military Misfortunes*, p. 46.
174 Handel, *War Strategy and Intelligence*, pp. 95, 96.
175 Ibid., p. 96.

3

The Battle of Sandfontein

Since the late 18th century, South Africa's value to Great Britain had been its strategic location at the southernmost tip of Africa. The geostrategic value of its sea ports was in that it allowed for British naval and commercial ships to rest, recuperate and re-supply en route to the East. The security of the Union's sea ports was considered fundamental to the British Naval strategy.[1] The GSWA campaign was the first involvement of the Union of South Africa in the First World War and was directly related to the control of British sea routes. British overseas colonies provided strategic depth to the Empire, which was brought forward through maritime power.

The German East Asiatic Squadron, commanded by Vice Admiral M. G. von Spee, had methodically disrupted the British naval trade and troop movements in the Indian Ocean in the early stages of the Great War.[2] In order to secure the supply of its own forces during the First World War, the British had to neutralise the German naval threat. The harbours in German South West Africa, namely Lüderitzbucht and Swakopmund, were possible refuelling and re-supply points for German naval shipping, and even more so for the raiders of Von Spee's East Asiatic Squadron.

The wireless stations in Lüderitzbucht, Windhoek and Swakopmund were also of strategic concern to the British Empire because they allowed for international communication (via a relay station in Togo) between German warships at sea and Berlin.[3] The control of the harbours and wireless stations in German South West

1   Department of Defence Archives (hereafter DOD Archives), Diverse (hereafter D), Box 8, 37, Report on the military situation in South Africa, 20 August 1910.
2   P.G. Halpern, 'The War at Sea', Chapter 8 in H. Strachan (ed.), *The Oxford Illustrated History of the First World War* (Oxford: Oxford University Press, 1998), p. 109.
3   G. L'ange, *Urgent Imperial Service* (Rivonia: Ashanti, 1991), p. 7; Anon., *Union of South Africa and the Great War, 1914-1918, Official History* (Pretoria: Government Printer, 1924), p. 10; H. Paterson, 'First Allied Victory: The South African Campaign in German South-West Africa, 1914–1915", *Military History Journal*, 13, 2, 2004, p. 1; Lentin, *Jan Smuts*, p. 31.

Africa became a matter or strategic importance, with Lewis Vernon Harcourt, the secretary for the colonies describing it as 'a great and urgent imperial service'.[4]

The strategic plan for the invasion of German South West Africa, prepared by Smuts included amphibious landings at Lüderitzbucht and Walvis Bay. One of the greatest military challenges for South Africa was that it did not have a staff system, which would ordinarily have planned for future conflicts.[5] Furthermore, the lack of a trained staff limited the organisational ability of the Union Defence Force while on campaign.[6] The proposed force at Walvis Bay was to advance via the shortest distance to Windhoek. The strategic plan as determined by Smuts was quashed by the British War Office which decided that the naval vessels could only transport troops as far as Lüderitzbucht. The invasion plan was thus changed and improvised to a less efficient one which Smuts was not entirely satisfied with.[7] The main form of direct military assistance provided by Britain in support of the campaign was the provision of naval transportation and an armoured car squadron.

In the end, the initial invasion comprised the amphibious landings of the South African forces at Lüderitzbucht and at Port Nolloth. The military force at Port Nolloth landed on 31 August 1914 and advanced across the Orange River into German South West Africa via Raman's Drift and Sandfontein.[8] The amphibious landing at Lüderitzbucht took place on 18 September 1914 and the port city was taken unopposed. Raman's Drift was occupied on 14 September 1914. The wireless station at Swakopmund was also destroyed on 14 September 1914 by naval shelling.[9]

The South African force grouping which took Raman's Drift continued its advance to Sandfontein where it was defeated by a German military force. This defeat coincided with the outbreak of the Afrikaner Rebellion in the Union. In an attempt to erase the defeat from history, the first commissioned draft of the historical record of the campaign, suggested that the history of operations in German South West Africa should be recorded from January 1915. However this was not to be the case, and the section intimating this suggestion on the original historical record's proof is crossed out with an ink marking.[10]

4   J.J. Collyer, *The Campaign in German South West Africa, 1914–1915* (Pretoria: Government Printer, 1937), p. 6.

5   Collyer, *The Campaign in German South West Africa, 1914–1915*, p. 6.

6   South African National Archives (hereafter SANA), Smuts Papers, Box 112, Major General Thompson: Report on a visit to German South West Africa, 20-27 March 1915.

7   I. Van der Waag, 'The Battle of Sandfontein, 26 September 1914: South African Military Reform and the German South-West Africa Campaign, 1914–1915', *First World War Studies*, 4, 2 (2013), p. 7.

8   DOD Archives, SD, Box 252, 17138, Reports of Force Commanders in German South West Africa, Operations in and around Sandfontein 25, 26 and 27 September 1914, 19 August 1915.

9   Nasson, *Springboks on the Somme*, p. 67.

10   DOD Archives, SD, Box 252, 17138, Historical Record of the Campaign in German South West Africa, 4 November 1919.

Hugh Wyndam who produced the first draft of the Official History of the campaign, echoed white society's fears that the deployment of the Union Defence Force, may have resulted in Black uprisings, without sufficient manpower at home to suppress such revolt.[11] The creation of a defence force was intimately related to the fear of Black aggression[12] However, Botha was certain that the Union could not be neutral while the British Empire was at war.[13] The state of the Union Defence Force was a complicated matter with much resistance to formal training camps, which manifested in 1914, when many Active Citizen Force members across the 15 military districts did not show up for their training camps.[14] The only uprising was in fact to be the 1914 Afrikaner Rebellion, an event complicated by divided political loyalties, economic considerations and a new military system - this will be discussed in further detail in chapters 4 and 5.

All further invasion efforts were consequently put on hold until the suppression of the rebellion was completed in late 1914,[15] although the force grouping at Lüderitzbucht remained in position until the invasion was resumed. The destruction of the German East Asiatic Squadron at the Battle of the Falkland Islands on 8 December 1914, gave the British unprecedented superiority at sea in the South Atlantic. This in turn allowed for freedom of movement and thus the amphibious invasion of German South West Africa.[16] The Union thus reverted to its initial strategic plan which included a deployment at Walvis Bay.

The second amphibious landing was executed and Walvis Bay was taken unopposed on 25 December 1914. Once the Union Defence Force was deployed, the physical geography of German South West Africa proved a great obstacle to the campaign by hampering the logistical supply of the troops. There were also two South African force groupings deployed from across the Union and German South West African border in March 1915. At the time, German South West Africa had no formal roads and was bordered in the south and the southeast by the Great Namaqualand and Kalahari Desert respectively. The terrain in German South West Africa was largely favourable for defence due to its extensive plateau which starts at sea level and rises to 1,060 metres in the interior. The desolate area receives little rainfall and is isolated by

11   I. Van Der Waag, *A Military History of Modern South* Africa (Johannesburg: Jonathan Ball Publishers, 2015), p. 93.
12   Correspondence between Smuts and Merriman, W.K. Hancock and J. van der Poel (eds), *Selections from the Smuts Papers, Volume III* (London: Cambridge University Press, 1966), p. 47.
13   Botha to Smuts, Hancock and Van der Poel (eds), *Selections from the Smuts Papers*, p. 282.
14   DOD Archives, South African Citizen Force (hereafter SACF), Box 59, Correspondence regarding the Units whose members did not attend the required training, 1914.
15   Van der Waag, 'The Battle of Sandfontein, 26 September 1914', p. 2.
16   B. Nasson, *Springboks on the Somme* (Johannesburg: Penguin, 2007), pp. 1-3; H.F. Trew, *Botha Treks* (London: Blackie & Son, 1936), p. 63

a desert belt on the western coast, of between 60 and 160 kilometres wide, which rises to the height of the plateau.[17]

The Namib Desert had two railway lines within the colony. These lines provided mobility from the coastal towns of Lüderitzbucht and Swakopmund to the interior. The line linked up with the north (Windhoek/Karibib) – south (Kalkfontein) railway line in the interior of German South West Africa.[18]

The Germans had the advantage of operating on interior lines which enabled them to concentrate superior numbers within most of the colony during the advance of the South African forces.[19] Despite having superior numbers, the Union Defence Force was unable to advance with its entire force at any one time, hence the Germans had the option of concentrating on the smaller South African advances on different lines of operations. Parts of the South African force were distributed on the lines of communication. The African experience in the Great War was one of supply and logistical challenges where the majority of forces experienced limited combat, often to the disappointment of the various regiments.[20]

Von Heydebreck, who was the commander of the German forces in German South West Africa, was a competent officer and he placed his forces strategically in and around Windhoek and Keetmanshoop. He held the central position and used his budding aviation corps to determine the location of the South African forces which assisted in the decision of where to launch his attacks.[21] The South African military planners had underestimated the competency of Von Heydebreck in their initial analysis of his command ability. Furthermore, the Defence Headquarters, believed Viktor Franke to be a strong and powerful commander, a prediction which also turned out to be incorrect.[22] Franke's addiction to opium and alcohol[23] had a negative effect on his bearing, and Botha noted on their first meeting that his hands shook terribly.[24]

17   DOD Archives, SD, Box 252, 17138, Historical Record of the Campaign in German South West Africa, 4 November 1919; Collyer, *The Campaign in German South West Africa, 1914–1915*, pp. 6, 7; Anon., *Official History*, p. 11; Van Der Waag, *A Military History*, p. 95; DOD Archives, SD, Box 252, 17138, Reports of Force Commanders in German South West Africa, Despatch number 4 by General Botha covering the period 15 May to 18 July 1915.

18   S.C. Buxton, *General Botha* (London: Hazel, Watson & Viney, 1924), p. 94; DOD Archives, SD, Box 252, 17138, Historical Record of the Campaign in German South West Africa, 4 November 1919.

19   Anon., *Official History*, 12, 13; Trew, *Botha Treks*, 94.

20   DOD Archives, SD, Box 252, Correspondence between Military District Headquarters and Defence Headquarters regarding Mentions – German South West Africa, 1917.

21   Van der Waag, 'The Battle of Sandfontein, 26 September 1914', p. 4; DOD Archives, SD, Box 252, 17138, Historical Record of the Campaign in German South West Africa, 4 November 1919.

22   Van Der Waag, *A Military History*, p. 95.

23   Ibid., p. 95.

24   Botha to Smuts, Hancock and Van der Poel (eds), *Selections from the Smuts Papers*, p. 283.

Major General Thompson on his inspection of German South West Africa stated, 'water remains the chief anxiety',[25] a sentiment that was rephrased by Botha in stating that 'water remains our greatest enemy'.[26] The advance routes of the Union Defence Force were determined by the availability of water.[27] The Germans found an ally in the desert and they exacerbated the general shortage of water supplies by poisoning the water wells with carbolic acid and sheep dip or tossing decomposing animals into the water.[28] The British and German general staffs considered that crossing the Namib Desert was impossible.[29] Botha understood the implications of crossing a desert with an Army and described German South West Africa as a natural fortress,[30] where certain terrain forms were ideally suited for ambushes and hit and run tactics.[31]

The Battle of Sandfontein

The initial invasion of German South West Africa was made up of three force groupings A, B and C Force. Lukin landed in Port Nolloth with the advanced party of A Force on 31 August 1914 and the remaining forces disembarked on 16 and 17 September 1914. The forces which embarked from Cape Town included the headquarters, the 10th Infantry (Witwatersrand Rifles), the Transvaal Horse Artillery (South African Mounted Riflemen), the 4th Permanent Battery (South African Mounted Riflemen), 1st, 4th and 5th Regiments South African Mounted Riflemen; and support sections, Ammunition Column, Signal Section (South African Mounted Riflemen), section of South African Engineer Corps, Water Boring section South African Engineer Corps as well as sections of the Railway Regiment, Post Corps and Ordinance respectively. These forces were transported on the S.S. Galway Castle, S.S. Monarch, S.S. City of Athens and the S.S. Colonial. From Durban the S.S. Commonwealth (troopship) and S.S. Logician (animal transport) transported the 2nd and 3rd Regiments of the South African Mounted Riflemen and the 2nd Permanent Battery (South African Mounted Riflemen).[32]

25   SANA, Smuts Papers, Box 112, Major General Thompson: Report on a visit to German South West Africa, 20-27 March 1915.
26   Botha to Smuts, Hancock and Van der Poel (eds), *Selections from the Smuts Papers*, p. 255.
27   For a complete analysis of water in the German South West African campaign, see, E. Kleynhans, "A Critical Analysis of the Impact of Water on the South African Campaign in German South West Africa, 1914 1915", *Historia*, 61, 2, 2016.
28   W. Whittal, *With Botha and Smuts in Africa* (Cassel, London, 1917), p. 137.
29   Trew, *Botha Treks*, p. 124.
30   Botha to Smuts, Hancock and Van der Poel (eds), *Selections from the Smuts Papers*, p. 255.
31   DOD Archives, SD, Box 252, Despatch number 4 by General Botha covering the period 15 May to 18 July 1915.
32   DOD Archives, SD, Box 252, 17138, Reports of Force Commanders in German South West Africa, 'A' Force operations during the initial stages of the German South West African campaign, 19 August 1915; Paterson, 'First Allied Victory', p. 1.

Lukin's advance with A Force, the first of the Force groupings, was hindered by B Force commander, Commandant Manie Maritz, who had defected in mid-1914 and from that time onwards was in collusion with the Germans.[33] The Germans were aware of the internal tensions in South Africa.[34] Walker discusses the extent of German influence in the Afrikaner Rebellion stating that the Kaiser had met with Beyers (commandant general of the Citizen Force) as early as 1913.[35] The Germans assisted in fomenting rebellion in South Africa with the express intention of delaying the invasion.[36] The tensions within South Africa were already running high at the outbreak of the First World War and the Germans supported Maritz and Beyers to promote rebellion. The *Cape Argus* reported on 3 February 1915 that 'the Rebellion, which the Germans engineered with such characteristic cunning and duplicity, was a scheme upon which they undoubtedly set great score'.[37] The invasion of German South West Africa coincided with the outbreak of the 1914 Afrikaner Rebellion and the Battle of Sandfontein.

The initial cross-country invasion was planned for Lukin's A Force and Maritz's B Force, where Maritz was supposed to have supported Lukin's invasion through Raman's Drift and Sandfontein. Collyer takes the view that even if everything had gone according to plan and with proper coordination, the advance would have been risky but that an advance of either force in isolation was akin to failure.[38] Botha's testimony in the Rebellion Enquiry claims that the government understood that Maritz would not have been able to support Lukin. This knowledge was not based on the political inclination of Maritz but rather on the time which would have been required to mobilise and the distance which was to be covered in order to arrive in the area of operations in time.[39] Botha's claim leaves many further questions regarding the first battle of the campaign and the lack of support for Lukin's advance. This theme requires further research.

33   Nasson, *Springboks on the Somme*, 43–44; R.C. Warwick, "The Battle of Sandfontein: The Role and Legacy of Major General Sir Henry Timson Lukin", *Scientia Militaria, South African Journal of Military Studies*, 34, 2, 2006, p. 74. See, DOD Archives, DG 1, Box 2, Evidence given in the Rebellion Commission of Enquiry.

34   DOD Archives, Diverse (hereafter D), Box 8, 37, Instructions from Headquarters, 20 Aug 1910.; Anon., *Official History*, p. 9.

35   DOD Archives, DG 1, Box 2, Rebellion Commission of Enquiry   Volume   1, Testimony by   Colonel Barend Daniel Bouwer, 117-119, 2 March 1916; H.F.B. Walker, *A Doctor's Diary in   Damaraland* (London: Edward Arnold, 1917), p. 158.

36   Collyer, *The Campaign in German South West Africa, 1914–1915*, p. 5; B. Farwell, *The Great War in Africa 1914–1918* (New York: Norton, 1986), p. 75.

37   R. Segal and R. First (eds), *South West Africa, Travesty of Trust: The Expert Papers and Findings of the International Conference on South West Africa* (London: Andre Deutsch, 1967), p. 8.

38   Collyer, *The Campaign in German South West Africa, 1914–1915*, p. 29.

39   DOD Archives, DG 1, Box 2, Rebellion Commission of Enquiry Volume 1, Testimony by General Louis Botha, June 1916.

Lukin was an experienced soldier and officer and led five South African Mounted Regiments, comprised of 1,800 riflemen with artillery support, from Port Nolloth northwards to the Orange River. There was railway transport available from Port Nolloth to Steinkopf, but from there onwards the only means of transportation and logistical supply were donkey and mule drawn wagons. The distance from Steinkopf to the Orange River was approximately 97 kilometres and had no natural water supply.[40] The Germans knew that the South Africans had to advance along predetermined routes in accordance with the availability of water.[41]

During Lukin's advance on Raman's Drift from Steinkopf in the south, there was a German force advancing simultaneously on Raman's Drift from the north. Lukin wanted to occupy the water sources before the arrival of the Germans,[42] and thus planned his advance through Raman's Drift, Warmbad, Kalkfontein and Seeheim.[43] The Germans had a blockhouse with negligible personnel at Raman's Drift which was easily taken by the 4th South African Mounted Regiment on 14 September 1914. Map 3.1 shows the advance route of the South African forces and the Battle of Sandfontein.

Lukin's cross border advance took place simultaneously with operations which stemmed from the amphibious landing at Lüderitzbucht. C Force harboured at Lüderitzbucht on 18 September shortly after the taking of Raman's Drift by Lukin's advance force. Lukin had sent up an advance detachment comprised of approximately 200 soldiers of the 4th and 5th Regiments of the South African Mounted Rifles which had advanced via Raman's Drift and then subsequently arrived at Sandfontein on 19 September 1914. Captain E Welby was sent up to Sandfontein with a squadron from Raman's Drift in support of the 4th and 5th Regiments of the South African Mounted Rifles.[44] Lukin's main force arrived at Raman's Drift on 24 September 1914. Colonel C.A.L. Berrange was part of A Force (Lukin's Force) and was sent to Houm's Drift to the east so as to cover the Union's advance on a wide front. [45]

C Force, landed on the night of 18 September 1914 and found Lüderitzbucht abandoned by the Germans. Beves's force took the German post at Grasplatz on 26 September, discovering that the German force had withdrawn destroying the railway

40   L'ange, *Urgent Imperial Service,* 19; DOD Archives, SD, Box 252, Report by Lukin on 'A' Force operations during the initial stages of the German South West African campaign, 19 August 1915.

41   DOD Archives, SD, Box 252, Report by Lukin on 'A' Force operations during the initial stages of the German South West African campaign, 19 August 1915.; Collyer, *The Campaign in German South West Africa, 1914–1915,* p. 23.

42   DOD Archives, SD, Box 252, Report by Lukin on 'A' Force operations during the initial stages of the German South West African campaign, 19 August 1915; L'ange, *Urgent Imperial Service,* p. 21.

43   Collyer, *The Campaign in German South West Africa, 1914–1915,* p. 31.

44   Van der Waag, 'The Battle of Sandfontein, 26 September 1914', p. 9.

45   DOD Archives, Adjutant General 1914 (hereafter AG 14), Box 13, 7, Report on the Battle of Sandfontein 26 September 1914.

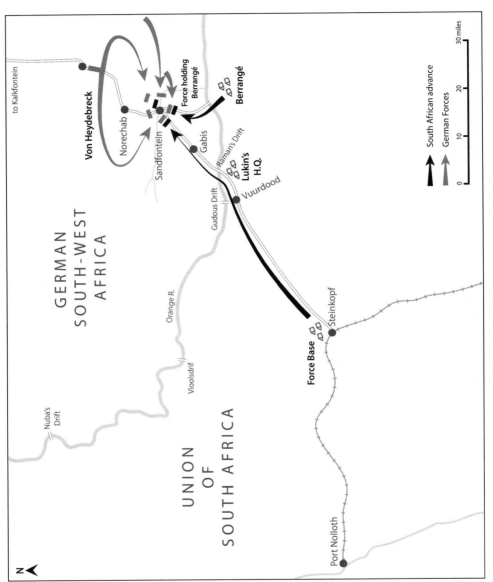

Map 3.1: The Battle of Sandfontein

to hamper Union mobility. The German retreat towards Aus was combined with an offensive on Sandfontein. The German force at Sandfontein withdrew around 23 or 24 September.[46] With hindsight, it becomes apparent, that where Von Heydebreck, aimed to hamper the mobility of 'C' Force in advancing across the Namib Desert, the retreat of the German detachment from Sandfontein was a feint, from which a strengthened German force would attack the advancing South Africans.

Defence headquarters wanted Lukin to move north of the Orange River to deter a possible German attack on the South African forces which landed at Lüderitzbucht, but Lukin was reluctant to send his forces north of the Orange River without the necessary logistical support. Defence headquarters ordered supplies up to Sandfontein to facilitate the advance on Warmbad.[47] This was in line with defence headquarters plan to take pressure off the force that had landed at Lüderitzbucht by requesting Lukin to advance from the south.[48]

Von Heydebreck had planned a daring attack on the advancing South Africans. He amassed his troops at Sandfontein on interior lines and intended to bring any South African invasion plans to a decisive halt.[49] Von Heydebreck had to consider the deployments of the Union Defence Force at Lüderitzbucht as well as those south of the Orange River.

The Germans decided to destroy the railway line running from Lüderitzbucht to the interior to delay the advance of the South Africans deployed at the port town. Von Heydebreck organised a large concentration of German resources for the Battle of Sandfontein, including those under Major D. von Rapport, Major H. Ritter and Major Viktor Franke,[50] who deployed with a column each on Sandfontein. Von Heydebreck commanded the German force personally.[51]

On 25 September 1914 at 17:00 the intelligence officer at Sandfontein reported that a German detachment had been seen in the vicinity of Aurus, as well as the movement of another German force in a southerly direction from Warmbad. On receiving the news, Lukin responded by sending Lieutenant Colonel R.C. Grant up to reinforce the detachment at Sandfontein under the command of Welby,[52] with one section of

46 DOD Archives, SD, Box 252, 17138, Reports of Force Commanders in German South West Africa, Operations in and around Sandfontein 25, 26 and 27 September 1914, 19 August 1915.
47 Collyer, *The Campaign in German South West Africa, 1914–1915*, p. 32.
48 DOD Archives, SD, Box 252, 17138, Reports of Force Commanders in German South West Africa, Telegraph from General Staff to General Lukin, 23 September 1914; Anon., *Official History*, p. 14; B. G. Simpkins, B.G., *Rand Light Infantry* (Cape Town: Howard Timmins, 1965), p. 17.
49 L'ange, *Urgent Imperial Service*, p. 26.
50 Franke later became a lieutenant colonel and commander of the German forces after the accidental death of Von Heydebreck on 2 November 1914. Von Heydebreck was accidentally struck by experimental ammunition during testing and subsequently died of his wounds.
51 Anon., *Official History*, p. 14.
52 Collyer, *The Campaign in German South West Africa, 1914–1915*, p. 78.

the Transvaal Horse Artillery, a machinegun section and one squadron of the 1st Regiment of the South African Mounted Rifles.[53]

In terms of the physical geography, the position at Sandfontein was untenable because it was encircled by high ground in the form of the surrounding hills.[54] The tactical disposition at Sandfontein was dire.[55] There were hills to the north, northeast and northwest that commanded the position; and the dry riverbed that ran from the southwest to the east gave the attacking force good cover.[56] The detachment of the Union Defence Force at Sandfontein was thus exposed and was positioned in low ground encircled by surrounding high ground which gave the enemy natural cover of advance, protection and various vantage points from which to deploy its forces.[57] Furthermore the force deployed there did not have a secure supply line and its rear was not protected.[58]

Grant arrived on the morning of 26 September 1914 and Von Heydebreck allowed his relief column to arrive at Sandfontein without opposition.[59] Von Heydebreck had good intelligence regarding the South African movements which included aerial reconnaissance and other sources, such as Maritz who was informing on the South African movements and plans. The German forces concentrated on Sandfontein with approximately 2,000 soldiers, four batteries of artillery and machine guns.[60] The Union's border area was also reconnoitred by German forces and were thus aware of water sources, or lack thereof on the desolate and arid axis of advance.[61]

As Grant arrived on the morning of 26 September, the Germans converged on Sandfontein with a large military force which had been massed in secret. The Germans attacked from the north, south, east and west,[62] commencing with an

53 DOD Archives, SD, Box 252, 17138, Reports of Force Commanders in German South West Africa, 'A' Force operations during the initial stages of the German South West African campaign, 19 August 1915.
54 DOD Archives, SD, Box 252, 17138, Reports of Force Commanders in German South West Africa, Operations in and around Sandfontein 25, 26 and 27 September 1914, 19 August 1915; DOD Archives, AG 14, Box 13, 7, Report on the Battle of Sandfontein 26 September 1914.
55 Van der Waag, 'The Battle of Sandfontein, 26 September 1914', p. 10.
56 Collyer, *The Campaign in German South West Africa, 1914–1915*, p. 38.
57 DOD Archives, AG 14, Box 13, 7, Report on the Battle of Sandfontein 26 September 1914.
58 L'ange, *Urgent Imperial Service*, p. 29.
59 E. Dane, *British Campaigns in Africa and the Pacific 1914-1918* (London: Hodder & Stoughton, 1919), p. 36.
60 Van der Waag, 'The Battle of Sandfontein, 26 September 1914', 10; DOD Archives, SD, Box 252, 17138 IO, General Botha's Despatch (GOC MC GSW Campaign) 9 July to 28 October 1920, Historical Record of the Campaign in German South West Africa, 4 November 1919.
61 DOD Archives, SD, Box 601, 95C, Reported fortifying of Kopje at Nakob by the Germans, 24 August 1914; DOD Archives, DG 1, Box 2, Rebellion Commission of Enquiry Volume 1, Testimony by Lieutenant Christiaan Rudolf Liebenberg, 207, 15 March 1916.
62 L'ange, *Urgent Imperial Service*, p. 28.

artillery bombardment which began shortly after Grants' arrival at 7:25.[63] Grant deployed his two artillery pieces at the base of the hill and the infantrymen made a line around the base of the high ground using rifle fire to keep the Germans at bay. The Germans bombarded the South African position, shelling the wagons, horses and mules as well as spraying shrapnel over the infantrymen.[64] Lieutenant F.B. Adler from the Transvaal Horse Artillery was in command of the guns and at 8:00 he was ordered to open fire on the German column advancing from the southwest.[65] Artillery fire was heard from Lukin's position in Raman's Drift at 8:00.[66]

The German force shelled the South African camp from all sides while the German infantry and machinegun sections had also encircled the Union's position.[67] The South African artillery scrambled and countered the German artillery attack from the northeast and then from the northwest.[68]

In response to the attack, Lukin sent a relief force from Raman's Drift and another from Houm's Drift. However, both columns were intercepted and pinned down by well-prepared German buffer forces. The Union relief force that advanced from Raman's Drift was anticipated by the Germans who promptly ambushed them, pinning them down with machinegun fire. The other Union relief force which advanced from Houm's Drift was met by infantrymen with machinegun support and was forced to withdraw.[69] The Union's artillery pieces at Sandfontein were destroyed by the German guns at approximately the same time that the relief force from Houm's Drift was checked by the Germans.[70]

Once the Union artillery was neutralised, the Germans intensified their bombardment of Sandfontein and after ten hours of fighting at 18:00, Grant raised the white flag.[71] He realised that no military objective could be reached by further resistance as their force was cut off and the relief forces had not managed to repel the Germans or provide them with reinforcements. Lukin was in agreement with Grant's decision to surrender after inspecting the battlefield on 27 September 1914.[72]

---

63 Farwell, *The Great War in Africa 1914–1918*, p. 78.
64 L'ange, *Urgent Imperial Service*, pp. 30-32.
65 N. Orpen, *The History of the Transvaal Horse Artillery 1904–1974* (Johannesburg: Alex White & Co., 1975), p. 17.
66 DOD Archives, SD, Box 252, 17138, Reports of Force Commanders in German South West Africa, Operations in and around Sandfontein 25, 26 and 27 September 1914, 19 August 1915.
67 Collyer, *The Campaign in German South West Africa, 1914–1915*, p. 41.
68 Orpen, *The History of the Transvaal Horse Artillery 1904–1974*, p. 17.
69 L'ange, *Urgent Imperial Service*, p. 33.
70 Collyer, *The Campaign in German South West Africa, 1914–1915*, p. 41.
71 Farwell, *The Great War in Africa 1914–1918*, 79; DOD Archives, SD, Box 252, 17138, Reports of Force Commanders in German South West Africa, Operations in and around Sandfontein 25, 26 and 27 September 1914, 19 August 1915
72 DOD Archives, SD, Box 252, 17138, Reports of Force Commanders in German South West Africa, Operations in and around Sandfontein 25, 26 and 27 September 1914, 19

During the battle the Union displayed reasonable strength at arms; they were severely outnumbered and outgunned but managed to hold out for over ten hours during an intense battle. The South African casualties were 18 killed, 42 wounded including Grant and 200 captured[73], while the German casualties numbered 23 killed, including the death of Von Rapport.[74] On the South African side, there was a large number of Black and Coloured casualties, including 6 dead, 3 injured and 19 captured.[75] This campaign history acknowledges the sacrifice of People of Colour, who were previously, to a large extent, invisible in the recording of the past. Black and Coloured casualties comprised 30 percent of the deaths, and approximately 10 percent of the captured and injured respectively. Their service and sacrifice must be given its due.

Many sources attribute the defeat at Sandfontein to the treachery of Maritz because he did not advance to support Lukin's cross-border operations.[76] Collyer assigns a great deal of blame to defence headquarters for ordering Lukin's force to advance despite the lack of resources to effectively invade South West Africa. He goes on to state that regardless of whether Maritz supported Lukin or not, the Germans could have amassed a larger force than the combined strength of Maritz and Lukin's forces.[77] In contrast, Warwick apportions most of the blame to Smuts for the undue haste of the Union's advance and for placing political objectives ahead of military considerations and realities.[78]

The secondary sources indicate that there was some negligence on the part of the reconnaissance parties and scouts who were sent out prior to the battle. They neither saw nor reported on any German troops in the vicinity of Sandfontein.[79] Another interesting point is that despite receiving intelligence on the movement of German troops to the south, defence headquarters did not inform Lukin of this in any great haste. The information was not telegraphed to Lukin – but was posted.[80] As for Smuts, he wanted to reaffirm the political decision to invade German South West Africa with military action on the ground.[81] I do not think that the intelligence which

August 1915; L'ange, *Urgent Imperial Service*, pp. 34–36.

73   DOD Archives, SD, Box 252, 17138, Report by Lukin, Annexture B: List of Killed, Wounded and Captured at and about Sandfontein, August 1915.

74   Anon., *Official History*, p. 15.

75   DOD Archives, SD, Box 252, 17138, Report by Lukin, Annexture B: List of Killed, Wounded and Captured at and about Sandfontein, August 1915.

76   Nasson, *Springboks on the Somme*, p. 67; Dane, *British Campaigns in Africa and the Pacific 1914-1918*, p. 35; J. Meintjes, *General Louis Botha* (London: Cassell & Co., 1970), p. 233; Paterson, 'First Allied Victory', p. 2.

77   Collyer, *The Campaign in German South West Africa, 1914–1915*, p. 47.

78   Warwick, 'The Role and Legacy of Major General Sir Henry Timson Lukin', p. 65.

79   Collyer, *The Campaign in German South West Africa, 1914-1915*, p. 36.

80   Farwell, *The Great War in Africa 1914-1918*, 80; L'ange, *Urgent Imperial Service*, pp. 21–23.

81   Warwick, 'The Role and Legacy of Major General Sir Henry Timson Lukin', p. 74. Van der Waag re-evaluates the loss at Sandfontein considering the complex study of military

Smuts received about German movements, to the south of the colony was new or novel enough to change the invasion plans of Lukin. Lukin was aware of the German threat, and there were reports of possible German incursions into the Union as early as 28 August 1914.[82] It would be difficult to attribute the entire defeat to a telegram confirming the presence of German forces in their own colony.

Analysis of the Battle of Sandfontein with reference to manoeuvre warfare theory

Analysing the South African approach: the Battle of Sandfontein demonstrates an example of static warfare which more closely resembles theory of attrition warfare. The column of the Union Defence Force advanced to Sandfontein, which was an untenable defensive position where they had to rely on firepower in response to the German attack. The South African force had not concentrated sufficient numbers, had insufficient resources to advance in such a way so as to constitute a threat and had failed in terms of intelligence gathering on the tactical and operational levels.

On the other hand, the Germans made excellent use of mobility by operating on internal lines of communication whereas the South Africans were using external lines of communication into largely unknown territories. Internal lines of operations theoretically allow a smaller force to concentrate rapidly on an objective,[83] however in the case of Sandfontein, the Germans were the larger force. The Germans mobilised approximately 2,000 soldiers from different parts of German South West Africa while the South African forces only numbered about 300.[84] Whereas the efficiency of internal lines of operations was demonstrated by the Germans at the Battle of Sandfontein; the Union Defence Force received their baptism of fire in terms of conventional operations. The German forces concentrated on Sandfontein with astonishing speed and surprise which overwhelmed the unsuspecting South African forces.

The speed of the German advance robbed the Union of its military initiative and they were forced onto the back foot in response to a completely dominant German attack. The operation was characterised by inefficient South African intelligence and

victories and defeats: Van der Waag, 'The Battle of Sandfontein, 26 September 1914'.

82   DOD Archives, SD, Box 252, 17138, Reports of Force Commanders in German South West Africa, Operations in and around Sandfontein 25, 26 and 27 September 1914, 19 August 1915.

83   B.T. Solberg, 'Maneuver Warfare: Consequences for Tactics and Organisation of the Norwegian Infantry' (MMAS thesis, United States Army Command and Staff College, Kansas, 2000), pp. 27, 28.

84   Van der Waag, 'The Battle of Sandfontein, 26 September 1914', p. 11.

predictable military advances.[85] Lukin justified his advance on Sandfontein by saying that he wanted to hold the only water supply in the area.[86]

Manoeuvre warfare theory is dependent on good intelligence and a rapid decision making cycle which is intended to gain and keep the initiative. At the Battle of Sandfontein it was the Germans who had good intelligence and a rapid decision making cycle. They demonstrated a well-planned attack and maintained the initiative by positioning blocking forces south of Sandfontein which stifled the Union's attempts to reinforce its pinned down detachments.

The Union's advance reached its culmination at Sandfontein. The advance of Lukin's entire force was extended from Sandfontein to Raman's Drift, Houm's Drift, Steinkopf and Port Nolloth.[87] It was advancing to no definable military operational objective while extending its logistical lines. As a result, Lukin was unable to effectively support the forces deployed at Sandfontein.[88]

At the tactical level the water supply was an objective, but it did not link up to an operational objective which would support the successful execution of the campaign. Tactical objectives should link up to an achievable operational objective. Furthermore, an advance on any given tactical and operational objective should have sufficient logistics to keep the troops supplied and mobile. In extending the advance beyond its capacity, the Union's force made itself susceptible to the rapid concentration of German forces. Prior to the battle, the Union forces were due for an operational pause in order to regroup, replenish and re-supply before deciding whether or not to advance on Sandfontein.

On the strategic level, the Union was required to advance into German South West Africa to show solidarity to the British war effort and the 'urgent imperial service'. On the operational level there was no conceptualisation of a definable decisive point or objective which theoretically should have led to the German centre of gravity. The operational advance was thus directed by a strategic consideration without realistic operational objectives and without sufficient logistical support.

The Union force at Sandfontein had reached its culmination point and was deployed in an untenable tactical position. Where manoeuvre warfare is intended to be offensive the Union's advance on Sandfontein was in stark contrast, as it offered no options for offensive action and required a defensive position to be taken – essentially it positioned a garrison in enemy territory. The Union force at Sandfontein was surrounded and cut off from its supply and communication lines and thus it was compelled to surrender.

85   Ibid., p. 8.
86   DOD Archives, SD, Box 252, 17138, Reports of Force Commanders in German South West Africa, Operations in and around Sandfontein 25, 26 and 27 September 1914, 19 August 1915.
87   Van der Waag, 'The Battle of Sandfontein, 26 September 1914', p. 10.
88   DOD Archives, SD, Box 252, 17138, Reports of Force Commanders in German South West Africa, Operations in and around Sandfontein 25, 26 and 27 September 1914, 19 August 1915.

4

The 1914 Afrikaner Rebellion

The loss at Sandfontein coincided with an explosion of internal tensions within the Union. The Afrikaner Rebellion grew from a combination of Boer republican ideology, economic disenfranchisement and personal interests against a conciliatory pro-British government. The rebellion was in many ways the manifestation of a clash of civilisations, between Briton and Boer, which arguably commenced in the early 1800s with significant flare ups during the Transvaal War of Independence, 1880-1881 and the Anglo-Boer War, 1899-1901.

The Afrikaner rebellion resulted in the delay of the invasion of German South West Africa as the Union Defence Force was diverted internally. Furthermore, there was collusion between the rebel leaders and the German South West African authorities. For this reason, the Rebellion is regarded as part of the German South West African campaign and this chapter addresses the political background and the causes of the rebellion which is linked to relative deprivation theory.

There has been considerable historical research conducted on the outbreak of the 1914 Afrikaner Rebellion. The causes for the uprising include political rivalries, the rise of Afrikaner nationalism and the advent of poor whitism. These elements are elaborated on in the course of this chapter. Furthermore, this chapter aims to add an analytical layer to this historical study by hypothesising that relative deprivation was a crucial factor in the motivation of the Afrikaner Rebellion.

This chapter examines three main challenges to Botha's concept of South Africanism, political, cultural and economic. These predisposing factors fostered the Afrikaner Rebellion of 1914. Political differences in terms of policy were epitomised by Botha's policy of conciliation which was opposed by Hertzog's two stream policy. Hertzog advocated separate 'streams' for English and Afrikaans speaking South Africans. While this was their key consideration at the time, the question of Black incorporation was beyond the norms of the day. Nonetheless there were the pioneering efforts of Dube, Plaatje, Ghandi and others to promote the rights of the marginalised.

The cultural challenges took form in the growth of Afrikaner nationalism which promoted the Afrikaans language and Afrikaner identity. Lastly, economic challenges in South African society included poor whitism, capitalism, black labour as well as urbanisation and the industrialisation of farming. These aspects were inextricably intertwined in the multi-faceted South African society of the day. This chapter discusses the various factors present in the Union which includes the political background, predisposing factors, political policy, Afrikaner nationalism, economics and class formation as well as the causes of the rebellion and links it to relative deprivation theory.

Political Background, Predisposing Factors and Relative Deprivation

Botha's political approach aimed to unite the white races in his attempts at a new South Africanism. He offered the idea of a united white nation which some believed to be good in principle but offered nothing concrete in practice except for the vague concept of a national unity.[1] Botha's policy has been termed 'frankly political' in that his efforts were mostly directed toward maintaining the votes of his constituency, which included war veterans in the Transvaal and rich farmers and landowners throughout South Africa. He was opposed by J.B.M. Hertzog whose political approach was regarded as 'racial', in that he viewed the South African political situation in terms of Afrikaner interests versus that of Empire. Hertzog, similarly to Botha, held power in his region through his power of influence which encompassed his supporters as well as those of M.T. Steyn, and General C.R. de Wet in the Orange Free State.[2]

In many ways the political differences between the two groupings echoed the sentiment of the 'bitter enders' of the Anglo-Boer War, where broadly speaking Botha and the Transvaal leaders were more inclined to pursue peace terms and a negotiated settlement earlier on, and where Steyn, De Wet and Hertzog represented the stoic fighters, struggling for complete independence. These differences, reflected the different societies of the Orange Free State and the Transvaal, where the prior had a largely homogenous Afrikaner population who were mostly dependent on farming; in contrast to the Transvaal which had English *uitlanders*[3] and Afrikaans communities, and a booming mining sector. The Black, Coloured and Indian populations were

---

1   D.W. Krüger, *The Age of the Generals* (Johannesburg: Dagbreek Book Store, 1958), pp. 66, 67. Botha's South Africanism is not to be confused with the pos-1994 New South Africa. The theme of Botha's attempts at reconciling the white races is further discussed in B. Williams, *Botha, Smuts and South Africa* (London: Hodder & Stoughton, 1946); D.H. Houghton, *The South African Economy* (Oxford: Oxford University Press, 1964); H.B. Giliomee, *The Afrikaners, A Biography of a People* (London: Hurst & Co, 2003); T.R.H. Davenport and C.C. Saunders, *South Africa, A Modern History* (New York: St. Martin's Press, 2000); M. Wilson and L.M. Thompson, *The Oxford History of South Africa* (Oxford: Oxford University Press, 1969); L.M. Thompson, *A History of South Africa* (New Haven: Yale University Press, 1990); S. Jones and A.L. Müller, *South African Economy, 1910 – 1990* (New York: St. Martin's Press, 1992); R. Ross, A.K. Mager and B. Nasson (eds), *The Cambridge History of South Africa, Volume 2 1885 – 1994* (Cambridge: Cambridge University Press, 2012).
2   O. Pirow, *James Barry Munnik Hertzog* (Cape Town: Howard Timmins, 1958), p. 59.
3   British settlers.

exploited and viewed paternalistically at this point, where they were awarded little to no rights.

The political dimensions and approaches coincided with the economic and social changes in South Africa during the period 1910 to 1914. This period was characterised by the growing poor white class, dependency on black labour, drought, increased capitalisation and industrialisation of farming[4], urbanisation and the rise of Afrikaner nationalism.[5] These predisposing factors were catalysed by the Union's entry into the First World War by virtue of being a dominion of the British Empire. In this analysis, predisposing factors are described as an essential ingredient but insufficient in itself to create rebellion.[6] The imperial service which manifested in the German South West African campaign, brought political rivalries to a head and ultimately resulted in the outbreak of the Afrikaner Rebellion in 1914. In order to explain the links between, relative deprivation and the Afrikaner Rebellion, I give an overview of the theory below.

Relative Deprivation is defined as 'a perceived discrepancy between men's value expectations (the conditions or goods which people believe that they are entitled to) and their value capabilities (goods and condition they think they are capable of attaining or maintaining given the social means available to them)'.[7] S.A. Stouffer proposed the theory of relative deprivation as a psychological concept to understand why people feel deprived, frustrated and even disgruntled in his 1946 analysis of Army affiliation based on Second World War case studies.[8] T.R. Gurr later built upon this theory by proposing that the frustration induced by relative deprivation leads to aggression which in turn results in political violence. The frustration aggression theory suggests that where discontent and frustration are politicised they manifest in political violence.[9]

Relative deprivation theory is proposed as a causative explanation for the Afrikaner Rebellion of 1914 by analysing the specific societal, economic and political variables and how these factors contributed to the outbreak of politically motivated civil violence. In the 40th anniversary edition of the book *Why Men Rebel*, Gurr mentions that

4   S. Swart, 'The "Five Shilling Rebellion", Rural White Male Anxiety and the 1914 Boer Rebellion', *South African Historical Journal*, 56, 1, 2006, pp. 94-96.
5   Department of Defence Archives (hereafter DOD Archives), Diverse Group 1 (hereafter DG 1), Box 2, Rebellion Commission of Enquiry Volume 1, Testimony by Deneys Reitz. 28 Feb 1916; H. Giliomee, 'Afrikaner Nationalism, 1902-1948', Chapter in Pretorius, *A History of South Africa* (Pretoria, Protea, 2014), p. 281.
6   S.G. McNall and M. Huggins, 'Guerilla Warfare, Predisposing and Precipitating Factors', Chapter in S.C. Sarkesian (ed.), *Revolutionary Guerilla Warfare* (Chicago: Precedent, 1975), p. 251.
7   T.R. Gurr, *Why Men Rebel* (Princeton: Princeton University Press, 1970), p. 13.
8   I. Walker and H.J. Smith, *Relative Deprivation, Specification, Development and Integration* (Cambridge: Cambridge University Press, 2004), 1; T. M. Pettigrew, 'Samuel Stouffer and Relative Deprivation', *Social Psychology Quarterly*, 78, 1, 2015, p. 11.
9   Gurr, *Why Men Rebel*, pp. 12, 13.

several writers have applied and modified his relative deprivation model to historical case studies including the Hungarian revolution of 1957 and the Tiananmen Square uprising of 1989.[10] In this spirit this chapter applies the theory of relative deprivation and frustration aggression to the case of the Afrikaner Rebellion, and uses it as a lens for the societal analysis[11] of the Union in 1914.

Political Policy

Botha's political approach and policy on reconciliation was based on the white demographic realities of the Union in the post Anglo-Boer War environment. The Orange Free State was mostly comprised of Afrikaner voters. In contrast, the Transvaal voting demographic was comprised of half English and half Afrikaans-speaking South Africans, which motivated Botha and Smuts' calls for reconciliation between the two white races.[12] Blacks, Coloureds and Indians found themselves marginalised after serving on both sides, Boer and British. Their fight however held no political capital. Where Britain had originally added concessions for People of Colour, in the initial peace terms at Middelburg in 1901, they were removed from the final Peace Treaty in Vereeniging in 1902. This point was diverted and the peace agreement stated, 'the question of granting the franchise to Natives will not be decided until after the introduction of self-government.[13] Upon the granting of self-government no franchise was granted, but instead stronger laws of oppression were passed which curtailed the political, economic and social freedoms of People of Colour.

During the first decade of the 20th century, Botha, Smuts and Hertzog came forward as the leaders of the Afrikaner people. The *Het Volk* formed by Botha and Smuts was virtually unopposed in 1910 and 1911.[14] Botha sought to placate the provinces and the different factions by incorporating a representative element from the various white groupings in parliament. The Union cabinet had an eclectic feel and indulged conservatives, liberals, republicans, imperialists and anti-British elements alike. The South African Party epitomised the compromise embedded in the Union's Constitution[15] and focussed on the reconciliation of the two white races under the British Empire in the interests of economic progress.[16]

10   T.R. Gurr, *Why Men Rebel 40th Anniversary Edition* (New York: Routledge, 2016), p. x.
11   For further discussion on South African society at the time of the rebellion, see, A. Grundlingh and S. Swart, *Radelose Rebellie, Dinamika van die 1914 – 1915 Afrikanerrebellie* (Pretoria: Protea, 2009), p. 11.
12   G.D. Scholtz, *Die Rebellie 1914-1915* (Pretoria, Protea, 2013), p. 17; Giliomee, 'Afrikaner Nationalism', p. 282.
13   TNA, F.O. 93, 107/9, Peace Terms between the British Government and the Governments of the South African Republic (Transvaal) and the Republic of the Orange Free State, 1902.
14   B. Freund, 'South Africa, The Union Years, 1910-1948 – Political and Economic Foundations', Chapter in Ross, Mager and Nasson, *Cambridge History*, p. 214.
15   Krüger, *Generals*, pp. 66, 67.
16   Giliomee, 'Afrikaner Nationalism', p. 287.

Plate 4.1: Middelburg Peace Talks

Botha's South Africanism was then challenged by Hertzog who championed Afrikaner Nationalism.[17] The difference in political ideology led to a rise in frustrations between republican and pro-British elements. G.D. Scholtz is of the opinion that the unification of South Africa led to the collision of the populations of the Transvaal and Orange Free State.[18]

Many Afrikaners viewed Botha as increasingly 'British' as the Prime Minister walked the tightrope of Imperial and Afrikaner interests. Hertzog capitalised on Botha's apparent 'Englishness' in particular following the 1911 Imperial Conference where Botha made various concessions and agreements regarding contributions to the Royal Navy[19] and state-aided British immigration, which Hertzog declared as anti-South African.[20] Botha's pro Rhodes speech was also frowned upon by many Afrikaners still hurting in the aftermath of the Anglo-Boer War.[21] Rhodes, Smuts's former role model, one of the central architects of the Jameson Raid and the Anglo-Boer War, was disliked and even hated by large portions of South African society.[22]

17   D.E. Reitz, *Trekking On* (London, Travel Book Club, 1947), pp. 16, 17.
18   Scholtz, *Die Rebellie*, p. 22.
19   Ibid., p. 24.
20   Pirow, *Hertzog*, p. 55.
21   Krüger, *Generals*, p. 67.
22   University of Cape Town Libraries, Archives and Manuscripts (hereafter UCT), Duncan Papers, BC 294, A.32. 63 .2, Second Report from the Select Committee on British South

Botha in turn regarded Hertzog's politicking as underhanded and counterproductive in his attempts at unity.[23]

Hertzog had little regard for the interests of Empire and the South African English-speaking population. He voiced his opposition to Botha's attempts to unite white South African society in a speech which he delivered at De Wildt in December 1912.[24] Hertzog advocated a 'two-stream policy' where English and Afrikaans South Africans would coexist side by side in parallel but not in an amalgamated way.[25] There was no mention of other races in Hertzog or Botha's 'streams', generally People of Colour were believed to varying degrees to be subordinate races to be overseen by a patriarchal white government. Hertzog's motto was summarised as 'South Africa first',[26] and his speeches caused considerable damage to the image of the South African Party.[27] The wave of Afrikaner nationalism, was anti-imperialist and anti-British. Where Afrikaner nationalism had a direct relation to the formation of an Apartheid state, the roots of African nationalism can be traced to the early 20th century. The formation of a truly united South Africa would only take place 90 years later, and this would be a new republic, not without its problems.

Botha took exception to Hertzog's proclamations, as the tension between the two generals, which had been mounting since the formation of the Union, came to a head.[28] The party split which led to a reshuffle of cabinet and the exclusion of Hertzog. In November 1913 in Cape Town, the political divide was formally completed through a vote to separate the party at the Union Congress of the South African Party. The vote found in favour of Botha by 131 votes to 90. Hertzog and his supporters subsequently launched the National Party in January 1914.[29]

The new generation of Afrikaners who had never experienced the freedom of the Republics increasingly viewed national unity as counter to the promotion of the Afrikaans speaking population.[30] Hertzog's National Party which led the Afrikaner Nationalist movement opposed Botha's South African Party and threw off the political balance. The new social movement slowly tipped the scales in favour of nationalism unbalancing the existing political equilibrium. The central principles of the National Party were essentially exclusivist and contrasted with the South African Party's concept of white amalgamation. The National Party was said to represent the 'national conviction and aspirations of the South African people... under the guidance

Africa, 13 July 1897.

23   W.K. Hancock and J. van der Poel (eds), *Selections from the Smuts Papers, Volume III* (London: Cambridge University Press, 1966), p. 45.
24   Scholtz, *Die Rebellie*, p. 25; Pirow, *Hertzog*, p. 61.
25   Krüger, *Generals*, p. 67; Reitz, *Trekking On*, p. 10.
26   Scholtz, *Die Rebellie*, p. 24
27   Giliomee, 'Afrikaner Nationalism', p. 288.
28   Hancock and Van der Poel (eds), *Smuts Papers*, p. 152.
29   Pirow, *Hertzog*, pp. 61, 62.
30   Krüger, *Generals*, p. 73.

The 1914 Afrikaner Rebellion   75

of God... the interests of the Union and its inhabitants must be placed before those of any other country or people'.[31] Hertzog's policy of putting South Africa first was represented by the English newspapers as one of racialism when compared to Botha's political approach of conciliation.[32] The divide between Hertzog and Botha's policies is regarded as a predisposing cause of the Afrikaner Rebellion.[33]

Following Botha's failure to amalgamate the white races into a single political party,[34] the formation of the National Party provided a political platform for the promotion of republican ideals and values. However not all republicans believed that the constitutional method would be sufficient to satisfy their needs for independence.[35] Military means were available to both political parties whether as an official organ of state or in traditional commando form.

The formation of the Union of South Africa was accompanied by the creation of the Union Defence Force, which was an amalgamation of the various colonial armed forces. In order to prevent a possible coup, the Botha government decided to split the power of the Defence Force by appointing Brigadier General H.T. Lukin as Inspector General of the Permanent Force and Brigadier General C.F. Beyers as Commandant General of the Citizen Forces.[36] This division of command, gave English and Afrikaans South Africans an equal split of the power.

Nonetheless the Union Defence Force mirrored the fragmentation present in South African society, epitomised by the split and competition of the white races, and the invisible yet essential service of People of Colour. Despite the societal schisms, Botha stood firm in his policy of a united white South Africa. In doing so he offended some of his Afrikaans supporters, who held on to republican ideals. Furthermore, the praise and lauding of the Empire did not sit well with many of the more conservative Afrikaners. Hertzog did not perceive the loss of independence of the Republics as a *fait accompli* and it was for that reason that he focussed on the language question as a representation of the identity of Afrikanerdom.[37] In the Vereeniging Peace Treaty, it was agreed that Afrikaans would be taught at schools in the Transvaal and the

31   Pirow, *Hertzog*, p. 62.
32   Krüger, *Generals*, p. 68.
33   Anon., *The Times History of the War* (London: The Times, 1915), pp. 484, 485; K. Fedorowich, 'Sleeping with the Lion? The Loyal Afrikaner and the South African Rebellion of 1914-1915', *South African Historical Journal*, 49, 1, 2009, p. 74; DOD Archives, DG 1, Box 2, Rebellion Commission of Enquiry Volume 1, Testimony by Deneys Reitz, 28 Feb 1916;
34   I. Van Der Waag, *A Military History of Modern South Africa* (Johannesburg: Jonathan Ball Publishers, 2015), p. 91.
35   A. Seegers, *The Military in the Making of Modern South Africa* (London: Tauris, 1996), p. 26.
36   I. Van Der Waag, 'Smuts's Generals, Towards a First Portrait of the South African High Command, 1912–1948', *War in History*, 81, 1, 2011, pp. 39, 40.
37   Krüger, *Generals*, p. 66.

Orange Free State on the instruction and wish of the the parents of pupils attending such schools.[38]

Afrikaner Nationalism: Language and Culture

The political differences between Botha-Smuts and Hertzog played out in the aftermath of the Anglo-Boer War. The Anglo-Boer War conceived the ideology of Afrikaner nationalism[39] which was nascent in 1899 but which became a prominent issue in the years prior to the start of the First World War.[40] The National Party embodied the Afrikaner ideology which offered the average Afrikaner more than just a political party but a movement which supported their language and culture. As a result, Botha's supporters were conflicted between their love for him as a leader and the love of their culture.[41] D. Reitz states that most Afrikaner families were divided between their loyalties towards Botha and Hertzog.[42]

The growth of Afrikaner Nationalism took place in the era of Milnerism and post Anglo-Boer War reconstruction. Milner became the antithesis of Afrikaner identity between 1899 and 1905,[43] as he attempted to force the English language and British cultural traditions on the Afrikaner population.[44] Prior to self-governance, Milner decided that English was the only official language and this met a firm cultural rebuff in favour of Afrikaner needs. Non-state organisations were set up to promote Afrikaner interests, such as the *Christelik-Nasionale Oderwys* (Christian National Education) organisation which was established through Dutch sponsorship,[45] and the Afrikaans language became the main symbol of Afrikaner Nationalism.[46] Dr D.F. Malan, who was a firm proponent of Afrikaner language and culture stated that 'Afrikanerdom had to defend itself against Anglicisation through the realisation that Afrikaners had their own legacy based on their own nationality, language and culture'.[47] Afrikaners strongly felt that *Die Taal* as the Afrikaans language was known, should carry the same weight as English.[48] Afrikaans as a surrogate of Afrikaner Nationalism found

38   TNA, F.O. 93, 107/9, Peace Terms between the British Government and the Governments of the South African Republic (Transvaal) and the Republic of the Orange Free State, 1902.
39   SANA, Leyds Archives (757), 7-12, President Steyn to President Kruger, 19 November 1899; J.C.G. Kemp, *Die Pad van die Veroweraar* (Cape Town: Nasionale Pers, 1946), p. 9.
40   Giliomee, 'Afrikaner Nationalism', p. 282.
41   Krüger, *Generals*, p. 72.
42   Reitz, *Trekking On*, p. 10.
43   Giliomee, *The Afrikaners*, p. 277.
44   L.M. Thompson, *The Unification of South Africa 1902-1910* (London: Oxford University Press, 1960), p. 7.
45   Giliomee, 'Afrikaner Nationalism', p. 282; Thompson, *Unification*, p. 19.
46   Freund, 'The Union Years', p. 230.
47   Giliomee, 'Afrikaner Nationalism', p. 284.
48   Scholtz, *Die Rebellie*, p.18.

its voice in the post Union dispensation.[49] Ironically where Botha was associated with Britishness after the Anglo-Boer War, it was in fact Botha who played an important role in terms of securing and managing Dutch support for teaching Afrikaans at schools.

The government of the Union of South Africa held a delicate balance between the importance of the Afrikaans language in the cultural sphere and the interests of South African capitalism. The urbanisation of many poor whites and *bywoners*[50] saw an increase of poor whites in urban centres.[51]

Economics and Class Formation

The Anglo-Boer War affected the rich and the poor in different ways. The landowners generally constituted the 'Bitter-enders' (who refused to surrender) and the poor Afrikaners were generally associated with being 'Joiners' (who fought on the side of the British). Approximately 72% of the Joiners were landless.[52] Many of the poorer Afrikaners regarded the Anglo-Boer War as a fortunate occurrence from an economic point of view.[53] This point is one dimensional and does not address the social and emotional impact of the conflict. Poverty and the pre-disposition to rebel was a legacy linked to the grave economic situation in the decades following the Anglo-Boer War.[54] Patrick Duncan declared in his investigation of the Afrikaner Rebellion, that 'in the long drought many of these people had lost what little they had and rebellion does not seem such a serous thing to desperate men'.[55]

Poor Whites were undermined and disposed of in the face of rising capitalisation of farms.[56] In the post Anglo-Boer War environment the poor farmer was to a large extent reliant on the landowner as well as Black labour.[57] People of Colour who were disenfranchised before and after the Anglo-Boer War were attempting to improve their economic and political situation. The political dialogue was forced to consider the situation as Afrikaners attempted to reshape their cultural identity through nationalist means. White families did not want to engage in what was regarded as 'Black jobs' which added an element of social classism to the economy of status.

---

49   P. Bonner, 'South African Society and Culture, 1910-1948', Chapter in Ross, Mager and Nasson, *Cambridge History*, p. 272. The author goes on to say that many elite Afrikaners spoke English at home, thus the point of the universality of Afrikaans should not be oversimplified.

50   This term refers to poor and landless Afrikaners. *Bywoners* were often tenants on farms and worked for the farm owner.

51   Freund, 'The Union Years', p. 213.

52   Swart, 'A Boer and his Gun', p. 739.

53   Bottomley, 'The South African Rebellion', p. 5.

54   Van der Waag, 'The Battle of Sandfontein', p. 7.

55   Grundlingh and Swart, *Radelose*, p. 26.

56   Bottomley, 'The South African Rebellion', p. 8.

57   Swart, 'A Boer and his Gun', p. 741.

Economic investment in the post Anglo-Boer War environment had favoured the mining industry in contrast to the agricultural sector which by 1910 was severely underdeveloped.[58] As a result the urbanisation of Afrikaners in the post Anglo-Boer War era was described as 'traumatic' in that they were removed from their position of familiarity and placed in an environment which they believed was below their station in society.[59] Poor Whites moved to the urban centres. The urbanisation of the Afrikaner population increased from 2.6% in 1899 to 24% 1911.[60] The poverty and depression in parts of South Africa facilitated Afrikaner Nationalist sentiment which was in a large part directed against the English-speaking population who held the economic power seat.[61]

Despite the lack of formal development in the agricultural sector, the sharecropping economy became an evolving rural industry with capitalist tendencies and experienced growth in the northern Orange Free State and the southern Transvaal during the 1890s.[62] The rebellion was geographically centralised in these very regions as a result of the economic condition present in Afrikaner society at the time.[63] In the decade following the Anglo-Boer War sharecropping was the most prominent form of agricultural production. This form of production was not the result of forced labour but rather the consequence of the interrelation between the sharecropper's production and output and the landowners' profits.[64] The sharecroppers' profits were thus directly proportional to that of the landlords', however there was a definite uneven power divide, where the landlord would generally oppress the Black, Indian and Coloured farmers.[65]

Many *Heeren-boeren* or wealthy landlords had arisen in the post Anglo-Boer War environment. Hertzog was one of these *Heeren-boeren* who had made his fortune through an inheritance. Despite this he tried to distance himself from the capitalist sphere. He gave the title and lifestyle a wide birth and politicked that Botha was the 'prime minister of imperialism'.[66] Botha held the support of many wealthy South

58   Freund, 'The Union Years', p. 211.
59   Giliomee, *The Afrikaners*, p. 324.
60   Grundlingh and Swart, *Radelose*, p. 39.
61   Giliomee, 'Afrikaner Nationalism', p. 281.
62   T. Keegan, 'The Sharecropping Economy, African Class Formation and the 1913 Natives' Land Act in the Highveld Maize Belt', Chapter in S. Marks and R. Rathbone (eds), *Industrialisation and Social Change in South Africa, African Class Formation, Culture and Consciousness 1870-1930* (London: Longman Group, 1982), p. 196.
63   Grundlingh and Swart, *Radelose*, p. 33. The northern Orange Free State and parts of the Transvaal experienced the highest rates of *burghers* (citizens) who disobeyed the call up to commando service in early 1914. The commandos were called up to suppress the industrial strikes of 1914, R. Geyer, 'The Union Defence Force and the 1914 Strike, The Dynamics of the Shadow of the Burgher', *Historia*, 59, 2, 2014, p. 140.
64   Keegan, 'The Sharecropping Economy', p. 196.
65   See, University of Witwatersrand, Cullen Library, Historical Papers, AG 2738, Tenancy and Sharecropping Project.
66   Giliomee, *The Afrikaners*, p. 327.

Africans who wanted peace at any cost.[67] However, the needs of the landowners were completely divergent from that of the poor Whites. Poor Afrikaners known as *bywoners* lived on farms as tenants and provided labour in a demanding rural existence.[68] People of Colour were also part of the rural agricultural equation, where oppression through collective violence and low wages was common practice and continued in various forms until the formal establishment of Apartheid.[69]

In the post Anglo-Boer War environment a strong sense of racial competition sprung up from the poor white population class who increasingly felt threated by black labour.[70] Malan was of the opinion that the poor white issue was fundamentally influenced by the promotion of Black education and development which led to direct competition with Whites for certain jobs and positions.[71] This type of thinking was a precursor to Apartheid rule and legislation.

The 1913 Natives' Land Act was the government response to the poor White problem[72] and the first post Union legislation which promoted segregation.[73] The Act was also an attempt to stop African land tenancy and black economic competition. There remained mixed feelings regarding sharecropping depending on the farmer's capital gain. Regardless of opinion the Act forever changed the direction of agrarian class formation. It prohibited Black sharecroppers from receiving cash for crops and only allowed the sale of labour, thereby forcing the capitalisation of farms so as to ensure their productivity (particularly in the Orange Free State).[74] *Bywoners* were no better off and they found themselves in a precarious position similar to that which they had faced following the Anglo-Boer War.

Escalating inflation and land prices led many landowners to forbid *bywoner* occupation and grazing of their cattle.[75] Class differentiation was fundamentally influenced by land ownership towards the end of the nineteenth century. The commercialisation and capitalisation of farms compromised the earning potential of

67 Pirow, *Hertzog*, p. 59.
68 E.J. Bottomley, *Poor White* (Cape Town: Tafelberg, 2012), p. 33.
69 See, J. Higginson, Collective Violence and the Agrarian Origins of South African Apartheid, 1900-1948 (Campbridge: Cambridge University Press, 2015).
70 Bonner, 'South African Society', p. 273.
71 Giliomee, *The Afrikaners*, p. 328.
72 S. Swart, "Desperate Men' The 1914 Rebellion and the Politics of Poverty', *South African Historical Journal*, 42, 1, 2000, p. 162.
73 L. Changuion and B. Steenkamp, *Disputed Land, The Historical Development of the South African Land Issue, 1652-2011* (Pretoria: Protea Book House, 2012), p. 133.
74 Keegan, 'The Sharecropping Economy', pp. 202-204.
75 E. J. Bottomley, 'The South African Rebellion of 1914, The Influence of Industrialisation, Poverty and 'Poor-Whitism", *African Studies Seminar Paper*, University of Witwatersrand, June 1980, p. 9.

poor Whites[76] and resulted in the reduction of social status of *bywoners*,[77] forming a social class which circumscribed their economic means and abilities. Poor Whites were either *bywoners* which encompassed rural dwellers or displaced *bywoners* who left the rural areas for urbanised and industrial centres.[78]

The fiscal insecurity of many farms and the disenfranchisement of *bywoners* led to their eventual expulsion and the state was allocated a part of the blame for this. Between the years 1904 and 1911 there was an exodus of poor Whites from the Orange Free State to other towns such as Kenhardt and Wolmaranstad in the north of the Cape Province and the north west of the Transvaal respectively. Kenhardt saw a population increase of 78.29% and the towns of Wolmaranstad and Lichtenburg in the North West Transvaal experienced a 43.43% population growth.[79] Furthermore the total percentage of Afrikaans miners increased from 14.6% in 1905 to 37.4% in 1910.[80]. The Afrikaners in rural and urban areas were divided in loyalty to the Botha administration and supporters of the rebels.[81] The *bywoner* exodus to the Western Transvaal in turn led to the political militancy of part of the region[82] as the movement of *bywoners* resulted in the transfer of their feelings of dissatisfaction about the government's inability to address their concerns.

The *bywoner* class searched for opportunity and escape and found it in their traditional and historical community based leadership and poor Whites became emboldened by the rise of Afrikaner Nationalism.[83] The *bywoners* found solace and a means of redress in their commandants who in turn became rebel leaders. The rank and file rebels were generally regarded to be poor Whites and or *bywoners*,[84] who were usually youngsters who were heavily indebted and not too concerned with politics but rather with the possibility of economic gain.[85]

An alternative point of view suggests that poor Whites were not necessarily becoming poorer but rather that they were remaining the same while other groupings around them were becoming wealthier. The rise in poverty was thus rather an increase in relative poverty when considering the economic upsurge of the middle and upper

76   Grundlingh and Swart, *Radelose*, p. 37.
77   S. Swart, "A Boer and his Gun and his Wife are Three Things Always Together', Republican Masculinity and the 1914 Rebellion', *Journal of Southern African Studies*, 24, 4, 2008, p. 741.
78   Carnegie Commission, *The Poor White Problem in South Africa* (Stellenbosch, Pro Ecclesia, 1932), pp. v, vi.
79   Bottomley, 'The South African Rebellion', pp. 8, 9.
80   Seegers, *The Military*, p. 43.
81   DOD Archives, Adjutant General 1914–1921 (hereafter AG 1914–1921), Box 8, Rebellion, Report by post office official at Millvale, 25 Oct 1914; DOD Archives, AG 1914–1921, Box 8, Armoured Trains, Smuts telegraph to Colonel Alberts, 22 Nov 1914.
82   Giliomee, *The Afrikaners*, p. 378.
83   Swart, 'A Boer and his Gun', pp. 741,742.
84   Bottomley, 'The South African Rebellion', p. 3.
85   Swart, 'Desperate Men', p. 167.

echelons of society.[86] The percentage of poor whites in the Afrikaner community increased from 5.2% in 1908 to 14.3% in 1916[87] and the identity of the *bywoner* and their social status became a pivotal point as white society fissured.[88] Poverty thus became a source of political instability, in the form of militant white labour in towns and disgruntled *bywoners* in the countryside.[89] Most of the rank and file rebels were poor whites as 90 % of Beyers' commando was comprised of *bywoners*.[90]

The Causes of the 1914 Afrikaner Rebellion

The Union's entry into the First World War and the concomitant commitment to the invasion of German South West Africa was the catalyst for the Afrikaner Rebellion[91] as the central issue of contention between English and Afrikaans South Africans.[92] Botha called a meeting on 14 August 1914 to discuss the invasion plans with his senior military officers.[93] At this meeting Commandant J. Kemp and Beyers opposed the idea of invading German South West Africa.[94] The division in South African society echoed within the military. Reitz, who was a veteran of the South African War and an ardent supporter of Smuts, stated that the political situation resulted in half the population not being on speaking terms.[95]

Commandants S.G. Maritz, Beyers and Kemp went into rebellion and Maritz declared a rebel republic in early October 1914.[96] The rebel leaders were the catalyst to political violence, where their motivations were mostly political and personal. Reitz indicates that the political and military situation within South Africa allowed Afrikaners to pursue the idea of old republicanism.[97]

Maritz, had little regard for the legitimacy of the German South West African invasion but rather went into rebellion in the hopes of forming an Afrikaner republic.[98] He was in cahoots with the Germans and refused to support the Union's advance

86   J. Fourie, 'The South African Poor White Problem in the Early 20th Century, Lessons for Poverty Today', *Stellenbosch Economic Working Papers, 14/6*. 2007, p. 2.
87   Bottomley, *Poor White*, p. 14.
88   Swart, 'The Five Shilling Rebellion', p. 96.
89   Giliomee, *The Afrikaners*, p. 330.
90   Grundlingh and Swart, *Radelose*, p. 25.
91   Ibid., p. 15.
92   Van Der Waag, *A Military History*, p. 91.
93   DOD Archives, DG 1, Box 2, Rebellion Commission of Enquiry Volume 1, Testimony by General Louis Botha, 29 June 1916. DOD Archives, DG 1, Box 2, Rebellion Commission of Enquiry Volume 1, Testimony by General Coenraad Jacobus Brits, 15 Mar 1916.
94   DOD, DG 1, Box 2, Rebellion Commission of Enquiry Volume 1, Testimony by General Louis Botha, 29 June 1916.
95   Reitz, *Trekking On*, p. 48.
96   Van Der Waag, *A Military History*, pp. 98, 99.
97   DOD Archives, DG 1, Box 2, Rebellion Commission of Enquiry Volume 1, Testimony by Deneys Reitz, 28 Feb 1916.
98   Scholtz, *Die Rebellie*, p. 41; L'ange, *Urgent Imperial Service*, p. 52.

on Sandfontein in late September 1914, which had consequences on the battle.[99] De Wet, a hero from the Anglo-Boer War who until the end refused to lay down arms, became one of the prominent rebel leaders in the Orange Free State.[100] He had clear nationalist and republican motivations for going into rebellion.[101] Beyers and Kemp resigned their commissions on 15 September 1914 and led the rebellion in the Transvaal.[102]

Kemp was of the opinion that a republic could be established through military means. In order to bring the fight to the Botha government he trekked across the Kalahari to join forces with Maritz in German South West Africa.[103] Beyers was not as determined and for the most part he viewed the rebellion as a protest to the German South West African campaign.[104] He was often wavering and undecided in the political and military uprising.[105] The rebel leaders became the centre of gravity for the Botha government and all Union military operations were directed at their respective forces.

The German authorities in German South West Africa were aware of the tensions in South Africa.[106] On 14 August 1914 at the military meeting in Pretoria, Maritz, Beyers and Kemp held a private conference,[107] where Maritz showed them German government correspondence which promised military support in the event of a rebellion.[108] Seeing this as an opportunity they could exploit, the German authorities incited rebellion by meeting with prominent republican-inclined Afrikaner military leaders who were heading up the rebellion.[109]

The Germans assisted in fomenting rebellion in South Africa with the express intention of delaying the invasion of German South West Africa.[110] British Imperial Defence Schemes had long known about the German influence on fomenting political uprisings in South Africa well prior to the formation of Union.[111]

99   Nasson, *Springboks on the Somme*, pp. 43–44;
100   Reitz, *Trekking On*, p. 50.
101   Scholtz, *Die Rebellie*, p. 135.
102   Van der Waag, 'The Battle of Sandfontein, 26 September 1914', p. 9.
103   Kemp, *Die Pad*, pp. 296, 297.
104   Scholtz, *Die Rebellie*, p. 135.
105   Van Der Waag, *A Military History*, p.100.
106   Anon., *Official History*, p. 9.
107   DOD Archives, DG 1, Box 2, Rebellion Commission of Enquiry Volume 1, Testimony by General Coenraad Jacobus Brits, 15 Mar 1916.
108   Anon., *The Times*, p. 498.
109   J.J. Collyer, *The Campaign in German South West Africa, 1914–1915* (Pretoria: Government Printer, 1937), p. 5; B. Farwell, *The Great War in Africa 1914–1918* (New York: Norton, 1986), p. 75.
110   Collyer, *The Campaign*, p. 5; Farwell, *The Great War*, p. 75.
111   DOD Archives, D, Box 8, 37, Instructions from Headquarters, 20 Aug 1910.

In regards to the outbreak of the First World War, Afrikaner nationalists were pro-neutrality[112] however Botha strongly opposed this option arguing that the Union of South Africa was part of the British Empire.[113] When the Great War eventually broke out and the Union committed to British nationalist ends, Botha struggled to unite the proponents of British and Afrikaner nationalisms. The entry into the War led to a fierce upsurge in Afrikaner nationalism.[114]

The generational cycle of poverty and reliance on older leadership was reframed in the Union's political and economic situation in 1914. This previous point is related to the idea that relative deprivation and frustration can remain present in a community or society for an indefinite amount of time. When there is an unsatisfied need, it remains present until one can satisfy it. In the case where relative deprivation is experienced for an extended period of time, myths are often transferred by an older generation to successive generations.[115] Young Afrikaners became enthralled with romantic tales of heroics on commando on the African veld.

The senior rebel leaders lived and fought for the Republics of the Orange Free State and the Transvaal during the Anglo-Boer War. The average age of the Anglo-Boer War new generation leader was 37; where the older generation leaders averaged at 58 years.[116] In 1914 the average age of the four senior rebel leaders, Beyers, De Wet, JH (Koos) de la Rey and Kemp was 53.5. The average age of the second tier rebel leaders who were tried with Kemp was 38.5.[117] Furthermore, the average age of the rebels caught with Jopie Fourie was 30 of which the youngest rebel aged 16 and the oldest 60.[118] The commando leaders embodied pertinent societal issues where an older generation led the younger. The commando system was symbolic of the Afrikaner community of the time and encapsulated concepts of Afrikaner identity.[119] The eminent military historian Ian Van Der Waag states that 'in 1914, seizing the opportunity presented by the war in Europe, the traditional elite called upon the commandos to defend, through armed protest, the traditional social order and therefore their political and military influence.'[120]

112 Nasson, *World War 1*, p. 66.
113 Seegers, *The Military*, pp. 29, 30; Giliomee, *The Afrikaners*, p. 360; Krüger, *The Age of the Generals*, p. 83.
114 Van Der Waag, *A Military History*, p. 92.
115 Gurr, *Why Men Rebel*, p. 83.
116 I. Van Der Waag, 'Boer Generalship and the Politics of Command', *War in History*, 12, 15, 2005, pp. 24, 37.
117 Grundlingh and Swart, *Radelose*, 76. For the latest statistical analysis of the Afrikaner Rebellion see, I. Van Der Waag and D. Katz, South African Historical Association conference paper on the Afrikaner Rebellion, Stellenbosch 2015. Forthcoming publication.
118 DOD Archives, Adjutant General, Box 13, Rebellion, Rebelle saam met Jopie Fourie gevang te Nooitgedacht 16 Desember 1914. The calculation was done using 44 of the 46 names indicated (2 names had no ages stipulated).
119 Grundlingh and Swart, *Radelose*, p. 45.
120 Van Der Waag, 'Smuts's Generals', p. 44.

The Rebel leaders 'were patriarchal which was socially transferred from the domestic unit into society. The rebel leaders included the economic and class issues into their political grievances.'[121] The patriarch was regarded as the overarching authority in the commando tradition and older Afrikaner culture.[122] The commando structure influenced the rebellion in that the leaders within the commando system were not only military leaders but were also community leaders and decision makers.[123] The leaders were regarded as the centre of gravity of the rebellion. The rank and file were regarded as mere followers and it was taken that it was their responsibility to follow their leaders. Within Afrikaner custom, the veldcornet would command a ward, and a commandant would be in charge of a town. These positions thus held military and economic power, and the burghers in the respective wards were obliged to follow the orders of their commandants. This was the historical and cultural tradition, which Botha, Smuts, Hertzog, De Wet, De La Rey and Kemp amongst others came from and thus fundamentally understood. It was assumed that the commandants served the highest political office of the republic/colony and thus burghers were taken as loyalists to the system of land ownership and state.

The rebellion trials are indicative of the understanding of the Botha government regarding the importance of leaders in the rebellion as opposed to the rank and file. The trials focussed on the leadership, court-marshalling 12 Union Defence Force officers of which Jopie Fourie was one of a small number of rebels executed.[124] Of Maritz's rebels who were convicted of high treason 13 were officers (Citizen Force) and 21 were citizens as well as one permanent force storeman.[125] The rebel leaders were revered by Hertzog as patriots who all participated in the Anglo-Boer War.[126] All of the rebels were believed to be Nationalists.[127]

Hertzog as a prominent leader and head of the National Party did not actively rebel, but the rebel leaders fought for his ideals and aspirations. Hertzog's name was mentioned by the different rebel leaders in motivating their defection. The cause of the rebellion is credited in part to the rift between Hertzog and Botha.[128]

The rebel leaders did not necessarily find a suitable place within Botha's South Africanism,[129] which they regarded as an unsatisfactory form of self-government, which was promised in the Peace of Vereeniging.[130] There were approximately 11,400

---

121   Swart, 'The Five Shilling Rebellion', p. 98.
122   Grundlingh and Swart, *Radelose*, p. 46.
123   Swart, 'A Boer and his Gun', p. 739.
124   Seegers, *The Military*, pp. 29, 30.
125   DOD Archives, DG 1, Box 1, Disposal of Maritz Rebels, 28 Aug 1915. These numbers were calculated from the lists available in the archival group.
126   Grundlingh and Swart, *Radelose*, p. 76
127   Reitz, *Trekking On*, p. 40.
128   Anon., *The Times*, 484, 485; Fedorowich, 'Sleeping with the Lion', p. 74.
129   Grundlingh and Swart, *Radelose*, pp. 75, 76.
130   TNA, F.O. 93, 107/9, Peace Terms between the British Government and the Governments of the South African Republic (Transvaal) and the Republic of the Orange Free State, 1902.

rebels of which 281 were leaders. The motivations of rebel leaders and rank and file rebels were divergent. Where the leaders focussed on political power, the rebel rank and file were oriented to economic motivations.[131] Obstacles which are perceived to influence the attainment of economic goals directly results in the discontentment of the grouping in question.[132] The Botha government's inability to address the needs of the poor Whites can be regarded as a further cause of the rebellion.[133]

The poor whites searched for answers from the Botha government but soon became discontented at the perception that Black labour was receiving increased economic opportunities through sharecropping.[134] However the truth was that where there were limited cases of Black sharecroppers and farmers attaining wealth and success, generally People of Colour were oppressed and deprived of economic and human rights. The disenchantment of the poor Whites gave Afrikaner Nationalism a mythical heroic appearance in the post Anglo-Boer War and post Union environments.[135] The political and economic issues manifested themselves in the military expression of collective grievance.

The collective feelings of discontent which arose as a result of relative deprivation amongst the poor Afrikaners led to frustration and aggression and was politically mobilised resulting in political violence. The rebel leaders were affected by the collective discontent and also by personal frustrations and ambitions which was later regarded as the overarching motivations for the rebellion. The following section addresses the underpinnings of relative deprivation theory.

Relative Deprivation Theory

Relative deprivation theory stipulates 'the primary causal sequence in political violence is first the development of discontent, second the politicisation of that discontent, and finally its actualisation in the violent action against political objects and actors.'[136] It is a social psychological theory which integrates the individual level of analysis with that of the collective by proposing a hypothesis which explains the behaviour of the individual.[137] Relative deprivation theory refers to the conception of political violence and rebellion, however it does not address the dynamics of political violence.[138] Relative deprivation describes the figurative distance between a person's current status

131 Swart, 'Desperate Men', p. 161.
132 T. R. Gurr, 'Psychological Factors in Civil Violence', *World Politics*, 20, 2, 1968, p. 79.
133 Swart, 'Desperate Men', p. 169.
134 Swart, 'The Five Shilling Rebellion', p. 96.
135 Swart, 'A Boer and his Gun', p. 743.
136 Gurr, *Why Men Rebel*, p. 12.
137 Pettigrew, 'Samuel Stouffer', p. 12.
138 A. Morris and C. Herring, 'Theory and Research in Social Movements, A Critical Review', *University of Michigan Center for Research on Social Organisation Working Paper Series*, Number 307, 1984, pp. 7,8.

and that of their expectations. Discontent results from the perceived gap between the aspirations and reality of a given population group and another comparable group.[139]

The first condition of relative deprivation as a causative theory of rebellion is the discontent caused by the perceived unfair treatment of a given group.[140] The related psychological processes include cognitive comparisons and appraisals which leads the in-group to believe that they were unfairly treated and which results in feelings of anger and frustration.[141] This anger can be experienced by an individual or a grouping within a state. The responsibility for the frustration is often transferred to the state when the needs and expectations of certain groupings aren't met.[142]

Frustration-aggression theory is a prominent theory on human aggression.[143] Aggression occurs as a result of predisposing tension and frustration.[144] J. Dollard et al proposed the frustration-aggression hypothesis which claims that aggressive behaviour results from previous frustrations,[145] is adapted and combined within relative deprivation theory. The frustration-aggression concept was further developed by later academics such as N.E. Miller[146] and L. Berkowitz.[147]

Frustration and aggression occur as a response to deprivation and discontent. Discontent occurs as a result of the gap between the resources which a given group possesses compared to that which they believe they should possess. The aggrieved individual or group often join social movements as a result of their discontent. In the context of a nation state, the frustration of a given people or community is generally linked to a large and rapid organisational change such as industrialisation and urbanisation. These changes influence the psychological state and expectation of the aggrieved groups. Their frustration often finds an outlet through political violence.[148] The poor whites in rural conditions found it difficult to adapt to a modernising South Africa which had new demands.[149] Impoverished Blacks experienced greater deprivation but lacked the organisational platforms to launch their resistance, during

139 A. Saleh, 'Relative Deprivation Theory, Nationalism, Ethnicity and Identity Conflicts', *Geopolitics Quarterly*, 8, 4 2013, p. 167.
140 Gurr, *Why Men Rebel*, p. 13.
141 Pettigrew, 'Samuel Stouffer', p. 12.
142 Saleh, 'Identity Conflicts', p. 166.
143 Gurr, 'Psychological Factors', p. 77.
144 Draman, 'Poverty and Conflict', p. 9.
145 Gurr, *Why Men Rebel*, p. 33. See J. Dollard, N.E. Miller, W. Leonard et al., *Frustration and Agression* (New Haven: Yale University, 1939).
146 N.E. Miller, 'The frustration-aggression hypothesis', *Psychological Review*, 48, 4, 1941.
147 L. Berkowitz, 'Frustration-Agression, Examination and Reformulation', *Psychological Bulletin*, 106, 1, 1989.
148 Morris and Herring, 'Social Movements', 25, 26; Gurr, 'Psychological Factors', p. 86.
149 Carnegie, *The Poor*, pp. ix, x.

the earlier part of the 20th century.[150] The changes in the political and economic landscape of South Africa was reflected through changes in society.

Social change is described as 'a permanent and rapid transformation of a given social organisation and its internal dynamics'.[151] Theories regarding the formation and development of societies are inextricably linked to relative deprivation theory. Relative deprivation theory merges with mass society theory in that the distance between the haves and the have nots is separated through insufficient societal bridging structures. When the societal structures and systems no longer address the needs of the people, new social movements are created. This often occurs at times of great societal change.[152]

Relative deprivation and the creation of political violence represents a causal chain of events in which each step is reliant on the previous one. The act of political violence is dependent on frustration-aggression which is in turn rooted in the discontent created by relative deprivation.[153] The development and increase of relative deprivation becomes the catalyst for political violence.[154]

Individual relative deprivation explains the subjective experience of the person whereas group relative deprivation refers to the collective experience of the social group.[155] The terminology for individual and collective deprivation can be reframed as fraternal and egoistic. Fraternal deprivation being the deprivation of a group whether real or perceived, in comparison to another group and egoistic deprivation describing the relative deprivation experienced between individuals.[156]

Economic and material differences within a society results in class and cultural differences.[157] Karl Marx, the revolutionary socialist and philosopher, claims that rebellion and revolution is a natural response to class divide.[158] When rural communities experience rapid development, their traditional political and economic agencies get subsumed in the greater political state. As such they become part of a larger society, and rely on the agency of state and not their previous traditional systems to resolve their problems.[159] If the problems of a group are not resolved by the state government, they often resort to their traditional and culturally respected systems and leaders. This was the case with the commandos which personified the identity

---

150 See, C. Van Onselen, *The Seed is Mine: The Life of Kas Maine, a South African Sharecropper, 1894-1985* (New York: Hill and Wang, 1997).
151 R. De La Sablonniere and F. Tougas, 'Relative Deprivation and Social Identity in Times of Dramatic Social Change, The Case of Nurses', *Journal of Applied Social Psychology*, 38, 9 2008, pp. 2293.
152 Morris and Herring, 'Social Movements', pp. 23, 24.
153 Gurr, *Why Men Rebel*, p. 14.
154 Ibid., 15.
155 Gurr, 'Psychological Factors', p. 82; Pettigrew, 'Samuel Stouffer', p. 13.
156 Draman, 'Poverty and Conflict', p. 9.
157 R. Wilkinson and K. Pickett, *The Spirit Level, Why Equality is Better for Everyone* (London: Penguin, 2010), p. 28.
158 Morris and Herring, 'Social Movements', p. 3.
159 Gurr, *Why Men Rebel*, p. 180.

of Afrikaners and their culture. The contest of legitimacy is thus between traditional forms of authority and the political leadership, where government in power holds the power to resolve economic deprivation and to accept or deny different ideological systems.[160] The balance is between political legitimacy, and economic empowerment and how the constituents identify both socially and politically.

Societal insecurity is created when the identity of a group is compromised and is defined as when 'people within a certain geographically defined state assume that their identity is threatened'.[161] The concept of identity, whether national or ethnic, is malleable and is formed in the socio-political and economic cauldron of the respective nation states. The identity of a given people is thus important for their social cohesion and the security of the state.[162] The importance of identity in terms of state security was espoused in the seminal study of S. Huntington, *Clash of Civilisations*.[163] Kemp wrote that the Anglo-Boer War was a 'clash between two opposite types of civilisation the one modern and progressive... and the other backward and repressive'.[164] In some ways the Afrikaner Rebellion was a continuation of the clash of Briton and Boer civilisations.

The identity of a people is often framed in an ideology. Ideology is defined as 'a set of attitudes, values and beliefs about the way things are and the way things ought to be'.[165] In terms of ideology and relative deprivation Gurr references Johnson who claims 'given sufficient time... an ideology will cause the disequilibrated society to divide into one group of allies seeking to change the structure of the system and another seeking to maintain it'.[166] A new ideology often calls into question the validity of other ideologies.[167] Ideological conflicts challenges the central concept of the legitimacy of a state and includes class conflicts.[168]

The 1914 Rebellion, and Internal Armed Conflict with reference to Relative Deprivation Theory

The participation in political violence is usually related to the pursuit of political objectives.[169] Reitz described the Afrikaner Rebellion as a difference between political parties and states that 'every member of the South African Party stood by Botha, and

---

160 Ibid., p. 148.
161 Saleh, 'Identity Conflicts', p. 166.
162 Ibid., p. 166.
163 S.P. Huntington, 'The Clash of Civilisations?', *Foreign Affairs*, 72, 3, 1993.
164 Kemp, *Die Pad*, p. 9.
165 McNall and Huggins, 'Guerilla Warfare', p. 247.
166 Gurr, *Why Men Rebel*, p. 139.
167 McNall and Huggins, 'Guerilla Warfare', p. 247.
168 J. Angstrom, 'Towards a Typology of Internal Armed Conflict, Synthesising a Decade of Conceptual Turmoil', *Civil Wars*, 4,3, 2001, p. 106.
169 Gurr, *Why Men Rebel*, p. 4.

while not every Nationalist was a rebel, it is literally true that every rebel, without a single exception, was a Nationalist.'[170]

A critical point of discontentment and frustration was the perception that an Afrikaner led government would provide poor Whites with a considerable amount of support. When this did not happen, poor Whites soon became disillusioned with the Botha government.[171] The theory holds that people are more likely to rebel where they are perceived to no longer be able to achieve their ambitions and hopes.[172] Ethnicity often becomes the medium for mobilisation where frustration and aggression is directed against the state. The main cause that provokes the politicisation of ethnic identity is a situation in which a state does not respond to ethnic demands.[173]

Botha's South Africanism was perceived as a threat to the identity of deprived Afrikaners. The livelihood of many was threatened. The relative deprivation experienced was related to the difference in value attainment between the *bywoners* and the wealthier farmers as well as the black sharecroppers. Black sharecroppers provided the same labour as *bywoners* but with greater efficiency and they were thus perceived as a threat to *bywoner* identity. The poor Whites felt a growing resentment against Black sharecroppers as White society fissured along class, race and labour lines.[174]

Political identity is formed and employed to merge people. Identity is linked to a sense and belief in common identity within a geographical locale.[175] The capitalisation of farming challenged the identity of the *bywoner*. During the 18th and 19th centuries it was socially acceptable to be a *bywoner*,[176] but in the early twentieth century with the advent of the mineral revolution in South Africa, the term *bywoner* took on a negative association.[177] The challenge on the identity of *bywoners* compromised South African societal security. The rebels were partially intoxicated by republican ideological nostalgia and the hopes of having their identity re-established.[178]

Due to the societal norms of the day *Bywoners* believed that they were entitled to certain rights and positions and thus felt dissatisfied when Black labour occupied certain posts. The rebel leaders included the economic and class issues of the *bywoner* into their political grievances. The previous point links strongly to Gurr's revolutionary theory which claims that leaders are able to direct the discontent of their followers and shape their anger into violent response.[179] A precursor to the Afrikaner Rebellion took place in 1913, where a commando under General Beyers, a future rebel leader, was

170 Reitz, *Trekking On*, p. 40.
171 Swart, 'The Five Shilling Rebellion', p. 96.
172 Saleh, 'Identity Conflicts', pp. 157, 165.
173 Ibid., pp. 165, 169.
174 Swart, 'A Boer and his Gun', p. 741; Swart, 'The Five Shilling Rebellion', p. 96.
175 Saleh, 'Identity Conflicts', pp. 158.
176 Swart, 'A Boer and his Gun', p. 741.
177 Grundlingh and Swart, *Radelose*, p. 32.
178 Grundlingh and Swart, *Radelose*, p. 30.
179 Gurr, 'Psychological Factors', p. 79.

called out to suppress an industrial strike in Johannesburg. En route to the striking proletariat, Reitz describes the mutinous talks of the men who proposed attacking Botha's men instead of suppressing the strike. There were further reports that Beyers had proposed arresting Botha and Smuts.[180]

The rebel leadership encompassed military and social structures and was framed in the commando system[181] which symbolised Afrikaner identity.[182] The 1912 Defence Act threatened the traditional links between powerful farmers and their rural constituencies[183] by placing traditional systems under centralised leadership.

In South Africa as in other states, ideologies often have a cultural and historical context in terms of the acceptability of political violence.[184] In the Republics of the Transvaal and the Orange Free State, armed protest was a regular and significant political method which had been used to achieve limited ends. Annette Seegers states that 'armed protest was a legitimate republican device: it rattled legislators' nerves'.[185] One example such example involves General J.J. Wolmarans, who in 1912, joined a group of farmers who opposed black sharecropping, was later charged for evicting a black man from the train on which he was travelling. Wolmarans subsequently mobilised a commando of 300 men who protested his charge leading to the withdrawal of the case.[186]

The classification of the Afrikaner Rebellion in regards to internal armed conflict is nuanced. In terms of the typology of conflict there are various categories including leadership, resource and ideological conflicts.[187] The Afrikaner Rebellion had elements of all three typologies. Insurgency can be defined as a struggle between ruling and non-ruling entities which uses political resources and includes violence to achieve their ends.[188] A non-ruling and contesting group often resorts to violence when they experience political, social or economic oppression.[189] The conflict between rebels and the Union government in the Afrikaner Rebellion of 1914 can thus be classified as an insurgency. An insurgency is a crisis of political legitimacy.[190] Similar to concepts of civil war, a rebellion takes a lesser form in terms of magnitude.[191] In

---

180 Reitz, *Trekking On*, pp. 11-15.
181 Swart, 'A Boer and his Gun', p. 741.
182 Grundlingh and Swart, *Radelose*, p. 45.
183 Van Der Waag, 'Smuts's Generals', p. 43.
184 Gurr, *Why Men Rebel*, pp. 194, 195.
185 Seegers, *The Military*, p. 4.
186 Swart, 'The Five Shilling Rebellion', p. 97.
187 Angstrom, 'Towards a Typology', pp. 105-108.
188 O'Neill, Insurgency', p. 13.
189 B.E. O'Neill, *Insurgency and Terrorism, Inside Modern Revolutionary Warfare*, (New York: Brasseys, 1990), p. 17.
190 O'Neill, Insurgency', p. 17.
191 A. Du Plessis and M. Hough, 'Civil War in South Africa?, Conceptual Framework, Ramifications and Proneness', Chapter in D.M. Snow, *Uncivil Wars* (London: Lynne Rienner, 1996), p. 100.

terms of its characteristics, a rebellion involves a violent and rapid challenge of the governing authority.[192] On the Afrikaner Rebellion, the historian Swart states, 'the movement grew from that of armed protest to a republican revolution'.[193] In terms of the classification of insurgency, the Afrikaner Rebellion can be termed a traditional insurgency which seeks to replace the political authority in power with an ancestral and or primordial political and value system.[194] Swart supports the argument for this categorisation when she states 'nostalgic republicanism was used as a mobilising device, as a balm for wounded identity; contradictions were masked, the myths reinforced.'[195]

Despite the appeal to historical and cultural traditions the Afrikaner Rebellion was limited in that it did not develop into full scale civil war. The Botha government was very sensitive to the escalation of hostilities. Smuts states that the lenient peace terms offered to the rebels was designed to mitigate any further attempts at revolution.[196] The Indemnity Act further promoted leniency and allowed for three types of amnesties, full, partial and minimum.[197] A large part of the English speaking South African population did not support the compassionate treatment of the rebels.[198]

Botha mostly used Afrikaners in the military suppression of the Rebellion.[199] He believed that it was an internal Afrikaner problem. People of Colour served as *agterryers*, support auxiliaries and scouts for both sides: the government and rebel commandos, as was the case in the Anglo-Boer War, received no political or economic reward for their service. The final casualty figures are represented in Table 4.1 and show an approximately 50 % difference in casualty figures. A prominent absence in the official casualty lists was that of the People of Colour.

	English South African Casualties	Afrikaans South African Casualties
Killed in Action	40	58
Died of Wounds	11	22
Wounded	94	183
Total Casualties	145	243

Table 4.1: Rebellion Casualties[200]

192 Du Plessis and Hough, 'Civil War', p. 105.
193 Swart, 'A Boer and his Gun', p. 751.
194 O'Neill, Insurgency', p. 18.
195 Swart, 'A Boer and his Gun', p. 751.
196 Hancock and Van der Poel, *Smuts Papers*, p. 220.
197 DOD Archives, DG 1, Box 1, Disposal of Maritz Rebels, 28 Aug 1915.
198 Hancock and Van der Poel, *Smuts Papers*, pp. 220, 221.
199 J. Meintjes, *General Louis Botha* (London: Cassell & Co., 1970), p. 239.
200 DOD Archives, Officer Commanding Records, Box 92, Statistics Re Casualties Rebellion, South West Africa, East and Central Africa and Europe, Letter from the Director

Conclusion

This chapter adds an analytical layer to the existing research on the Afrikaner Rebellion by merging the genesis of the conflict with relative deprivation theory. Relative deprivation theory encapsulates the perceived disconnect between the value capabilities and the value expectations of an individual or group. Individuals and or groups believe themselves to be entitled to certain goods and conditions which are referred to as value expectations. The value capabilities are the goods and conditions which they are capable of attaining. The disconnect between expectations and capabilities results in discontentment and is linked to the frustration-aggression theory. The politicisation of the discontent and aggression is the final phase of political violence.[201]

In the case of the rebellion the discontent of the rebel leaders and their followers targeted Botha's South Africanism. Issues of economic disenfranchisement and loss of identity were coupled to the Botha government. The socio-economic relative deprivation experienced by the rebels is considered to be a predisposing cause of the 1914 Afrikaner Rebellion. *Bywoners* were greatly affected by increased poverty which resulted in displacement. As a result of the societal changes, the *bywoner* social class and identity was called into question. The rise of Afrikaner nationalism and the political split between Botha and Hertzog were further predisposing factors. The trigger for activating the predisposing causes into violence was South Africa's entry into the First World War. The following chapter addresses the Botha government's response to the Afrikaner Rebellion.

Information Bureau to the Minister of Defence, 15 July 1915.
201 Gurr, *Why Men Rebel*, pp. 12, 13.

5

Suppression of the 1914 Afrikaner Rebellion

The Afrikaner Rebellion resulted in a brief halt in operations in German South West Africa while the Union Defence Force engaged in quelling the rebellion inside the Union. British intelligence had been aware that the Germans were considering fomenting rebellion in South Africa since 1908.[1] The German authorities counted on the rebellion to distract the Union government and divert its forces which they hoped would translate into the military advantage by weakening the cohesion of the Union Defence Force and gaining time.[2] Von Heydebreck aimed to hold up the Union's forces for as long as possible so as to delay their redeployment to other theatres of the war. The German command in Berlin had ordered its colonial forces to operate strictly on the defensive in this regard.

After refusing to support the Union's advance on Sandfontein in late September 1914, Maritz signed a treaty with the Germans and took refuge with his fellow defectors in German South West Africa. C.R. De Wet, who was a commandant in the Anglo-Boer War, became one of the rebel leaders in the Orange Free State.[3] Beyers resigned his commission on 15 September 1914 along with Kemp and these two former officers of the Union Defence Force and their supporters were prominent figures in the Afrikaner Rebellion.[4]

The Germans ordered Maritz to attack Upington, while Union defence headquarters instructed Brits to check Maritz's advances. Maritz was defeated by a force under Brits at Keimoes on 22 October 1914 and then again at Kakamas in the Northern Cape, close to the German South West African border. Withdrewing to German South

1   DOD Archives, Diverse (hereafter D), Box 8, 37, Instructions from Headquarters, 20 August 1910.
2   J.J. Collyer, *The Campaign in German South West Africa, 1914–1915* (Pretoria: Government Printer, 1937), p. 5.
3   D.E. Reitz, *Trekking On* (London, Travel Book Club, 1947), p. 50.
4   I. Van der Waag, 'The Battle of Sandfontein, 26 September 1914: South African Military Reform and the German South-West Africa Campaign, 1914–1915', *First World War Studies*, 4, 2 2013, p. 9.

West Africa after being wounded in the knee, Maritz retreated with an estimated 1,000 rebels.[5] The rebel leadership comprised Beyers and Kemp in the Transvaal, De Wet in the Free State and Maritz in the Northern Cape and UDF military operations were directed at their respective forces. Due to the nature of the rebellion (insurgency), the rebel leaders became the centre of gravity.

On 12 October 1914, Smuts declared martial law in support of the suppression of the rebellion.[6] There were 15 military districts which reported to defence headquarters, and Smuts used them to gather intelligence on the formation and movement of the different rebel groupings. Botha declined the British offer of military assistance to suppress the rebellion and for the most part used Afrikaners[7] when he took to the field with 32,000 troops.[8] This was done in order to minimise the simmering tension between English and Afrikaans-speaking South Africans.

Operational Strategy of the Central Position

The strategy of the UDF entailed rapid movement from a central position to rebel strongholds via internal lines, using trains (and motorcars to some extent) for operational movement (over large distances) and horses for tactical movement (over shorter distances related to battle). Botha and Smuts decided to concentrate their forces in and around Pretoria and to deploy on internal lines to the areas where they were most required.[9] The Union faced a threat from Maritz in German South West Africa and the Northern Cape; Beyers and Kemp in the Transvaal; and De Wet in the Orange Free State. The fulcrum of the strategy of the central position was Pretoria with deployments of the UDF projected to the key operational areas namely the Transvaal, Orange Free State and the Northern Cape. The operational strategy hinged on the dual aspects of military intelligence which identified targets and operational/tactical mobility which in turn provided the means to reach and defeat the rebel forces.

The operational movement of the UDF was achieved through the construction and maintenance of additional railway lines which allowed for the rapid deployment of troops. The South African Railway Service constructed 227 kilometres of new railway

5   G. L'ange, *Urgent Imperial Service* (Rivonia: Ashanti, 1991), p. 57; Anon., *Union of South Africa and the Great War, 1914-1918, Official History* (Pretoria: Government Printer, 1924), p. 15.
6   L'ange, *Urgent Imperial Service*, p. 56; Ritchie states that the proclamation of martial law was on 22 October 1914: M.E. Ritchie, *With Botha in the Field* (London: Longmans, 1915), p. 4.
7   J. Meintjes, *General Louis Botha* (London: Cassell & Co., 1970), p. 239; K. Fedorowich, 'Sleeping with the Lion? The Loyal Afrikaner and the South African Rebellion of 1914-1915', *South African Historical Journal*, 49, 1, 2009, p. 80.
8   B. Nasson, *Springboks on the Somme* (Johannesburg: Penguin, 2007), pp. 43–45.
9   H.F. Trew, *Botha Treks* (London: Blackie & Son, 1936), p. 29.

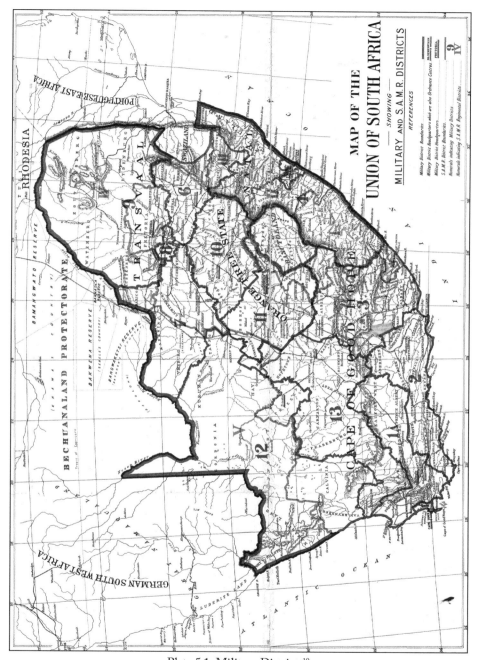

Plate 5.1: Military Districts[10]

10   DOD Archives, Secretary of Defence (hereafter SD), Box 39, Strike Precautionary Measures, 1914.

between Prieska and Upington which facilitated the projection of Union forces into the different operational theatres.[11] Armoured trains which were used to deploy troops were protected with armoured plating and were equipped with a 12 pounder gun, a machinegun section and a searchlight.[12] The horses were entrained with saddles and bridles which had the dual purpose of saving space and allowing for a quick reaction time.[13] Mobility was further promoted by the formation of a motorcar contingent comprised of 110 automobiles (fitted with machineguns) provided by the Transvaal Automobile Club and 500 soldiers of the 2nd Transvaal Scottish.[14] The operational movement of troops was aided by the provision of accurate intelligence.

The Union government had a Union wide intelligence network which included the police, magistrates and other sources such as the Railway Rifle Associations which guarded the railways and bridges. Sir Hugh Wyndham was in charge of gathering and processing information into reliable intelligence which was effectively capitalised on by the Union Defence Force.[15] Thus military intelligence and operational mobility were effectively employed from the hub of Pretoria to put down the rebellion.

Rebellion in the Northern Cape

Botha called a meeting on 14 August 1914 to clarify the Union's position in terms of the outbreak of the Great War, to gather support from the Union's military leaders[16] and to discuss the operational plans, logistical requirements and possible contingencies for the pending German South West African campaign.[17] Maritz attended the meeting along with many other commandants.[18]

Botha informed the meeting that the duty of all officers was to follow orders regardless of their personal feelings about the campaign. Kemp and Beyers nonetheless opposed the invasion plans [19] and while in Pretoria Maritz, Beyers and Kemp along with the other conspirators held a private meeting,[20] at which Maritz showed them

11   Fedorowich, 'The Loyal Afrikaner and the South African Rebellion of 1914-1915', p. 83.
12   Department of Defence Archives (hereafter DOD Archives). Adjutant General 1914–1921 (hereafter AG 1914–1921), Box 8, Armoured Trains, Telegram from Defence Staff to Captain Wallace Officer Commanding No. 1 Armoured Train, 22 November 1914.
13   Trew, *Botha Treks*, p. 30.
14   Fedorowich, 'The Loyal Afrikaner and the South African Rebellion of 1914-1915', p. 83.
15   Ibid., p. 83.
16   DOD Archives, Diverse Group 1 (hereafter DG 1), Box 2, Rebellion Commission of Enquiry Volume 1, Testimony by General Louis Botha, 956, 29 June 1916.
17   DOD Archives, DG 1, Box 2, Rebellion Commission of Enquiry Volume 1, Testimony by General Coenraad Jacobus Brits, 144, 15 March 1916.
18   Ibid.
19   DOD, DG 1, Box 2, Rebellion Commission of Enquiry Volume 1, Testimony by General Louis Botha, 958, 29 June 1916.
20   DOD Archives, DG 1, Box 2, Rebellion Commission of Enquiry Volume 1, Testimony by General Coenraad Jacobus Brits, 144, 15 March 1916.

correspondence from the German government which guaranteed German military support for the rebellion.[21] At the same time there was increased German military activity on the border of the Union.

The Germans initially sent a small force which occupied a hill close to Nakob from 15-18 August 1915.[22] What was at first thought to be an invasion turned out to be the occupation of a hill in the widely desolate border area which happened to be within the territory of the Union. The German reconnaissance mission positioned itself so as to overlook the waterhole at Nakob.[23] On 22 August 1914 Lieutenant C.R. Liebenberg (Active Citizen Force) who was a farmer in German South West Africa, was fleeing to the Union when he was confronted by three German soldiers. A shootout ensued in which one German soldier was killed and one soldier was injured.[24] This incident was used by the Union to justify the invasion of German South West Africa.[25]

After this incident Maritz crossed the border at Schuit's Drift from where he went to the German military post at Stolzenfels on 24 August 1914. Maritz telephoned a German official named Max Teinert and apologised for the incident at Nakob explaining that he was not in any way responsible.[26] Maritz also discussed the issue of German weapon supply for the rebels. Following this discussion P. de Wet (the brother of Andries de Wet leader of the *Vrij Korps*) and Max Teinert approached the German Governor, Dr T. Seitz, in Windhoek who agreed to provide the rebels with rifles but not artillery.[27]

On the side of the Germans there was already a small number of dissident South Africans who formed the *Vrij Korps*: renegade Afrikaners and commandos from the Anglo-Boer War who under the command of A. de Wet promoted the German cause in the Northern Cape.[28] On 18 September 1914 the *Vrij Korps* comprising 300 soldiers supported by a machine gun section captured the Union military post at Nakob.[29] They subsequently captured the Rietfontein police station which was a small and

21 Anon., *The Times History of the War* (London: The Times, 1915), p. 498.
22 DOD Archives, SD, Box 601, 95C, Reported fortifying of Kopje at Nakob by the Germans, 24 August 1914; DOD, DG 1, Box 2, Rebellion Commission of Enquiry Volume 1, Testimony by Mr Frederick Carruthers Cornel, 14, 16 February 1916.
23 Collyer, *The Campaign in German South West Africa, 1914–1915*, 22; DOD Archives, SD, Box 601, 95C, Reported fortifying of Kopje at Nakob by the Germans, 24 August 1914.
24 DOD Archives, DG 1, Box 2, Rebellion Commission of Enquiry Volume 1, Testimony by Lieutenant Christiaan Rudolf Liebenberg, 207, 15 March 1916.
25 L'ange, *Urgent Imperial Service*, pp. 11, 12.
26 DOD Archives, DG 1, Box 2, Rebellion Commission of Enquiry Volume 1, Testimony by Captain Alfred Ernest Trigger, 3, 15 February 1916; DOD Archives, DG 1, Box 2, Rebellion Commission of Enquiry Volume 1, Testimony by Mr Pieter de Wet, 213, 28 March 1916; Anon., *The Times History of the War*, p. 499.
27 DOD Archives, DG 1, Box 2, Rebellion Commission of Enquiry Volume 1, Testimony by Mr Pieter de Wet, 214, 28 March 1916.
28 L'ange, *Urgent Imperial Service*, p. 51.
29 DOD, DG 1, Box 2, Rebellion Commission of Enquiry Volume 1, Testimony by Mr Frederick Carruthers Cornel, 14, 16 February 1916.

secluded post on the border of German South West Africa .[30] These activities and limited actions predated the Union's failed cross border invasion which culminated in the Battle of Sandfontein, and increasingly pressurised the Union government to pursue offensive operations.

On 25 September 1914, Defence Headquarters ordered Maritz up to support Lukin (later Sir, Major General Lukin) with his advance on Sandfontein. Maritz promptly refused the order,[31] claiming that his Force was insufficiently supplied in comparison with that of Lukin.[32] Maritz was then ordered back to Pretoria but refused. On the orders of Smuts, Major B. Enslin was sent to Upington on 27 September 1914 to determine if Maritz had in fact defected. Enslin wired Smuts stating that Maritz was in collusion with the Germans and that he required 2,000 commandos to deal with Maritz's forces.[33] While awaiting further direction from Pretoria, Enslin remained in Upington with Maritz and acted as his chief-of-staff, in an attempt to keep a close eye on his activities.[34]

In response to Maritz's defection, Botha held a meeting with 35 commandants and informed them that he would lead the German South West Africa campaign and the operations against the rebellion. For a brief moment, it was a throwback to the days of the Anglo-Boer War, where the romantic idea of life on commando and serving one's commandant, general and president combined a sense of duty and adventure. All of the commandants naturally agreed to follow Botha.[35]

Botha recommended to Cabinet that he be made commandant general as Beyers had resigned and gone into rebellion, and he was subsequently appointed as commander-in-chief of the expeditionary force for German South West Africa by special commission, under Section 81 of the Defence Act of 1912.[36] Botha asked for Colonel J.J. Alberts, Commandants Collins, Mentz, Cilliers and General M.W. Myburgh to raise 1,000 men each for the campaign. At the outbreak of the rebellion Botha moved these men throughout the Union by train so as to suppress the rebellion at key points.[37]

30 L'ange, *Urgent Imperial Service*, p. 53.
31 Anon., *The Times History of the War*, p. 502.
32 DOD Archives, DG 1, Box 2, Rebellion Commission of Enquiry Volume 1, Testimony by General Barend Gottfried Leopold Enslin, 394, 17 April 1916.
33 P.J. Sampson, *The Capture of De Wet: The South African Rebellion 1914* (London: Edward Arnold, 1915), p. 78; Anon., *The Times History of the War*, p. 502.
34 Sampson, *The capture of De Wet: The South African Rebellion 1914*, p. 78.
35 DOD Archives, DG 1, Box 2, Rebellion Commission of Enquiry Volume 1, Testimony by General Louis Botha, 967, 968, 29 June 1916. See, Reitz, *On Commando*; Reitz, *Trekking On*.
36 DOD Archives, Adjutant General 1914-1921 (hereafter AG 1914–1921), Box 8, Commander-in-chief, Government notice for the next issue of the *Union Gazette*, 18 October 1914.
37 DOD Archives, DG 1, Box 2, Rebellion Commission of Enquiry Volume 1, Testimony by General Louis Botha, 968, 29 June 1916.

On 30 September, Maritz was again ordered back to Pretoria, which he refused.[38] Commandant C. Brits (later brigadier general) was sent up to Upington and was appointed as the commander of the entire area of the Northern Cape, [39] arriving in Upington with his staff on the morning of 6 October 1914.[40] Enslin had recommended Brits's appointment as he held considerable influence in the Northern Cape. On Brits's assumption of duty, Enslin became his chief-of-staff and was given specific orders to arrest Maritz.[41]

In response to the news of Brits's deployment, Maritz left Upington with his supporters (approximately 900) on 2 October and made for Vanrooisvlei 40 kilometres west of Upington.[42] Enslin remained in Upington when Maritz departed to Vanrooisvlei.[43] Maritz trekked up to German South West Africa between 5 and 6 October 1914[44] and with the *Vrij Korps* proceeded to Ukamos in German South West Africa where they met with the commander of the *Schutztruppe*,[45] Colonel J von Heydebreck.[46] The grouping discussed the type of artillery support which would be given to Maritz. Following the meeting with Von Heydebreck, Maritz returned to Vanrooisvlei in the Union of South Africa on 8 October 1914. A. de Wet subsequently joined Maritz at Vanrooisvlei on 9 October with the *Vrij Corps* and German artillery support.[47]

The *Vrij Korps* had approximately 92 members with German artillery support which included four '96 model' and two pom-poms which were supported by 80 German soldiers.[48] Maritz captured a Union gun section at Vanrooisvlei and made a speech where he claimed to be liberating the Union of South Africa from Britain.[49] A total of 62 Union soldiers were taken prisoner and were sent off to German South West

---

38 L'ange, *Urgent Imperial Service,* p. 54.
39 Ibid., p. 53.
40 DOD Archives, DG 1, Box 2, Rebellion Commission of Enquiry Volume 1, Testimony by General Barend Gottfried Leopold Enslin, 400, 401, 17 April 1916.
41 Sampson, *The capture of De Wet: The South African Rebellion 1914,* pp. 82, 83.
42 Anon., *The Times History of the War,* p. 503; L'ange, *Urgent Imperial Service,* p. 54.
43 DOD Archives, DG 1, Box 2, Rebellion Commission of Enquiry Volume 1, Testimony by General Barend Gottfried Leopold Enslin, 399, 17 April 1916.
44 Sampson, *The capture of De Wet: The South African Rebellion 1914,* p. 84; Anon., *The Times History of the War,* p. 503; L'ange, *Urgent Imperial Service,* p. 54.
45 The *Schutztruppe* were the colonial forces of imperial Germany.
46 DOD Archives, DG 1, Box 2, Rebellion Commission of Enquiry Volume 1, Testimony by Mr Pieter de Wet, 218, 28 March 1916.
47 DOD Archives, DG 1, Box 2, Rebellion Commission of Enquiry Volume 1, Testimony by Captain Alfred Ernest Trigger, 3, 4, 15 February 1916; Anon., *The Times History of the War,* p. 503; L'ange, *Urgent Imperial Service,* p. 54.
48 DOD Archives, DG 1, Box 2, Rebellion Commission of Enquiry Volume 1, Testimony by Mr Pieter de Wet, 218, 28 March 1916. Alternative sources give the Union prisoners at 60: Anon., *The Times History of the War,* p. 503; L'ange, *Urgent Imperial Service,* p. 54.
49 Sampson, *The capture of De Wet: The South African Rebellion 1914,* pp. 84, 85.

Africa.[50] Maritz's defection made the Union susceptible to invasion from a German/rebel force from the direction of the border of the Northern Cape.[51]

Enslin sent a telegram to Smuts recommending that another military force be sent up to the Northern Cape to protect the interests of the Union from Maritz and any possible attacks which may come from German South West Africa.[52] Botha and Smuts proceeded to send a detachment of the Active Citizen Force Regiment, Enslin's Horse to Upington which arrived on 9 October 1914[53] in addition to the Durban Light Infantry and the Imperial Light Horse which arrived in Upington on 18 October 1914.[54] These units were to form a buffer force in the event of an invasion of the Union or an attack on the Union forces from the German/rebel forces on the border.[55] Smuts later reinforced the contingent in Upington with a heavy battery of artillery.[56]

On 9 October 1914 Colonel B.D. Bouwer was sent to Maritz's position with a message from Brits requesting him to hand over his command. Bouwer reached Maritz on 10 October after he had given his speech at Vanrooisvlei[57] and was taken prisoner by Maritz,[58] who showed Bouwer German documents and correspondence dating back to June 1913. This revealed that Maritz, at that point, had been in contact and possibly in collusion with the Germans for over a year.[59]

The German authorities requested Maritz to attack Upington during the month of October 1914 but Maritz did not comply with this request as he was unsure what the Afrikaner reaction would be to such an attack. Instead Maritz and his rebel force captured Keimoes (temporarily) and then Kakamas.[60] Maritz was seen with his force

50   DOD, DG 1, Box 2, Rebellion Commission of Enquiry Volume 1, Testimony by Mr Daniel Pieter Rousseau, 19 - 26, 17 February 1916.
51   Anon., *The Times History of the War*, p. 503.
52   DOD Archives, DG 1, Box 2, Rebellion Commission of Enquiry Volume 1, Testimony by General Barend Gottfried Leopold Enslin, 399, 17 April 1916.
53   DOD Archives, DG 1, Box 2, Rebellion Commission of Enquiry Volume 1, Testimony by General Barend Gottfried Leopold Enslin, 402, 17 April 1916.
54   DOD Archives, DG 1, Box 2, Rebellion Commission of Enquiry Volume 1, Testimony by General Barend Gottfried Leopold Enslin, 403, 17 April 1916; L'ange, *Urgent Imperial Service*, p. 53.
55   DOD, DG 1, Box 2, Rebellion Commission of Enquiry Volume 1, Testimony by General Louis Botha, 968, 29 June 1916.
56   DOD Archives, DG 1, Box 57, General Botha's Operations Against the Rebels, Order from Defence Headquarters, 21 November October 1914.
57   DOD Archives, DG 1, Box 2, Rebellion Commission of Enquiry Volume 1, Testimony by Colonel Barend Daniel Bouwer, 117, 118, 2 March 1916; DOD Archives, DG1, Rebellion Commission of Enquiry Volume 1, Testimony by General Coenraad Jacobus Brits, 142, 15 March 1916.
58   DOD Archives, DG 1, Box 2, Rebellion Commission of Enquiry Volume 1, Testimony by General Barend Gottfried Leopold Enslin, 401, 17 April 1916.
59   DOD Archives, DG 1, Box 2, Rebellion Commission of Enquiry Volume 1, Testimony by Colonel Barend Daniel Bouwer, 117 - 119, 2 March 1916.
60   L'ange, *Urgent Imperial Service*, p. 57.

en route to Keimoes with 600 rebels,[61] the combined rebel force comprising South African rebels, the *Vrij Corps* and German artillery on 11 October 1914. On arrival he declared a new Republic of South Africa.[62] Maritz's forces then left Keimoes and proceeded to Kakamas. Maritz didn't have sufficient forces to occupy many positions simultaneously and the Union Defence Force subsequently retook the desolate town of Keimoes.

On the morning of 22 October 1914, Maritz's forces returned and attacked the Union's military post at Keimoes with approximately 800 soldiers[63] of which 120 soldiers were German.[64] There were initially 150 Union soldiers in Keimoes who were later reinforced by 200 of the Durban Light Infantry and 200 more soldiers of the Imperial Light Horse.[65] P. de Wet was ordered to take a hill which overlooked the outpost at Keimoes. A group of rebels later charged the Union forces at Keimoes where two rebels were killed. Maritz was informed about the failed charge and proceeded to inspect the terrain by approaching the military post and observing the situation through his field glasses. During this inspection Maritz came within firing range and was shot in the leg.[66] A group of South African military historians joked that it was possible that Maritz was looking through his field glasses the wrong way round and seeing a smaller picture, proceeded to walk forward at which point he received a gunshot. Maritz was then evacuated to Jerusalem in German South West Africa.[67]

The Union forces defended their post in Keimoes and the rebel forces withdrew. The Union forces subsequently pursued the rebels to Kakamas where the rebels were again forced to flee.[68] Brits's forces advanced on Kakamas on 24 October 1914[69] and Commandant Stadler and a number of rebels formed a blocking force so as to delay the advance of the Union forces.[70] Brits's force advanced on Kakamas from three directions. Although the rebels had taken the hills north of Kakamas and engaged

61   DOD Archives, AG 1914 – 1921, Box 8, Letter from Upington magistrate to Defence Headquarters, 10 October 1914.
62   DOD Archives, DG 1, Box 2, Rebellion Commission of Enquiry Volume 1, Testimony by Captain Alfred Ernest Trigger, 4, 5, 15 February 1916.
63   DOD Archives, DG 1, Box 2, Rebellion Commission of Enquiry Volume 1, Testimony by General Barend Gottfried Leopold Enslin, 404, 17 April 1916; L'ange, *Urgent Imperial Service*, p. 57.
64   Sampson, *The capture of De Wet: The South African Rebellion 1914*, p. 90.
65   Ibid., p. 110.
66   DOD Archives, DG 1, Box 2, Rebellion Commission of Enquiry Volume 1, Testimony by Mr Pieter de Wet, 219, 220, 28 March 1916.
67   L'ange, *Urgent Imperial Service*, p. 58.
68   DOD Archives, DG 1, Box 2, Rebellion Commission of Enquiry Volume 1, Testimony by General Coenraad Jacobus Brits, 143, 15 March 1916.
69   DOD Archives, DG 1, Box 2, Rebellion Commission of Enquiry Volume 1, Testimony by General Barend Gottfried Leopold Enslin, 404, 17 April 1916; L'ange, *Urgent Imperial Service*, p. 57.
70   DOD Archives, DG 1, Box 2, Rebellion Commission of Enquiry Volume 1, Testimony by Mr Pieter de Wet, 220, 28 March 1916.

the Union forces as they advanced; the Union Defence Force returned fire and rushed the rebel held positions forcing them to flee.[71] The rebels then fled to Schuits Drift. At this point Brits was recalled to Pretoria.[72] The remnants of Maritz's force was scattered at Schuits Drift[73] one of the few negotiable fords across the Orange River.[74]

On 25 October 1914 Major P.A. Vermaas captured 32 rebels at Brandvlei close to Calvinia. Maritz's lieutenants had been attempting to gather support for the rebellion in and around Calvinia, however, Vermaas managed to capture the majority of these rebels and various smaller rebel detachments were forced to retreat.[75] Following the retreat of the rebels from around Calvinia, Vermaas was sent to Pella on 29 October 1914 from where he deployed to Raman's Drift where he had several skirmishes with the Germans forces.[76] With the initial defeat of Maritz at Keimoes and Kakamas, the focus of the rebellion changed to Beyers and Kemp and C.R. De Wet.

Operations in the Transvaal and Orange Free State

The Union Defence Force received word on 25 October 1914 that Beyers was marching on Rustenburg with approximately 4,000 rebels. A Mr J. Watt reported the incident to defence headquarters.[77] Botha and his bodyguard subsequently deployed to Rustenburg in pursuit of Beyers.[78] Major (later Lieutenant Colonel) Trew commanded Botha's bodyguard, which initially comprised 50 and later grew to around 100 men. Botha insisted that the bodyguard be made up of English and Afrikaans South Africans.[79]

Before Botha took to the field, armed with the state commandos and a Mauser pistol[80], he sent a personal message to his wife Annie: 'I have said goodbye to you in many difficult circumstances, but never on such a painful occasion as this.

71   DOD Archives, DG 1, Box 2, Rebellion Commission of Enquiry Volume 1, Testimony by General Barend Gottfried Leopold Enslin, 404, 17 April 1916.
72   DOD Archives, DG 1, Box 2, Rebellion Commission of Enquiry Volume 1, Testimony by General Coenraad Jacobus Brits, 143, 15 March 1916.
73   Anon., *The Times History of the War,* p. 503.
74   Ibid., p. 499.
75   DOD Archives, DG 1, Box 2, Rebellion Commission of Enquiry Volume 1, Testimony by Major Pieter Arnoldus Vermaas, 1008, 30 June 1916.
76   DOD Archives, DG 1, Box 2, Rebellion Commission of Enquiry Volume 1, Testimony by Major Pieter Arnoldus Vermaas, 1009, 30 June 1916.
77   DOD Archives, AG 1914–1921, Box 8, Rebellion, Report by post office official at Millvale, 25 October 1914.
78   DOD Archives, DG 1, Box 57, General Botha's Operations Against the Rebels, Telegram to Defence Headquarters, 26 October 1914.
79   DOD Archives, SD 2, Box 632, General Botha, Defence Headquarters to Quartermaster General, 3 October, 1914.
80   DOD Archives, SD 2, Box 632, General Botha, Letter Superintendent Ordinance Store, 8 October, 1914.

God give me strength to do my duty.'[81] With this emotional message sent, Botha's bodyguard entrained in Pretoria on 26 October complete with horses, saddles and all the necessary equipment. Botha and his bodyguard detrained in Rustenburg with his commando on 27 October 1914. Deploying his forces to Kommissie Drift after receiving an intelligence report confirming the whereabouts of Beyers, Botha's troops then marched through Olifantsnek where they engaged[82] and scattered Beyers's force.[83] Beyers and the remnants of his force were pursued to the Vaal River where the majority of the rebels surrendered. Rather than face defeat, Beyers fled.[84] With the rebel force effectively dispersed, Botha returned to Pretoria to focus on the uprising in the Free State.[85]

Just prior to the scattering of Beyers' force, he was in negotiations with the government for his surrender and that of his rebels. Smuts allowed Beyers to be in contact with De Wet via telegraph but refused that messengers be allowed to cross through Union lines.[86] No decisive result was achieved in the negotiations.[87] Beyers also wanted to hold talks with De Wet in person and requested to be allowed to cross into the Orange Free State. While Botha was directly pursuing De Wet, Smuts took the decision to deny Beyers' proposed consultation with De Wet on 11 November 1914, the day before the Battle of Mushroom Valley.[88] After being on the run for a month, after the dispersal of his forces Beyers met an unfortunate end on 8 December when he drowned in the Vaal River while fleeing from Union forces.[89]

Kemp was the other significant threat in the Transvaal. Colonel J.J. Alberts was despatched to Treurfontein where Kemp had been active. Alberts arrived in Treurfontein on 29 October and sent out a reconnaissance team which made contact with a group of Kemp's rebels. The rebels captured the reconnaissance group after luring them in under the guise of a white flag.[90]

81 Trew, *Botha Treks*, p. 29.
82 Ritchie, *With Botha in the Field*, p. 4; Trew, *Botha Treks*, p. 29.
83 DOD Archives, DG 1, Box 57, General Botha's Operations Against the Rebels, Telegram to Defence Headquarters, 27 October 1914; Anon., *Official History*, pp. 16, 23; Meintjes, *General Louis Botha*, p. 241; Trew, *Botha Treks*, p. 29.
84 L'ange, *Urgent Imperial Service*, pp. 59, 60.
85 Ritchie, *With Botha in the Field*, p. 5; Trew, *Botha Treks*, p. 30.
86 DOD Archives, AG 1914–1921, Box 8, Rebellion, Secret telegraph between Pretoria headquarters and Mr Conradie at Prieska post office, 20 October 1914.
87 Smuts to Merriman, W.K. Hancock and J. van der Poel (eds), *Selections from the Smuts Papers, Volume III* (London: Cambridge University Press, 1966), p. 214.
88 DOD Archives, DG 1, Box 57, General Botha's Operations Against the Rebels, Telegram Smuts to Botha, 11 November 1914.
89 Nasson, *Springboks on the Somme*, p. 46.
90 DOD Archives, AG 1914–1921, Box 8, Armoured Trains, Colonel Alberts report to General Smuts after the action at Treurfontein, 19 October 1914.

The main body of Alberts' force engaged Kemp's force and captured 240 rebels – the bulk of Kemp's commando.[91] The Union forces reported 13 rebels killed and 36 injured in the action at Treurfontein.[92] Smuts then proceeded with administrating the mopping-up operations. He sent Alberts on a wide front from Treurfontein to Wolmaranstad where he received the support of commandos loyal to the Union.[93] Kemp managed to escape and eventually crossed the German South West African border where he joined Maritz and other defectors. In total, the Union forces took approximately 400 prisoners in their operations against Beyers and Kemp.[94] The Union Defence Force then shifted its focus to the Orange Free State where the rebellion had gained popularity.

Botha had planned a meeting in Vereeniging to mobilise the required commandos for operations in the Orange Free State and he took personal command of the Union force against De Wet.[95] Botha departed from Pretoria on 9 November with his personal bodyguard and arrived in Winburg on 11 November 1914.[96] De Wet and his followers had left the town shortly before their arrival. [97] Ritchie claims that the Union force arrived in Winburg two hours after De Wet had left and found the inhabitants in a state of panic. De Wet and his followers had told them that the government was on the verge of being toppled and that Germany had defeated Britain.[98]

Botha was en route to telegraph Smuts when he received a telephone call at the local post office, where he learnt that De Wet was at Mushroom Valley. The caller was being held captive at the farm in Mushroom Valley.[99] Botha planned the encirclement of Mushroom Valley with his trusted commanders Myburgh, Lukin, Brits and Colonel G. Brand. Brits and Lukin were cooperating on Botha's right flank.[100] The entire force marched through the night and at dawn on 12 November the artillery opened fire on De Wet's forces which scattered in disarray at the sound of the first shell exploding.[101]

Myburgh attacked through the centre while Brand enveloped the rebels to the right.[102] De Wet's forces were caught unawares and almost instantly broke into retreat.

91   Anon., *Official History*, p. 16.
92   DOD Archives, AG 1914–1921, Box 8, Armoured Trains, Colonel Alberts report to General Smuts after the action at Treurfontein, 19 October 1914.
93   DOD Archives, AG 1914–1921, Box 8, Armoured Trains, Smuts telegraph to Colonel Alberts, 22 November 1914.
94   Nasson, *Springboks on the Somme*, p. 46.
95   L'ange, *Urgent Imperial Service*, p. 66.
96   DOD Archives, DG 1, Box 57, General Botha's Operations Against the Rebels, Telegram from Quartermaster General to Defence Headquarters, 12 November 1914.
97   Ritchie, *With Botha in the Field*, p. 6.
98   Ibid., pp. 7, 8.
99   Meintjes, *General Louis Botha*, p. 242; Trew, *Botha Treks*, p. 29.
100   Trew, *Botha Treks*, p. 31.
101   DOD Archives, DG 1, Box 57, General Botha's Operations Against the Rebels, Telegram Botha to Smuts, 13 November 1914; Ritchie, *With Botha in the Field*, p. 9.
102   Trew, *Botha Treks*, p. 32.

Brits was in command of the cut off force that was positioned to intercept the retreating rebels. Reitz, who was one of the subordinate officers under Brits, maintained that they were unable to cut off the fleeing rebels.[103] While the fighting ensued, Trew as head of Botha's bodyguard, was trying to keep the Prime Minister away from the front.[104]

Lukin was deployed in support of the cut off force but was unable to intercept the rebels as they fled through the Koraanberg.[105] Lukin was not in position at the pivotal point when the rebels passed by in full flight.[106] It should be added that the heliographer didn't relay the message to Lukin as instructed by Botha.[107] Botha stated that a wretched miscommunication was the cause of delay between Brits and Lukin.[108] After the battle, Botha inspected the battlefield with deep sorrow and commented, 'you English will never understand how hard this is for me'.[109]

The battle ended with 22 rebels dead and this action for the most part neutralised the rebellion in the Orange Free State.[110] The Union casualties were 10 dead and 24 injured.[111] The number of rebels captured which according so some sources are estimated at 3,000 have been exaggerated and the true number is around 300.[112] De Wet was not one of the rebels captured at Mushroom Valley and he made his escape with the speed and cunning on which his reputation was built during the Anglo-Boer War. He had skilfully eluded capture fourteen years earlier in a similar fashion at Surrender Hill in the Brandwater Basin where General Prinsloo had surrendered.[113]

Botha complained to Smuts that many of the rebels were in possession of white arm bands, which was used by government forces to distinguish themselves from rebels.[114] The commandos still operated in the old way, where their uniforms were the clothes on their backs.

103 Reitz, *Trekking On*, p. 60.
104 Trew, *Botha Treks*, p. 32.
105 Sampson, *The Capture of De Wet*, p. 172.
106 Trew, *Botha Treks*, p. 32.
107 E.W. Nortier, 'Major General Sir Henry Timson Lukin (1860–1925): The Making of a South African Hero' (M Mil, Military Academy Stellenbosch University, Stellenbosch, 2005), p. 23.
108 DOD Archives, DG 1, Box 57, General Botha's Operations Against the Rebels, Telegram Botha to Smuts, 13 November 1914.
109 Trew, *Botha Treks*, p. 32.
110 L'ange, *Urgent Imperial Service*, p. 68.
111 DOD Archives, AG 14-21, Box 166. Report on Akrikaner Rebellion casualties to the High Commissioner for South Africa, 8 December 1914.
112 DOD Archives, DG 1, Box 57, General Botha's Operations Against the Rebels, Telegram Botha to Smuts, 13 November 1914.
113 See, F. Pretorius, *The Great Escape of the Boer Pimpernel, Christiaan De Wet: The Making of a Legend* (Pietermaritzburg: University of Natal Press, 2001).
114 DOD Archives, DG 1, Box 57, General Botha's Operations Against the Rebels, Telegram Botha to Smuts, 13 November 1914.

Following the Battle of Mushroom Valley, Botha gave orders to Lukin, Brand and the other commandants to relentlessly pursue De Wet without giving him a moments rest.[115] Botha mentioned that a large amount of supplies and ammunition was lost and many of the rebels were returning home after the battle.[116] This was standard practice for commandos in the field, where burghers would merely return to their homes or farms when the military situation no longer suited them.

WHERE DE WET'S FORCES WERE SCATTERED.
General Botha (on left) and staff at Mushroom Valley, where the rebel forces were completely defeated and routed.

Plate 5.2: Following the Battle of Mushroom Valley[117]

Trekking to Clocolan, Botha entrained on 18 November and headed for Kimberley via Bloemfontein.[118] Botha and his bodyguard returned to Kroonstad on 29 November to finalise the required mopping up operations of the remnants of the Afrikaner Rebellion. Botha met with Smuts on 30 November at Kroonstad from where Botha and his men moved to Bethlehem.[119] Smuts managed the administration of the ministry of war from Pretoria, while Botha coordinated operations in the field. Their operational partnership mirrored their interaction during the conventional phase of

---

115 DOD Archives, DG 1, Box 57, General Botha's Operations Against the Rebels, Telegram to Defence Headquarters, 17 November 1914.
116 DOD Archives, DG 1, Box 57, General Botha's Operations Against the Rebels, Telegram Botha to Smuts, 13 November 1914.
117 DOD Archives.
118 Ritchie, *With Botha in the Field*, p. 10.
119 Ritchie, *With Botha in the Field*, pp. 10, 13.

the Anglo-Boer War, where Smuts remained in Pretoria until 1900, before taking to the field. The first formal operational correspondence between Botha and Smuts, was believed to be dated, 2 April 1900.[120] Earlier correspondence between Botha and Smuts can be found in the N.J. De Wet Archive in the South African National Archives.

De Wet attempted to cross the Northern Cape into German South West Africa, and Brits, who had exchanged horse for motorcar in his cross-country chase, eventually caught up with the rebel leader in Bechuanaland at the dry riverbed of the Molopo River.[121]   De Wet was captured by Brits on 1 December 1914 to which Reitz nostalgically commented, 'when I heard how the obstinate old guerrilla leader had been run to earth with the help of these mechanical contrivances I was almost sorry, for it spelt the end of our picturesque South African commando system.'[122] It is interesting to note that the hardy guerrilla leader De Wet, also had a motorcar which was captured after the Battle of Mushroom Valley.[123]

The remaining rebel commandos surrendered on 10 December 1914 at Loskop in the Orange Free State.[124] By December 1914, the rebellion withered away and the only rebels who posed a threat were those under Maritz and Kemp who were still at large in German South West Africa.

Jopie Fourie was one of the few hard-line rebels in the Transvaal who remained at large. Smuts called Trew in to assist Colonel Pretorius with the attack on Fourie's commando that was encamped at Roodekoppies. Fourie's commando later moved from Roodekoppies to the farm, Nooitgedacht.[125] On 16 December 1914, at 16:30, Trew and Pretorius defeated Fourie's commando with a double envelopment attack. After some resistance the rebels surrendered.[126] Fourie was subsequently tried and executed.

Operations against Kemp spill over into the Northern Cape

During late October 1914 Kemp was on the run and headed for German South West Africa through the Northern Cape, after being defeated by the Union forces close to Treurfontein. On 6 November Kemp passed Vryburg and then made for Kuruman.

120 See, Botha to Smuts, W.K. Hancock and J. van der Poel eds., *Selections from the Smuts Papers, Volume I* (London: Cambridge University Press, 1966), pp. 313, 331.
121 L'ange, *Urgent Imperial Service*, p. 69; Anon., *Official History*, p. 22.
122 Reitz, *Trekking On*, p. 63.
123 DOD Archives, DG 1, Box 57, General Botha's Operations Against the Rebels, Telegram Botha to Smuts, 13 November 1914.
124 Sampson, *The Capture of De Wet*, p. 220.
125 DOD Archives, Adjutant General (hereafter AG), Box 13, Rebellion, Rebelle saam met Jopie Fourie gevang te Nooitgedacht, 16 December 1914.
126 DOD Archives, AG, Box 13, Rebellion, Rebelle saam met Jopie Fourie gevang te Nooitgedacht 16 December 1914; Trew, *Botha Treks*, pp. 44-48; Ritchie, *With Botha in the Field*, pp. 16–19.

By 7 November the communication lines to Kuruman was cut and the next day the town was captured by Kemp,[127] after which it was reported that his force had moved towards Upington.[128] Continuing his retreat, Kemp moved to Klein Witzand and took a position which had the only water source in the area. The Union forces attacked Kemp at Klein Witzand on 16 November 1914 but were repulsed.[129]

Kemp and his men then made a dash for German South West Africa by first heading northeast to the edge of the Kalahari Desert where he reached Rooidam on 25 November. Following a brief engagement with the Union Forces the rebels headed westwards towards the German South West African border. The Union forces engaged the rebels with artillery to which the rebels returned fire with small arms targeting the horses of the Union forces.[130] The Natal Carbineers and the SAMR were also in the area of operations but they never managed to capture him. There was one final stand before Kemp made good his escape: Kemp had left a rear-guard to cover his final escape and while the Union forces were engaged with this force, Kemp managed to circle back past the rear of the Union forces and make good his escape to German South West Africa.[131] After Kemp left Rooidam, P. de Wet met up with the fleeing rebel force close to Grondneus from where the *Vrij Korps* escorted them into German South West Africa.[132]

Skirmishes on the Orange River

Van Deventer took over command of the forces in the Northern Cape in December 1914.[133] Commandant P.L. Du Plessis's Cradock commando was sent up to Upington where they served under Colonel Bouwer.[134] On 10 December Bouwer deployed Du Plessis's commando to capture a grouping of rebels who were in and around the Orange River border area. The Union and rebel forces engaged and after a skirmish several Union soldiers were wounded and the rebels managed to escape.[135] Du Plessis

127 DOD Archives, DG 1, Box 1, Special Criminal Court Judgement of Abraham Petrus Jacobus Bezuidenhout, 28 June 1915.

128 DOD Archives, DG 1, Box 57, General Botha's Operations Against the Rebels, Telegram Smuts to Botha, 11 November 1914.

129 Anon., *The Times History of the War*, p. 512.

130 L'ange, *Urgent Imperial Service*, p. 62.

131 Sampson, *The capture of De Wet: The South African Rebellion 1914*, pp. 132, 134.

132 DOD Archives, DG 1, Box 2, Rebellion Commission of Enquiry Volume 1, Testimony by Mr Pieter de Wet, 221, 28 March 1916.

133 DOD Archives, DG 1, Box 2, Rebellion Commission of Enquiry Volume 1, Testimony by Colonel Barend Daniel Bouwer, 121, 2 March 1916.

134 DOD Archives, DG 1, Box 2, Rebellion Commission of Enquiry Volume 1, Testimony by Commandant Phillipus Lodivicus Du Plessis, 415, 18 April 1916.

135 DOD Archives, DG 1, Box 2, Rebellion Commission of Enquiry Volume 1, Testimony by Commandant Phillipus Lodivicus Du Plessis, 416, 18 April 1916.

and ten of his soldiers were subsequently captured by the rebels and taken to Schuits Drift.[136]

On 22 December 1914 a Union commando under the command Lieutenant Colonel Van Zijl and Commandant Breedt were captured by rebel forces at Nous. The rebels attacked the Union camp and it was discovered that Van Zijl had not deployed his forces in the correct positions and an all-round defensive perimeter was not established to defend the camp from possible attack.[137] The rebels captured approximately 130 Union soldiers at Nous.[138]

In an attempt to show strength and dominate the area, Van Deventer subsequently sent the Vermaas Scouts and the Calvinia Ruiters to Schuits Drift. On their arrival on 22 December and on hearing the sound of cannon fire they found Commandant Van Niekerk and approximately 500 Union soldiers on the back foot as they were surrounded by Maritz's rebels. The arrival of the Vermaas Scouts and Calvinia Ruiters shifted the initiative to the side of the Union forces and Maritz's rebels soon retreated.[139]

There was substantial German and rebel activity on the border of German South West Africa in late December 1914 and January 1915. The remoteness of many of the positions in the arid Northern Cape and its concomitant lack of water served as justification to not permanently deploy Union commandos in many of the rural and distant locations. Further reasons for the centralisation of Union forces for an advance into German South West Africa was that any pockets of localised rebel or German forces in rural locations would have their communication lines cut by the invasion force.

Van Deventer wrote to Smuts on 27 December 1914 stating that there was a concentration of German and rebels at Schuits Drift. This deployment was confirmed to be the strongest German/rebel position.[140] Furthermore the German and rebel forces had been seen at Nydesputs. On receipt of this information Van Deventer deployed his forces accordingly;[141] 400 Union soldiers were deployed to Nydesputs. On 18 January 1915 the Union Defence Force position at Nydesputs was surrounded

136 DOD Archives, DG 1, Box 2, Rebellion Commission of Enquiry Volume 1, Testimony by Commandant Phillipus Lodivicus Du Plessis, 416, 18 April 1916.
137 DOD Archives, SD, Box 252, Telegram from Colonel Van Deventer to General Smuts, 23 December 1914.
138 DOD Archives, DG 1, Box 2, Rebellion Commission of Enquiry Volume 1, Testimony by Commandant Phillipus Lodivicus Du Plessis, 416, 18 April 1916.
139 DOD Archives, DG 1, Box 2, Rebellion Commission of Enquiry Volume 1, Testimony by Major Pieter Arnoldus Vermaas, 1011, 30 June 1916.
140 DOD Archives, SD, Box 252, Telegram from Zuidcom to General Smuts, 4 January 1915.
141 DOD Archives, SD, Box 252, Telegram from Colonel Van Deventer to General Smuts, 27 December 1914.

by a rebel/German force. During the engagement that ensued, 9 Union soldiers were killed, 20 wounded and 170 were taken prisoner.[142]

The remaining Union soldiers retreated to Vanrooisvlei. The casualties of the German/rebel force are not known. The German/rebel force was 700 to 800 strong with three pom-poms and three maxims.[143] The presence of the *Vrij Korps* at the Battle of Nydesputs is confirmed by Pieter de Wet.[144]

Van Deventer attributes the loss at Nydesputs to the inadequate orders given by the Union officers which offered an all-round defence but did not provide for protection from flank attacks which in turn allowed the Union position to be surrounded. Furthermore Van Deventer adds that the officers gave orders for the Union soldiers to retreat without giving them specific instructions on what was required of them which caused confusion and contributed to the resultant losses. The prisoners of war were left behind by the German/rebel forces, and were subsequently reorganised into other Union Defence Force units.[145]

The Battle of Nydesputs angered Van Deventer as the Union forces suffered a large amount of casualties.[146] Bouwer had reservations about the quality of the commandos deployed at the border of German South West Africa and he requested Defence headquarters to have them replaced.[147] It is unclear whether the abilities and qualities of the deployed commandos had a direct impact on the loss at Nydesputs.

Following the Battle at Nydesputs, Maritz was told by the German authorities that the South African rebels were not allowed to fall back into German South West Africa as the colony was running low on rations and supplies. Maritz tried to make contact with Van Deventer in Upington to discuss terms but received no response. Following this Maritz and his rebels attacked Upington.[148]

Maritz attacked Upington with approximately 1,000 men, four guns, two pom-poms and two machine guns on 24 January 1915. Maritz and Kemp attacked from the northeast; and the rebel forces led by Stadler which attacked from the west along the Orange riverbed, advanced forward under the cover of pom-pom fire. The

142 DOD Archives, AG 14-21, Box 166, Casualty List, February 1915; Other statistics for the battle is given as 10 killed and 18 wounded: DOD Archives, SD, Box 252, Telegram from Colonel Van Deventer to General Smuts, 20 January 1915.

143 DOD Archives, SD, Box 252, Telegram from Colonel Van Deventer to General Smuts, 18 January 1915.

144 DOD Archives, DG 1, Box 2, Rebellion Commission of Enquiry Volume 1, Testimony by Mr Pieter de Wet, 222, 28 March 1916.

145 DOD Archives, SD, Box 252, Telegram from Colonel Van Deventer to General Smuts, 20 January 1915.

146 DOD Archives, DG 1, Box 2, Rebellion Commission of Enquiry Volume 1, Testimony by Colonel Johann Robert Francois Kirsten, 493, 24 April 1916.

147 DOD Archives, SD, Box 252, Telegram from Colonel Bouwer to General Smuts, 26 December 1915.

148 DOD Archives, DG 1, Box 2, Rebellion Commission of Enquiry Volume 1, Testimony by Mr Pieter de Wet, 223, 28 March 1916.

Union defenders delivered a high volume of accurate fire which prevented the rebels from entering the town.[149]

The rebels became desperate in not being able to penetrate the defences of the town. In their frustration Maritz and Kemp attempted a mounted charge[150] but were repulsed by the Cape Field Artillery who fired at the advancing rebels at a range of approximately 1,000 yards.[151]

The rebels were firmly repulsed. The Union artillery fired 243 rounds during the exchange and the German artillery fired approximately 150 shells. The rebel casualties were: 12 killed, 23 wounded and 97 captured to the Union's three killed and 22 wounded.[152] The rebel assault on the town of Upington on 24 January 1915 lasted six hours and Van Deventer[153] who was in command ensured a decisive victory for the Union.[154] The rebels subsequently surrendered handing themselves over to the Union government.

The failed attack by Maritz on Upington brought an effective end to any rebel participation in the German South West African campaign. Major H. Ritter subsequently attacked the Union force based at Kakamas on 4 February 1915 but was repulsed by a stout South African defence.[155] Ritter's offensive on Kakamas was the last attack that the Germans would make within Union territory. During the attack on Kakamas the Germans suffered 12 killed and 12 soldiers captured.[156]

Analysis and conclusion

The headquarters of the UDF had the advantage of efficient intelligence gathering and processing systems during the Afrikaner Rebellion. This gave the Union forces access to information that made a rapid decision making cycle possible; furthermore they made maximum use of mobility to concentrate on the rebels and ensure surprise.

The strategy of the central position was effectively employed. The Union made use of internal lines of operations to combat the military threat of the Afrikaner Rebellion; Botha's forces used railways, armoured trains and motorcars for internal operational movement within the Union's borders. In addition horses were used for tactical movement against the rebels. The Union forces had 33,308 mounted troops

149 L'ange, *Urgent Imperial Service*, p. 79.
150 Dane, *British Campaigns in Africa and the Pacific 1914-1918*, pp. 44, 45.
151 L'ange, *Urgent Imperial Service*, p. 79.
152 L'ange, *Urgent Imperial Service*, p. 80, Statistics have indicated that the Union casualties were: 6 dead and 23 casualties: DOD Archives, AG 14-21, Box 166, Casualty List, February 1915;
153 Van Deventer went on to become a Lieutenant General and was later knighted for his exploits in German East Africa.
154 Anon., *Official History*, p. 52; DOD Archives, SD, Box 252, Telegram from General Smuts to Colonel Van Deventer, 26 January 1915.
155 Collyer, *The Campaign in German South West Africa, 1914-1915*, p. 80.
156 Nasson, *Springboks on the Somme*, p. 69.

which were mobilised for the German South West African campaign; a large number of these troops were used in operations against the rebels (refer to graph 5.1).[157]

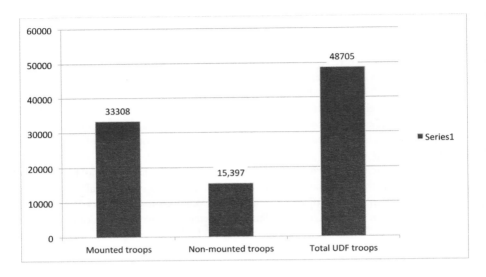

Graph 5.1: UDF troops used in operations to suppress the rebellion[158]

Van Deventer attributes the success of his operations against the rebels to the rapidity with which the Union forces deployed and positioning of his commandos; which induced the rebels to surrender.[159] Furthermore, the UDF was able to defeat the rebel forces because of their superior operational and tactical mobility and their rapid decision making cycle which in turn ensured surprise. The UDF gained and maintained the initiative throughout the military operations against the rebels.

According to Lord S Buxton, the governor general of South Africa, the rebels had no clear campaign plan, no staff work, no cooperation and no definite objectives.[160] Following the failed attempt at Upington the rebels based in German South West Africa surrendered on 30 January 1915. Smuts gave the official figures of the rebellion as 130 government soldiers killed and 275 wounded; and 190 rebels killed and 400 wounded.[161] The casualties of People of Colour in the suppression of the rebellion

157 DOD Archives, AG 1914–1921, Box 150, Strengths, List of all Union Defence Forces on active duty, 23 November 1914.
158 DOD Archives, AG 1914–1921, Box 150, Strengths, List of all Union Defence Forces on active duty, 23 November 1914.
159 Trew, *Botha Treks*, p. 154.
160 S.C. Buxton, *General Botha* (London: Hazel, Watson & Viney, 1924), p. 66.
161 Nasson, *Springboks on the Somme*, pp. 48–50.

is unknown, and requires further research. The total number of rebels who were captured and surrendered is indicated in Table 5.1.

Province	Captured	Surrendered	Total
Orange Free State	3,138	3,985	7,123
Transvaal	2,350	648	2,998
Cape	398	192	590
Totals	5,886	4,825	10,711

Table 5.1: Rebels captured and surrendered[162]

There were significant engagements in the Northern Cape, Orange Free State and Transvaal. These engagements ensured that the UDF maintained the initiative in their operations against the rebels.

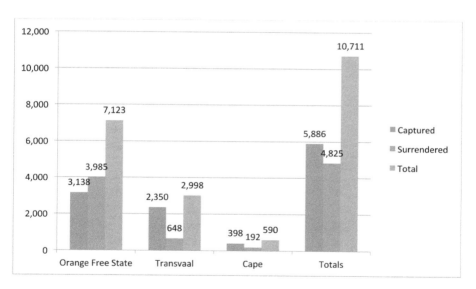

Graph 5.2: Rebels captured and surrendered[163]

162 DOD Archives, D, Box 1, Treason trials, Rebels captured and surrendered. Note these statistics exclude the Battle of Upington.
163 DOD Archives, D, Box 1, Treason trials, Rebels captured and surrendered. Note these statistics exclude the Battle of Upington.

Northern Cape Engagements	
Union victories	Rebel victories
Keimoes	Schuits Drift
Kakamas	Nous
Schuits Drift	Nydesputs
Upington	

Table 5.2: Significant Northern Cape engagements

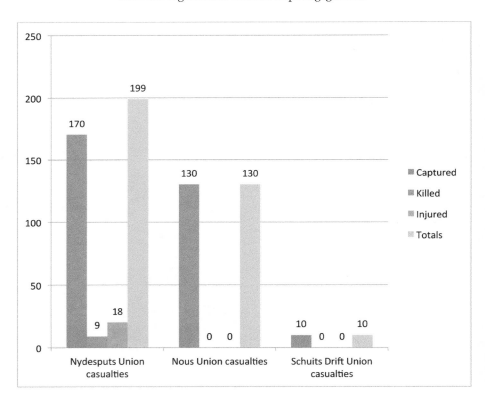

Graph 5.3: Union casualties at significant Northern Cape Engagements

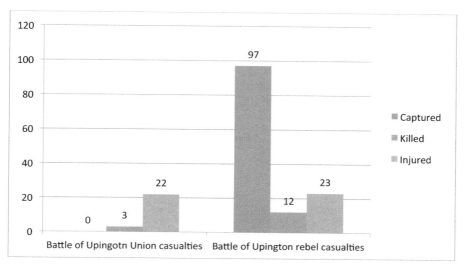

Graph 5.4: Battle of Upington Casualties

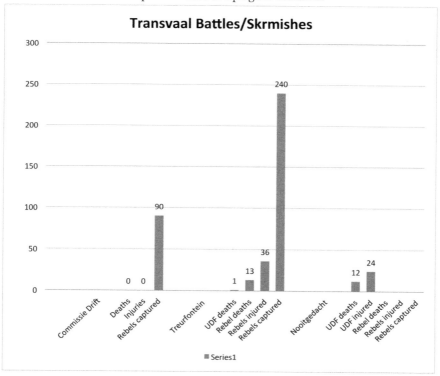

Graph 5.5: Transvaal Battles/Skirmishes[164]

164 Anon., *Judicial Commission of Inquiry*, p. 66. Anon., *Official History*, pp. 16–17.

The rebellion provided the UDF – especially the commandos – with the means to rehearse their doctrine, drills and tactics. The rebels unwittingly gave the UDF valuable training in the execution of operational and tactical movements and in the review of their battle drills before recommencing the invasion of German South West Africa.

The Union raised a total of 48,705 troops for the rebellion and the German South West African campaign of which 33,308 were mounted troops and 15,397 were non-mounted troops.[165] The rebellion gave the UDF insight into its deficiencies as far as supplies were concerned and the UDF subsequently acquired 20,000 Portuguese Mauser rifles and 10,000,000 rounds of ammunition.[166]

After the Battle of Sandfontein and the Afrikaner Rebellion, the UDF was solidified under a unified leadership structure. The re-invasion of German South West Africa followed four axes of advance which included the Northern, Southern, Eastern and Central forces. This invasion concept was similar to the one Smuts initially envisioned.[167] The next chapter discusses the invasion effort of the Northern Force.

165 DOD Archives, AG 1914–1921, Box 150, Strengths, List of all Union Defence Forces on active duty, 23 November 1914.
166 Buxton, *General Botha*, p. 102.
167 Van der Waag, 'The Battle of Sandfontein, 26 September 1914', p. 15.

6

The Northern Offensive until 31 March 1915

The Northern Force, was central to the Union's invasion plans of German South West Africa. Where the proposed amphibious landings at Swakopmund was denied by the British Admiralty and the abortive terrestrial invasion resulted in the Battle of Sandfontein, the reinvasion, following the establishment of British dominance of the sea, allowed for a northerly line of advance. The Union forces took Walvis Bay on 25 December 1914 without a shot fired in anger, and Swakopmund was subsequently captured in January 1915. Colonel P.C.B. Skinner led the initial invasion of Walvis Bay which was unopposed by the Germans except for sporadic skirmishing and some booby traps and mines left behind.[1] Botha, as prime minister of the Union was appointed as commander-in-chief of the expeditionary force by special commission, Section 81 of the Defence Act of 1912,[2] arrived in Walvis Bay in February 1915 and took over command of the Northern Force with the clear intention of advancing eastwards towards Windhoek.

The Union's amphibious landings in Walvis Bay and Lüderitzbucht meant that the Germans had a wide front to defend.[3] Walvis Bay and Swakopmund were also extended forward bases to be supplied by the Union via naval support. Botha had a large number of troops at his disposal in the north, including the 1st Mounted Brigade under command of Brits with approximately 2,200 soldiers; the 2nd Mounted Brigade with approximately 2,500 soldiers under the command of Alberts; and two infantry brigades under the respective commands of Skinner and Colonel J.S. Wylie. He also had two unabridged infantry battalions, one mounted regiment, one battery and one section of heavy artillery.[4]

1   G. L'ange, *Urgent Imperial Service* (Rivonia: Ashanti, 1991), pp. 138, 139.
2   DOD Archives, AG 1914–1921, Box 8, G5/305/9199, Commander-in-chief, Government notice for the next issue of the *Union Gazette*, 18 October 1914.
3   B. Nasson, *Springboks on the Somme* (Johannesburg: Penguin, 2007), pp. 69, 70.
4   J.J. Collyer, *The Campaign in German South West Africa, 1914–1915* (Pretoria: Government Printer, 1937), p. 55.

The main thrust of the strategy of the Union Defence Force took place in the northern region of German South West Africa. The advance of the Northern Army was directed at Windhoek and at the headquarters of the *Schutztruppe*.

Botha's plan was to take Windhoek by capturing a number of intermediate German positions en route. The first objectives on the advance included Nonidas and Goanikontes which were followed by the positions of Usakos and Husab.[5] The first substantial defence offered by the German forces were the engagements at Riet, Pforte, and Jakkalsfontein.[6] Map 6.1 indicates the direction of the Northern Army's and Central force's advance.

The Union commenced its advance on Nonidas on 23 February.[7] This attack was in the form of a double envelopment. The Germans retreated and poisoned the wells while making their withdrawal.[8] Goanikontes was one of the subsequent German positions to fall to the South African advance. The Germans commented that they were astonished at the extraordinary mobility of the South Africans.[9]

Botha wrote to Smuts on 27 February after the capture of Nonidas and discussed the operational needs of the campaign. Botha stated that the horses needed fresh water and the soldiers required compasses for night navigation. The Germans had managed to escape from Nonidas because the Union cut off force commanded by Alberts had lost its way on the night of the operation.[10]

Usakos was the next German position to be taken on the advance. There were two broad options: advancing along the railway or along the dry Swakop riverbed. Advancing without the railway would require many more wagons as well as oxen and mules but nonetheless Botha decided to use the Swakop riverbed for his primary advance sacrificing logistics for mobility and displaying faith in the abilities and robustness of the commandos.[11] Whereas the tactical operations and advance on Usakos could be executed with horse, ox and waggons, the construction of the railway continued and became essential for the re-supply of the troops in the later stages of the campaign.[12]

5   DOD Archives, SD, Box 252, 17138, Historical Record of the Campaign in German South West Africa, 4 November 1919.
6   While Map 6 and Map 7 both use the name Jakkalswater (in Map 7 the spelling is Jakalswater) in the text of this book Jakkalsfontein is used instead, which is the name used in some of the secondary material as well as the Department of Defence Archives where archival sources on the campaign were consulted.
7   M.E. Ritchie, *With Botha in the Field* (London: Longmans, 1915), p. 32.
8   Trew, *Botha Treks* (London: Blackie & Son, 1936), pp. 91, 92.
9   L'ange, *Urgent Imperial Service*, p. 175.
10   Botha to Smuts, W.K. Hancock and J. van der Poel (eds), *Selections from the Smuts Papers, Volume III* (London: Cambridge University Press, 1966), p. 242.
11   Collyer, *The Campaign in German South West Africa, 1914–1915*, p. 59.
12   SANA, Smuts Papers, Box 112, Major General Thompson: Report on a visit to German South West Africa, 20-27 March 1915.

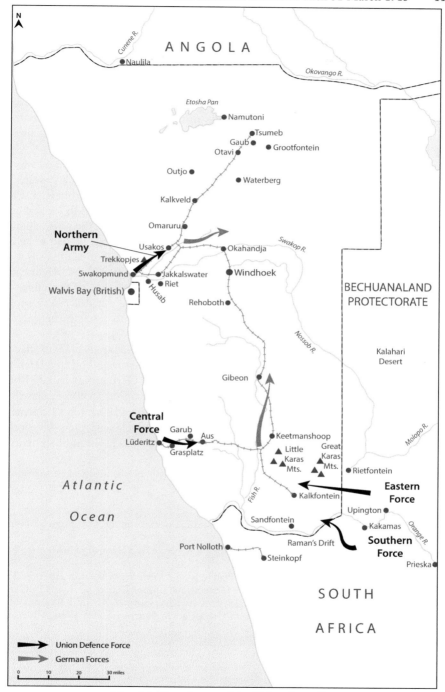

Map 6.1: The advance of the Union Forces[13]

Botha planned an ingenious method of placing advanced logistical supplies beyond the forward base of the Union forces. In this regard he placed a five day supply at Husab prior to the advance on Riet. The central idea was to keep the fighting forces at a position where they could be easily maintained in terms of rations and water prior to the advance and then when they advanced, to have a logistical supply in place to facilitate their extensive movements.[14] It was difficult for some British staff officers to understand Botha's irregular, dynamic and daring thinking and he complained to Smuts, infuriated by officers almost stifling his logistical plans.[15]

Besides resupply, the fundamental consideration during the campaign was the shortage of water[16] and the South African forces advanced from waterhole to waterhole along the Swakop riverbed.[17] After taking Usakos, the defensive line from Riet, Pforte and to Jakkalsfontein was the next logical step on the advance to Windhoek and it was also of strategic importance as water source. Ritchie says that 'Botha's principle task was to take an army right across the Namib Desert and to do that he had to capture every water-hole and keep it'.[18]

Botha expected that the Germans would be in and around the Riet, Pforte, and Jakkalsfontein area. The Union had intercepted information to the effect that the Germans were in a strong position at Riet and that they had artillery support and a competent commander. Botha immediately planned to envelop the defensive position.[19]

The expeditionary force was ready to advance by mid-March 1915: Botha had mobilised all the transport and supplies of the Northern Army and by 16 March they had five and a half days supplies for the advance on the Germans at Riet.[20] Botha's forces made use of, 59 ammunition wagons, 110 wagons and 51 water carts.[21] The commander-in-chief departed from Swakopmund at 14:30 on 18 March 1915 reaching Goanikontes by 23:00 that same day. Botha and his bodyguard then advanced to Husab where they arrived on the morning of 19 March 1915. Botha marched with

Campaign) 9 July to 28 October 1920, Historical Record of the Campaign in German South West Africa, 4 November 1919.

14   DOD Archives, SD, Box 252, 17138, Historical Record of the Campaign in German South West Africa, 4 November 1919.
15   Botha to Smuts, Hancock and Van der Poel (eds), *Selections from the Smuts Papers*, p. 257.
16   SANA, Smuts Papers, Box 112, Major General Thompson: Report on a visit to German South West Africa, 20-27 March 1915. See, E. Kleynhans, "A Critical Analysis of the Impact of Water on the South African Campaign in German South West Africa, 1914 1915", *Historia*, 61, 2, 2016.
17   J. Meintjes, *General Louis Botha* (London: Cassell & Co., 1970), p. 261.
18   Ritchie, *With Botha in the Field*, p. 33.
19   Hancock and Van der Poel (eds), *Selections from the Smuts Papers*, p. 243.
20   Collyer, *The Campaign in German South West Africa, 1914–1915*, p. 62.
21   DOD Archives, AG 1914–1921, Box 182, Mounted Strengths, Field state, 12 April 1915.

great haste and as a result there were no luxuries for his staff: they suffered similar hardships as the rest of the men.[22]

Plate 6.1: Botha attends his horses in the early morning

On 19 March 1915, Botha departed from Husab and proceeded with staged operations on the Riet, Pforte, Jakkalsfontein defensive line,[23] with Husab as the launching base from where the advance to battle commenced. The 1st and 2nd Mounted Brigades were used for the attack.

The Germans held a strong defensive position from Riet, Pforte and Jakkalsfontein, which extended for 48 kilometres.[24] They made optimum use of the terrain and high ground and deployed 2,000 soldiers and four artillery pieces. The Langer Heinrich hills on the eastern bank of the river provided a strong defensive position for the German forces,[25] and they also occupied the Husabberg, Pforteberg and Geisberg hills to the north of the river.[26]

The German position was well fortified and had good lines of communication between the various sections of the defensive line up to and including Jakkalsfontein,

22 Trew, *Botha Treks*, pp. 95, 96.
23 Nasson, *Springboks on the Somme*, p. 70.
24 Meintjes, *General Louis Botha*, p. 261.
25 H. Paterson, 'First Allied Victory: The South African Campaign in German South-West Africa, 1914–1915", *Military History Journal*, 13, 2, 2004, p. 5.
26 L'ange, *Urgent Imperial Service*, p. 181.

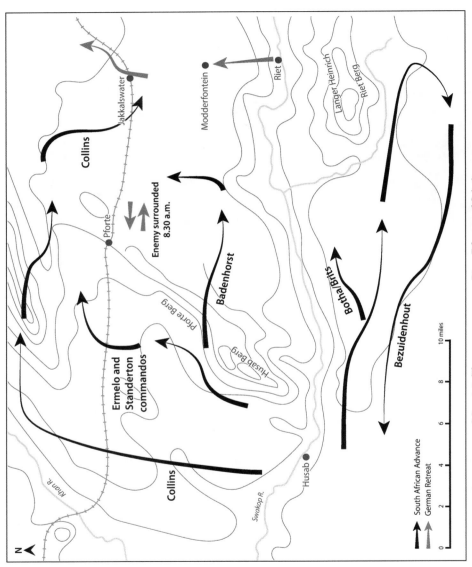

Map 6.2: The engagements at Riet, Pforte and Jakalswater

where the German reserve was placed. The German position was particularly strong to the east and had rocky outcrops which were largely impregnable.[27] The German right flank was on the Pforteberg mountain range and their left flank was on the Langer Heinrich hills.[28]

Botha was renowned for his night marches[29] and during the night advance from Husab to Riet, in order to promote secrecy and surprise he did not allow smoking as the glow of cigarettes could be seen for a considerable distance at night. At the same time Brits's force advanced in parallel columns so as to prevent raising excessive dust.[30] The secretive advance on Riet was to be followed by an outflanking and enveloping attack on the defensive line (refer to Map 6.3). Botha intended to attack and outflank the forces at Riet, Pforte and Jakkalsfontein simultaneously so as to prevent the German forces from reinforcing a particular front.[31]

The advance on Riet began at 19:00 on 19 March 1915 and continued through the night. Alberts was ordered to envelop the Pforteberg range from the north and Brits would attack the German position at Langer Heinrich. In the early hours of the morning of 20 March Brits's scouts made contact with the German position. The initial contact was followed by the South African artillery engaging the German positions at Riet.[32] The Transvaal Horse Artillery arrived at Riet at approximately 6:00 and provided accurate fire on the German position.[33] The artillery range was approximately 2.5 kilometres but the Germans struggled to bring their guns to bear.[34] Major S.S. Taylor of the Transvaal Horse Artillery was cited for his actions as an artillery commander at the engagement at Riet and received a mention in despatches.[35] However, the Black and Coloured drivers which served as part of the various artillery units, received no mention.

Brits and his force attacked the German emplacements in the Langer Heinrich hills. The well placed German position gave stiff resistance to the Union's direct attack. The Potchefstroom commando under the command of Brits made slow progress and eventually managed to take a ridge en route to the German emplacements.[36] The

27 Collyer, *The Campaign in German South West Africa, 1914–1915*, p. 67.
28 DOD Archives, SD, Box 252, 17138, Historical Record of the Campaign in German South West Africa, 4 November 1919; Trew, *Botha Treks*, p. 96.
29 Ritchie, *With Botha in the Field*, p. 8.
30 Meintjes, *General Louis Botha*, 261, 262; Trew, *Botha Treks*, p. 97.
31 H.F.B. Walker, *A Doctor's Diary in Damaraland* (London: Edward Arnold, 1917), p. 42.
32 Trew, *Botha Treks*, 97–102; Ritchie, *With Botha in the Field*, pp. 34, 35.
33 N. Orpen, *The History of the Transvaal Horse Artillery 1904–1974* (Johannesburg: Alex White & Co., 1975), p. 25.
34 Ritchie, *With Botha in the Field*, p. 35.
35 DOD Archives, World War 1 German South West Africa (hereafter WW1 GSWA), Box 23a, Citations, German South West Africa, Northern Army 1st Mounted Brigade Transvaal Horse Artillery, 17 February 1918.
36 DOD Archives, WW1 GSWA, Box 23a, Citations, German South West Africa, Northern Army 1st Mounted Brigade Potchefstroom 'B' Commando, 17 February 1918.

artillery shelling supported the direct attack on Riet, which fixed the German forces as the mobile forces proceeded with flanking operations.

During the offensive, Commandant Bezuidenhout was sent to envelop the German position at Rietfontein. The map that Bezuidenhout used to navigate his route over a mountain pass turned out to be inaccurate, and this topographical error led to the failure of his attempted envelopment.[37] Maps were issued to Van Deventer and Brits from the topographical branch before the military operations in GSWA commenced.[38] The gap in the mountains through which Bezuidenhout was supposed to advance simply did not exist. The shortage and quality of maps was an issue of concern prior to the reinvasion of German South West Africa.[39] Furthermore, on his return, Bezuidenhout made the mistake of not informing Brits or Botha or any of the other command staff that his envelopment had failed.[40]

While the battle ensued, Trew, having had a similar problem during the Afrikaner Rebellion, requested that Botha withdraw to a safe position, but he refused believing his withdrawal might have resulted in a negative influence on the morale of the troops.[41] Brits sent another grouping of 300 reserve troops to envelop the position at Riet but this met with little success due to the ruggedness of the terrain.[42] This force was supposed to have cut the German left flank on the Langer Heinrich hills but failed to do so. The clash at Riet was essentially a deadlock and the day ended with an attrition-like artillery shelling of alternate positions. The Germans were in a strong position at Riet which rendered direct attack infeasible.

Brits waited for Bezuidenhout to turn the German position which was not achieved due to erroneous terrain intelligence. The artillery duel continued,[43] and the attack remained relatively stationary.[44] Botha's chief fear was not getting water at Riet because this would have completely disabled his fighting force. By 18:30 on 20 March, the fighting died down considerably allowing the soldiers and horses a chance to rest and acquire adequate water supplies,[45] which they did by digging in the Swakop Riverbed. Many of the soldiers had to move to Gawieb to get sufficient water and Botha and his

37   L'ange, *Urgent Imperial Service*, p. 184; Anon., *Official History*, p. 40. Walker states that Bezuidenhout was able to follow a route that led to Salem: Walker, *A Doctor's Diary in Damaraland*, p. 43; DOD Archives, SD, Box 252, 17138, Historical Record of the Campaign in German South West Africa, 4 November 1919.

38   DOD Archives, AG 1914–1921, Box 162, G219/310/9199, Letter from the Defence Topographical Section to Commando Staff Office, 26 January 1915.

39   DOD Archives, SD2, Box 260, Correspondence Topographical Section to Defence Headquarters, December 1914.

40   Collyer, *The Campaign in German South West Africa, 1914–1915*, p. 69.

41   Trew, *Botha Treks*, p. 103.

42   Collyer, *The Campaign in German South West Africa, 1914–1915*, p. 67; Anon., *Official History*, p. 41.

43   Trew, *Botha Treks*, p. 105.

44   Collyer, *The Campaign in German South West Africa, 1914–1915*, p. 68.

45   Trew, *Botha Treks*, pp. 105–109.

bodyguard moved two kilometres away along the road from Riet to Husab where they encamped for the night.[46]

Alberts had a much more successful day around Pforte. He sent the Standerton and Ermelo commandos to engage the Germans directly at Pforte while deploying Swarts's scouts and two other commandos through the gap between Hussabberg and Pforteberg. The commandos hurried through under artillery fire from the Germans and enabled the railway between Pforte and Jakkalsfontein to be cut, thereby isolating the forward German detachments.[47] The envelopment cut the German communications to the west of Jakkalsfontein,[48] and the action at Pforte also culminated in an artillery duel. Captain J.F. Wolmarans, commander of the 4th Permanent Battery of the South African Mounted Rifles was commended for his actions at Pforte and received the Distinguished Service Order medal.[49] The Black, Coloured and Indian drivers of the artillery battery were not recognised for their efforts. Alberts eventually captured the entire force at Pforte, who surrendered at 15:00 on 20 March 1915 as a result of having their lines of retreat and communications cut. [50]

The surprised German commander at Pforte later told the story of how the South Africans came at them from all sides, especially from behind and that the commandos were seen firing from the saddle.[51] The success of the manoeuvre was attributed to the swiftness of the commandos.[52] The total loss for the South African forces was 13 dead, 41 wounded and 43 prisoners of war. German losses amounted to 16 dead, 21 wounded and 284 prisoners of war.[53]

While the battle at Riet ensued, the commando wing of Commandant Collins's force had successfully engaged the German forces at Jakkalsfontein which eventually retreated. Collins's men pursued the fleeing Germans who responded with strong and direct artillery fire, forcing the commandos to withdraw leaving 43 soldiers as prisoners of war.[54] These men had their horses shot down and were thus left stranded. The German forces at Riet withdrew under the cover of darkness as a result of the actions a Pforte and Jakkalsfontein.

A German commander told Trew that he was surprised at how fast the South Africans could advance. The Germans had calculated that it should have taken another day to set up a forward supply base at Husab and that it was unimaginable that the

46   Ritchie, *With Botha in the Field*, p. 36.
47   DOD Archives, SD, Box 252, 17138, Historical Record of the Campaign in German South West Africa, 4 November 1919; L'ange, *Urgent Imperial Service*, p. 186.
48   Paterson, 'First Allied Victory', p. 5.
49   DOD Archives, WW1 GSWA, Box 23a, Citations, German South West Africa, Northern Army 2nd Mounted Brigade 4th Permanent Battery SAMR, 17 February 1918.
50   Trew, *Botha Treks*, p. 114.
51   Trew, *Botha Treks*, p. 117.
52   Collyer, *The Campaign in German South West Africa, 1914–1915*, p. 70.
53   DOD Archives, SD, Box 252, 17138, Historical Record of the Campaign in German South West Africa, 4 November 1919; L'ange, *Urgent Imperial Service*, p. 188.
54   Collyer, *The Campaign in German South West Africa, 1914–1915*, p. 72.

Union would press forward without proper supplies.[55] The tactical surprise was crucial to the South African victory and can also be regarded as a German intelligence failure.

Following the occupation of Riet, important documents were found which provided information that for the most part the Germans were concentrated in the north of the colony. Information regarding German mines, booby-traps and their intention to poison various water wells was also found.[56]

Following the battle Riet became the forward supply depot for the South African forces from which further advances would be launched.[57] These water wells were left intact by the Germans – but not for a lack of trying. The German engineer section that was sent to destroy the wells following their retreat from Riet was shot down by two commando scouts.[58]

At this stage the commandos and the rest of the forces did not have the logistical requirements to continue the campaign.[59] The horses of the South African commandos were exhausted and thus the victory at Riet, Pforte and Jakkalsfontein could not be exploited by pursuing the Germans any further.[60] There were reports which indicated that the terrain at Riet may have had good grazing for the horses,[61] however this was not the case.

The Germans' secret code was found at Pforte enabling the South African forces to decode German messages.[62] This proved a crucial find as it allowed the South African forces to decrypt German messages about the movement of their forces. Following the victory at Riet, Pforte and Jakkalsfontein on 20 March, there was very little activity in the northern part of German South West Africa until the end of April 1915. Botha and the South African forces took an operational pause so as to replenish their logistics which was required to continue the advance on Windhoek.[63]

A manoeuvre warfare theory analysis of the northern operations until the Battle of Riet, Pforte and Jakkalsfontein

In considering the overlap between strategic and tactical dimensions of the campaign, Botha was the commander-in-chief of South Africa's expeditionary force in German South West Africa as well as prime minister of the Union. Because of

55 Trew, *Botha Treks*, p. 115.
56 A.C. Martin, *The Durban Light Infantry, Volume 1, 1854 to 1934* (Durban: Hayne & Gibson Ltd, 1969), p. 171.
57 Ritchie, *With Botha in the Field*, p. 39.
58 Trew, *Botha Treks*, p. 113.
59 SANA, Smuts Papers, Box 112, Major General Thompson: Report on a visit to German South West Africa, 20-27 March 1915; Nasson, *Springboks on the Somme*, pp. 70, 71.
60 Nasson, *Springboks on the Somme*, p. 71; Paterson, 'First Allied Victory', p. 6.
61 Paterson, 'First Allied Victory', p. 5.
62 Trew, *Botha Treks*, p. 114.
63 SANA, Smuts Papers, Box 112, Major General Thompson: Report on a visit to German South West Africa, 20-27 March 1915.

his unique position he had a clear idea of what was needed on the different levels of war and he understood the needs of the campaign on the strategic, operational and tactical levels. Botha had outlined the strategic importance of the campaign when he addressed parliament and appealed for the approval of the campaign,[64] which were linked to British war aims. Prior to parliamentary approval, the Defence headquarters powered by the brain power of Smuts, had already started mobilising forces for the invasion.

There was a merging of the strategic and operational levels of war. Botha (prime minister) and Smuts (minister of defence and acting prime minister while Botha was on campaign) were in political control and also in military command of the Union. Thus the operational and strategic levels of war were amalgamated in their leadership. Their objectives at the levels of war targeted the German centre of gravity which was the *Schutztruppe* headquarters. Neutralising of the German forces was crucial to their political ends and included the imperial objectives dictated by the British war strategy. By defeating the *Schutztruppe* Botha would complete his responsibility to the British Empire and allow the Union Defence Force to be redeployed to other theatres of the war. A rapid victory would also be important for the 1915 elections. However the 1914 Afrikaner Rebellion, the redeployment of loyal troops (away from voting booths) and a fragmented white society would lead to a complicated electoral victory which was only made possible through uncomfortable alliances.

As the prime minister, Botha had a clear idea of the political interests of Britain and South Africa. Botha acted as both politician, understanding the importance of a rapid conclusion to the campaign, and as a general who understood the logistical complexities of operations. Tzu argues that politicians should not command soldiers as this generally leads to confusion.[65] However, in the case of the German South West Africa campaign Botha was an exception; he was well suited to command the military force because of his previous experience and abilities, and his personality which united English and Afrikaans- speaking South Africans.[66]

Botha did not focus on the tactical level; instead he kept his aim firmly fixed on the operational objectives of the campaign. Botha and Smuts through their dual roles as political and military leaders centralised the strategic and operational levels, thereby uniting the objectives, vision and efforts of the Union's forces.

The Union Defence Force advanced on four divergent axes. By advancing on separate routes it weakened the German forces and prevented them from linking up and operating effectively on in internal lines.

---

64   L'ange, *Urgent Imperial Service*, p. 14.
65   S. Tzu, tr. Sadler, A.L., *The Art of War* (Tokyo: Tuttle, 2009), p. 6.
66   SANA, Smuts Papers, Box 112, Major General Thompson: Report on a visit to German South West Africa, 20-27 March 1915.

Graph 6.1 demonstrates the strength of the different forces on their respective axes of advance. The numerical superiority of the Union forces allowed for the deployment of troops and materiel on four divergent axes.

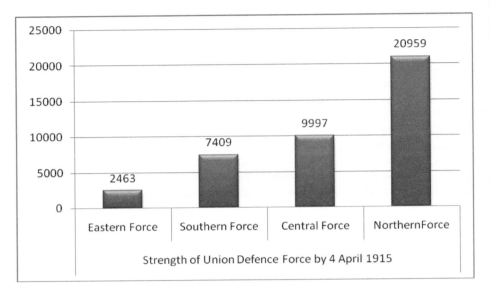

Graph 6.1: Strength of the Eastern, Southern, Central and Northern forces (including forces in field and en route to the theatre of operations)[67]

The events at Riet, if taken in isolation, could be regarded as attrition-based. The envelopments at Pforte however qualify the operations throughout the entire defensive line as congruent with the principles of manoeuvre warfare. The battle at Riet and Pforte began as a direct attack on the German position. The terrain prevented the turning of the German left flank and thus the engagement resulted in a stalemate. The terrain at Pforte lent itself to extensive movements which was exploited by the mobility of the commandos.[68] The attack of the Union Defence Force on the German forces at Pforte and Jakkalsfontein was in part an envelopment of the German forces at Riet. As a result the German forces at Riet were cut off and withdrew.

Botha allowed his forces to operate on their own initiative in a decentralised fashion.[69] They understood the objectives and used their initiative in realising the

67 DOD Archives, AG 1914–1921, Box 150, Strengths, General Summary, 4 April 1915.
68 Collyer, *The Campaign in German South West Africa, 1914–1915*, p. 74.
69 DOD Archives, SD, Box 252, 17138, Reports of Force Commanders in German South West Africa, Despatch number 4 by General Botha covering the period 15 May to 18 July 1915; Collyer, *The Campaign in German South West Africa, 1914–1915*, 114. DOD Archives,

commander's intent. The Unions' envelopment of Pforte and Jakkalsfontein robbed the Germans of the initiative and forced them to retreat. The Union forces executed a rapid OODA loop on the tactical and operational levels which essentially disrupted the German defence. Botha thus gained the initiative. Chapter 7 proceeds with a discussion on the operations in the south of German South West Africa.

SD, Box 252, 17138 IO, General Botha's Despatch (GOC MC GSW Campaign) 9 July to 28 October 1920, Historical Record of the Campaign in German South West Africa, 4 November 1919.

7

Operations in the South of German South West Africa

The offensive in the south of German South West Africa, commenced in September 1914, however it delayed because of the Afrikaner Rebellion. The Southern Army was a combination of C Force (which later became the Central Force) and the Southern and Eastern Forces. The aim of the Southern Army was to capture Kalkfontein, Aus, Keetmanshoop and Gibeon so as to nullify the German force's ability to concentrate its forces in the south of the colony.

The force at Lüderitzbucht, originally C Force, landed on the night of 18 September 1914 and was led by Colonel P.S. Beves. Expecting to receive resistance from the Germans, Beves deployed a small force to envelop the German port and cut its railway line to force a retreat,[1] however this proved to be unnecessary as Lüderitzbucht was abandoned by the Germans.

Beves' force comprised the 1st Transvaal Scottish, the Witwatersrand Rifles, one squadron of the Imperial Light Horse, and seven guns from the 7th Citizen Force Battery.[2] Its total strength was approximately 1,824 soldiers.[3] C Force took the German post at Grasplatz on 26 September without much incident. The Germans had withdrawn from the vicinity of the coast towards Aus and had destroyed the railway piecemeal during their retreat as a means to slow down the South African advance. It was later discovered that the Germans were concentrating their efforts on Sandfontein (refer to chapter 3).

General D. Mackenzie took command of the force at Lüderitzbucht in October 1914, after which it became known as the Central Force. The Central Force took Tschaukaib on 8 November 1914 and then in mid-December attempted to take Garub where they were repulsed by the Germans who put up a stout defence. Following the

---

1   G. L'ange, *Urgent Imperial Service* (Rivonia: Ashanti, 1991), pp. 91, 92.
2   Ibid., p. 94.
3   I. Van der Waag, 'The Battle of Sandfontein, 26 September 1914: South African Military Reform and the German South-West Africa Campaign, 1914–1915', *First World War Studies*, 4, 2 2013, p. 9.

failed attempt, Mackenzie's force then returned to Tschaukaib.[4] The Union's plan of attack included the capture of Aus, Keetmanshoop and Gibeon.

The strength of Mackenzie's force on 22 December was 2,183 mounted men and 5,754 infantrymen.[5] The Southern Force was opposed by the German commander, Major Ritter, who had a battery of artillery and four mounted regiments at his disposal. He also had the support of Maritz with approximately 800 rebels.[6] The German force was estimated at approximately 1,000 soldiers.

Mackenzie's force numbers increased to 10,830 on 24 March 1915 of whom 3,842 were mounted soldiers and 5,777 were infantrymen.[7] The Central Force comprised two field batteries of artillery, along with two mounted brigades. A third brigade was sent to Lüderitzbucht in early March 1915 which comprised seven infantry battalions and two batteries of heavy artillery.[8] Graph 7.1 demonstrates the increase in troops of the Central Force from September 1914 until March 1915.

The Southern and Eastern forces deployed from Upington and Kakamas respectively and were commanded by Van Deventer (Southern Force) and Colonel CAL Berrange (Eastern Force). Berrange had four mounted regiments and one section of heavy artillery under his charge, while Van Deventer had one battery of heavy artillery and 29 commandos. Van Deventer's force had a numerical strength of 6,958 men, of whom 6,176 were mounted soldiers.[9]

Berrange's force comprised mounted riflemen to the strength of 1,992 men.[10] Both forces were supported by a small section of artillery and their rendezvous point was Keetmanshoop.[11] The Southern and Eastern forces formed part of the invasion force that would cross the German South West African border and link up with the Central Force, thus forming part of the Southern Army. Smuts assumed overall command of the Southern Army in April 1915.

Berrange moved from Kakamas to Kuruman and then travelled 403 kilometres from Kuruman and crossed the German South West African border in March 1915.

4   H. Paterson, 'First Allied Victory: The South African Campaign in German South-West Africa, 1914–1915", *Military History Journal*, 13, 2, 2004, p. 2; B. Nasson, *Springboks on the Somme* (Johannesburg: Penguin, 2007), p. 68.
5   DOD Archives, AG 1914–1921, Box 150, Strengths, Strength return of the Central Force, 22 December 1914.
6   J.J. Collyer, *The Campaign in German South West Africa, 1914–1915* (Pretoria: Government Printer, 1937), p. 80.
7   DOD Archives, AG 1914–1921, Box 150, Strengths, General Summary Central Force, 24 March 1915.
8   Collyer, *The Campaign in German South West Africa, 1914-1915*, p. 55.
9   DOD Archives, AG 1914–1921, Box 150, Strengths, General Summary, Southern Force, 4 April 1915.
10   DOD Archives, AG 1914–1921, Box 150, Strengths, General Summary, Eastern Force 14 April 1915.
11   L'ange, *Urgent Imperial Service*, p. 142.

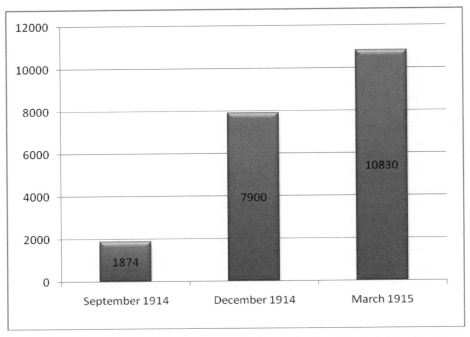

Graph 7.1: Central Force increase in troops (including the forces in the field and 1,815 soldiers en route in March 1915)[12]

An advanced logistical system was put in place with forward water points established by motor vehicles to facilitate the movement of the mounted men.[13] The mechanical transport section of the Eastern Force kept the advanced troops supplied with water and equipment by driving vast distances from the Union to the front lines. They were exposed to substantial risk because the extended communication lines were generally unprotected and were susceptible to German ambushes.[14]

Berrange advanced from Kuruman and forced the Germans to abandon Kiries West on 16 March 1915. One of Berrange's sections took Rietfontein on 19 March 1915 with only a minor skirmish.[15] The Eastern Force used the Kalahari Horse as its scouts

12   DOD Archives, AG 1914 – 1921, Box 150, Strength of the Central Force, 22 December 1914; DOD Archives, AG 1914–1921, Box 150, Strengths, General Summary Central Force, 24 March 1915; Van Der Waag, 'The battle of Sandfontein, 26 September 1914', p. 9.
13   Anon., *Union of South Africa and the Great War, 1914-1918, Official History* (Pretoria: Government Printer, 1924), p. 57; DOD Archives, WW1 GSWA, Box 20, Report, Berrange's report on the operations of the Eastern Force, 15 May 1915.
14   DOD Archives, WW1 GSWA, Box 23a, Citations, German South West Africa, Southern Army Eastern Force Mechanical Transport, 17 February 1918.
15   Anon., *Official History*, p. 81.

for forward reconnaissance. They did excellent work and were highly commended for their speed, scouting and ability to conduct efficient mobile warfare.[16]

Van Deventer marched from Upington in late February 1915. His first objectives as he headed into German South West Africa were Schuit's Drift and Nakob. The advance of the mounted forces across the Kalahari placed forces at the fording points on the Orange River.[17]

The mounted troops under Van Deventer, who had captured Schuit Drift, numbered 1,364 men. There were also ten artillerymen and 154 administrative staff. The administrative staff included an army post office, field cashier, an engineering section, pioneers, a telegraph corps, and also staff to deal with transport, remounts, ordinance, sanitation and supplies.[18] Van Deventer took Nakob with little resistance on 26 February 1915.[19] His force advanced at a rapid pace and one of his detachments took Nabas on 8 March 1915. The German commander at Nabas retreated after resisting for half a day leaving all his supplies and transport behind. Van Deventer's brother, Colonel D. van Deventer, took Platbeen on 27 March where the German commander retreated, leaving behind 14 Union prisoners of war who were subsequently freed.[20]

While the central force pushed forward, Botha went to see Mackenzie on 29 March 1915 to discuss the necessity of his advance on Aus. However the Germans evacuated Aus on 31 March 1915[21] which allowed the South African forces to take Aus unopposed. The *Official History* states that Aus was evacuated due to strategic pressure within German South West Africa.[22]

Van Deventer took Kalkfontein on 5 April 1915. The Germans had assumed a strong position in the Karas Mountains outside Kalkfontein, but Van Deventer deployed a double envelopment that forced the German forces to retreat. After putting up a brief fight the Germans withdrew to Keetmanshoop.[23]

Kalkfontein was an important military base and military objective as it housed an important railway junction. The capture of the position allowed the South Africans access to the German railway systems that joined the major towns in German South West Africa and thus provided the Union with improved operational mobility.

16 DOD Archives, WW1 GSWA, Box 23a, Citations, German South West Africa, Southern Army Eastern Force Kalahari Horse, 17 February 1918.
17 L'ange, *Urgent Imperial Service*, p. 153.
18 DOD Archives, AG 1914–1921, Box 150, Strengths, Southern Force at Steinkopf, 23 February 1915.
19 E. Dane, *British Campaigns in Africa and the Pacific 1914-1918* (London: Hodder & Stoughton, 1919), p. 50.
20 Collyer, *The Campaign in German South West Africa, 1914–1915*, pp. 52–54.
21 Ibid., p. 79.
22 Anon., *Official History*, p. 47.
23 L'ange, *Urgent Imperial Service*, pp. 151–154.

The number of men under Berrange and Van Deventer totalled 8,950 on 14 April 1915. Most of the fighting soldiers were mounted and totalled 7,506, while there were some administrative and supporting personnel.[24] On 16 April 1915 Smuts took over command of the entire Union force at Kalkfontein, with Berrange and Van Deventer's forces having linked up. Mackenzie's command was superseded by that of Smuts, who remained in command until the capture of Gibeon.

Following the capture of Kalkfontein on 5 April 1915, the South African railway line was joined from Prieska to the one in Kalkfontein.[25] The German forces consequently evacuated Aus and Kalkfontein and retreated to Kabus and Keetmanhoop. Berrange and Van Deventer arranged for a cut-off force to envelop the German position north of Keetmanshoop on 19 April 1915 and Kabus was subsequently taken on 20 April 1915 with the cooperation of Van Deventer and Berrange's forces. On the same day the German forces retreated from Kabus and Keetmanshoop to Gibeon.[26]

Mackenzie's force advanced from Aus on 14 April and arrived in Gibeon less than two weeks later.[27] The 8th and 9th Mounted Brigades with a section of the 12th Permanent Battery of the South African Mounted Rifles took Berseba just south of Gibeon on 22 April along with 20 German prisoners.[28] The German force which retreated from Berseba united with the main German force in Gibeon. Smuts wrote to Botha from Aus to inform him that the Germans were retreating at a rapid pace and he doubted whether they would be able to catch up to them.[29]

On 26 April 1915 as the South African force approached Gibeon they tapped the telegraph line at Grundorns which the German force had left intact. The Union Defence Force received valuable information in the form of the German plan for the evacuation of Gibeon.[30]

The Germans were planning to retreat northwards by train, and the evacuation was planned for that particular evening, 26 April 1915. Captain H.O. von Kleist was the officer in charge of the German retreat. Mackenzie immediately put plans in place to cut off the German retreat by placing a force behind Gibeon so as to blow up the

24   DOD Archives, AG 1914–1921, Box 150, Strengths, General Summary, 14 April 1915.

25   Nasson, *Springboks on the Somme*, p. 72.

26   DOD Archives, WW1 GSWA, Box 20, Report, Berrange's report on the operations of the Eastern Force, 15 May 1915.

27   Nasson, *Springboks on the Somme*, p. 72.

28   DOD Archives, SD, Box 252, 17138, Reports of Force Commanders in German South West Africa, Operations of the Central Force from 15 to 27 April 1915 including the action at Gibeon station, 15 May 1915; Collyer, *The Campaign in German South West Africa, 1914–1915*, p. 88; Paterson, 'First Allied Victory', p. 3.

29   W.K. Hancock and J. van der Poel (eds), *Selections from the Smuts Papers, Volume III* (London: Cambridge University Press, 1966), p. 272.

30   DOD Archives, SD, Box 252, 17138, Reports of Force Commanders in German South West Africa, Operations of the Central Force from 15 to 27 April 1915 including the action at Gibeon station, 15 May 1915.

railway line.[31] Lieutenant Colonel J.R. Royston, affectionately known as Galloping Jack, was sent with one regiment of the 8th Mounted Brigade, supplemented by a grouping of the 9th Mounted Brigade, to cut off the German retreat. A scouting party and engineer section was also sent to destroy the railway north of Gibeon. Royston received orders to go wide around to the east of the German position and then close in so as to place his force astride the German line of retreat.[32]

Galloping Jack placed his forces in an open position and as a result they were easily discovered and defeated by the Germans who enfiladed their position with machinegun fire. The position was poorly selected in terms of its ability to provide cover and defence.[33] The total losses were 26 killed and 59 wounded. Of the injured there were also two People of Colour drivers who were severely wounded.[34] Although a part of Royston's force managed to retreat, 70 of his soldiers were captured by the Germans.[35]

The German victory was short lived because Mackenzie launched a frontal attack with a double envelopment on the morning of 27 April 1915 which sent the Germans into full retreat. Galloping Jack's prisoners of war were recovered in the running fight which ensued.[36] The cavalrymen and commandos were in hot pursuit and Von Kleist left a rear-guard to cover his withdrawal. After their rapid advance from Aus the South African horses were exhausted and could not effectively pursue the retreating German force. The Southern Army had covered 320 kilometres in 12 days to converge on the German forces at Gibeon: a great feat of mobility.[37] A German soldier who had fought at Gibeon commented that the South African soldiers were the bravest and worst equipped soldiers that he had ever seen.[38]

31 DOD Archives, SD, Box 252, 17138, Reports of Force Commanders in German South West Africa, Operations of the Central Force from 15 to 27 April 1915 including the action at Gibeon station, 15 May 1915; L'ange, *Urgent Imperial Service*, p. 212; Paterson, 'First Allied Victory', p 3.
32 DOD Archives, SD, Box 252, 17138, Reports of Force Commanders in German South West Africa, Operations of the Central Force from 15 to 27 April 1915 including the action at Gibeon station, 15 May 1915; Collyer, *The Campaign in German South West Africa, 1914–1915*, p. 89.
33 DOD Archives, SD, Box 252, 17138, Reports of Force Commanders in German South West Africa, Operations of the Central Force from 15 to 27 April 1915 including the action at Gibeon station, 15 May 1915; Paterson, 'First Allied Victory', p. 3.
34 DOD Archives, SD, Box 252, Casualties at Gibeon, 15 May 1915; L'ange gives the casualties as 23 killed and 48 injured: L'ange, *Urgent Imperial Service*, p. 217.
35 DOD Archives, SD, Box 252, 17138, Reports of Force Commanders in German South West Africa, Operations of the Central Force from 15 to 27 April 1915 including the action at Gibeon station, 15 May 1915.
36 DOD Archives, SD, Box 252, 17138, Reports of Force Commanders in German South West Africa, Operations of the Central Force from 15 to 27 April 1915 including the action at Gibeon station, 15 May 1915.
37 Collyer, *The Campaign in German South West Africa, 1914–1915*, pp. 91, 92.
38 H.F.B. Walker, *A Doctor's Diary in Damaraland* (London: Edward Arnold, 1917), p. 175.

Collyer maintains that the German withdrawal from Gibeon was not related to the actions of Mackenzie's force, but that it was rather the result of the overall strategic situation.[39] The final tallies for the Battle of Gibeon, including the losses suffered by Galloping Jack's regiment, were 27 killed and 61 wounded while Royston's prisoners of war were recovered. The Germans had 11 dead, 30 wounded and 188 taken as prisoners of war.[40]

Manoeuvre warfare analysis of the operations in the south of German South West Africa

The divergent advances of the Central, Southern and Eastern forces in the south of German South West Africa was indicative of the characteristics of manoeuvre warfare. These diverging advances robbed the German forces of all initiative. The German force had previously demonstrated its prowess by using internal lines to concentrate a large military force on Sandfontein but the option of using internal lines in the south was nullified by the various advances of the Union Defence Force along divergent axes. Had the Germans considered concentrating their forces on one of the Union's advancing groupings, they would have risked being enveloped and cut off by one of the Union's other advancing forces.

The German force therefore had little option in terms of seeking out and defeating the Union Defence Force piecemeal. Map 7.1 shows the various lines of advance of the Central, Southern and Eastern Forces. The German response to the advancing Union forces was to withdraw from Aus and Kalkfontein to Keetmanshoop.

In addition to the Union's advance on diverging axes, the German forces were also heavily outnumbered in the south. The Germans had approximately 1,000 soldiers in the south of the colony. Graph 7.2 demonstrates the numerical superiority of the South African forces.

The Central Force was relatively inactive in the capture of Aus. The Germans withdrew from Aus due to the overall operational situation in the south of the colony. Their position at Aus was untenable because they faced the possibility of being enveloped and cut off by the Southern and Eastern forces. Graph 7.3 indicates the disparity between mounted and non-mounted soldiers as part of the Southern, Eastern and Central forces. The mounted soldiers provided a high degree of mobility for the Southern and Eastern Forces.

39   Collyer, *The Campaign in German South West Africa, 1914–1915*, p. 92.
40   DOD Archives, SD, Box 252, 17138, Reports of Force Commanders in German South West Africa, Operations of the Central Force from 15 to 27 April 1915 including the action at Gibeon station, 15 May 1915.

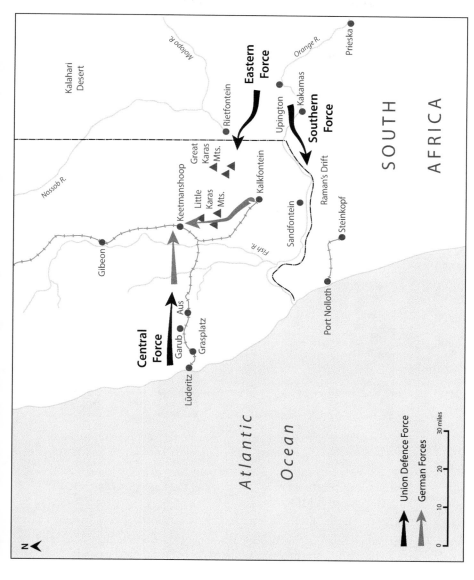

Map 7.1: The divergent advance of the Union Defence Force in the south of German South West Africa

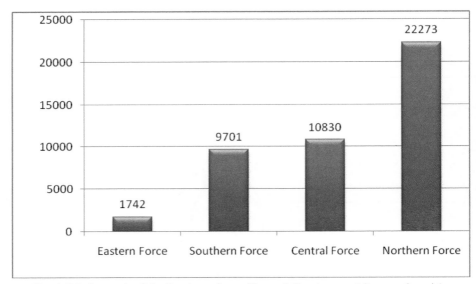

Graph 7.2: Strength of the Southern Army (Central, Southern and Eastern forces) by March1915 (inclusive of the forces in the field and 5,895 soldiers en route)[41]

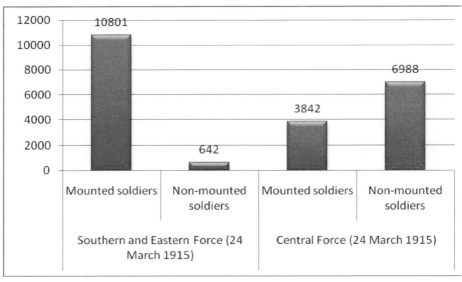

Graph 7.3: Comparison between mounted and non-mounted soldiers in the Central and Southern and Eastern forces (inclusive of the forces in the field and en route)[42]

41   Bar graph compiled from DOD Archives, AG 1914–1921, Box 150, Strengths, General Summary Central Force, 24 March 1915.
42   DOD Archives, AG 1914–1921, Box 150, Strengths, General Summary Central Force, 24 March 1915.

The above graphs include 1,815 mounted soldiers (destined to join the Central Force) and 4,080 mounted soldiers (for the Southern Force) who were still mobilising for the operation.[43] Their high mobility and rapid advance was in complete contradiction to the cautious approach of the Central Force. Their rapid advance gave the Germans less time to consider defence alternatives. Considering the entire theatre of operations, the rapid and divergent advances of the South African forces ensured that the initiative stayed with the Union Defence Force.

The capture of Kalkfontein by the Eastern and Southern forces resulted in the retreat of the German forces stationed there and communicated sufficient threat of envelopment to the German forces at Aus which forced their withdrawal to Keetmanshoop. When this town was subsequently taken, the Germans further retreated to Gibeon. The Union Defence Force attempted to cut off the German force at Gibeon but after giving battle the German force escaped.

Botha's advance and capture of the Riet, Pforte, Jakkalsfontein defensive line in the north had made the Germans aware of the mobility of the South African forces. The South African threat in the north was very prominent and the Germans thus chose to abandon their defence of the south in favour of a northerly defence.

The *Schutztruppe* headquarters only deployed a force of approximately 800 men in the south.[44] This was a mere token resistance. The German defensive strategy was to withdraw until a suitable time and place where they could deliver a decisive blow to the South African forces.[45]

When analysing the final operations in the south in the light of the competing theories of attrition and manoeuvre, a superficial view might lead one to argue that it was the superiority in numbers alone that led to the German retreat. However, the defensive posture of the German forces; the divergent advances of the Union Defence Force on three axes in the south; and the Union's advance in the north, all played a role in the retreat of the German forces to Gibeon and then further north to Windhoek. The final battle did not take place in the south of German South West Africa but was planned for the north where the German forces had more resources.

The value of superior numbers is not devalued. The quantitative value of a military force must be evaluated in relation to qualitative factors such as doctrine and organisational qualities and values as well as strategy and tactics of the opposing forces. Where superior numbers gave the Union Defence Force tactical strength, the

43   Ibid.
44   DOD Archives, SD, Box 252, 17138, Reports of Force Commanders in German South West Africa, Operations of the Central Force from 15 to 27 April 1915 including the action at Gibeon station, 15 May 1915.
45   DOD Archives, SD, Box 252, 17138, Reports of Force Commanders in German South West Africa, Translation of an appeal by Lieutenant Colonel Franke, the commander-in-chief of the Protectorate, 28 June 1915.

divergent advances led to an overload of the German force's OODA cycle. Furthermore the divergent advances on decisive points annulled the Germans ability to concentrate on interior lines, a tactic which proved effective earlier in the campaign (the Battle of Sandfontein).

8

The Final Envelopment

The fall of Gibeon and the retreat of the German forces signalled the advance of the Northern Army on Karibib and Windhoek on 26 April 1915. The German forces in the south retreated in a northerly direction following their defeat at Gibeon and Botha attempted to intercept the retreating force with a rapid advance on Karibib before they could amalgamate with the bulk of the German force in the north. Karibib held the railway junction which connected the south of German South West Africa to the north.

The same date, 26 April 1915, was also significant because it marked the day that the Germans attempted to capture Trekkoppies, a railway post in the northern region of German South West Africa that was part of the Union Defence Force's northerly lines of communication. In an attempt at offense, the Germans attacked the position at Trekkoppies with infantry and artillery,[1] intending to delay the South African general advance. However a stout defence managed to repulse the attack.

The Battle of Trekkoppies

Skinner, who led the initial landing at Walvis Bay and Swakopmund, was in command at Trekkoppies. The Union believed that the Germans would in all likelihood not attack the post at Trekkoppies and therefore decided to withdraw the two guns that were stationed there.[2]

The tactical disposition of Trekkoppies was not well suited for defence. The Union forces were encamped in low ground which was surrounded by a ridge to the east and

---

1   B. Nasson, *Springboks on the Somme* (Johannesburg: Penguin, 2007), p. 74; H. Paterson, 'First Allied Victory: The South African Campaign in German South-West Africa, 1914–1915", *Military History Journal*, 13, 2, 2004, p. 6.
2   W. Whittal, *With Botha and Smuts in Africa* (Cassel, London, 1917), p. 27; DOD Archives, SD, Box 252, 17138, Historical Record of the Campaign in German South West Africa, 4 November 1919.

high ground to the north.[3] The position had hills covering possible enemy advance routes. Furthermore the ground was hard and only allowed for shallow trenches.[4]

Whittal, the British naval Lieutenant Commander was deployed at Trekkoppies with the Royal Navy Armoured Car Division No. 1. The armoured cars were essentially fortified cars with mounted machine guns. Due to questions about the ability of these vehicles to negotiate the sandy terrain in German South West Africa they were posted in a more defensive role.[5] The British Navy contributed to the campaign by the shipping of Union's forces, the provision of supplies by naval vessels and the deployment of an armoured car squadron.

The Germans made use of aerial reconnaissance to verify the South African movements and disposition. The German pilot, Von Scheele did an aerial reconnaissance mission on Trekkoppies on 23 April and returned to conduct a rudimentary air bombing raid but was deterred by anti-aircraft artillery fire.[6] The anti-aircraft piece, was a converted Armstrong field gun, affectionately named 'Skinny-Liz' which never managed to hit a German plane.[7]

The result of the reconnaissance was that Ritter, gained intelligence on the South African tactical position and as a result Franke ordered a demolition team to destroy the railway behind Trekkoppies. In response to the air reconnaissance, Skinner was proactive and led the Imperial Light Horse and a detachment of the 2nd Transvaal Scottish on a reconnaissance mission where they spotted Ritter's force marching towards the South African camp.[8] On returning to Trekkoppies on the morning of 26 April, Skinner called for reinforcements from Arandis and deployed the infantry in shallow trenches around the railway.[9]

The armoured cars were deployed between and in front of the trenches. Five armoured cars were deployed to the front of the trenches, two were deployed between the trenches and two were held in reserve in the event of a retreat.[10] As they could not

3   Nasson, *Springboks on the Somme*, p. 234.
4   Whittal, *With Botha and Smuts*, p. 33.
5   Ibid., p. 21.
6   J.O.E.O. Mahncke, "Aircraft operations in the German Colonies 1911-1916: The Fliegertruppe of the Imperial German Army", *Military History Journal*, 12, 2, 2001, p. 10.
7   DOD Archives, SD, Box 252, 17138, Historical Record of the Campaign in German South West Africa, 4 November 1919.
8   DOD Archives, SD, Box 252, 17138, Historical Record of the Campaign in German South West Africa, 4 November 1919; J.J. Collyer, *The Campaign in German South West Africa, 1914–1915* (Pretoria: Government Printer, 1937), p. 93; Anon., *Union of South Africa and the Great War, 1914–1918, Official History* (Pretoria: Government Printer, 1924), p. 44; H.F. Trew, *Botha Treks* (London: Blackie & Son, 1936), p. 122; Whittal, *With Botha and Smuts*, p. 34.
9   G. L'ange, *Urgent Imperial Service* (Rivonia: Ashanti, 1991), p. 237; Whittal, *With Botha and Smuts*, p. 34.
10   L'ange, *Urgent Imperial Service*, p. 238.

effectively manoeuvre in the sand they were mostly used on the railway embankment.[11] Fortunately for the South African forces, the German aerial reconnaissance had mistaken the armoured cars for water trucks.

On 26 April 1915 the northern post of Trekkoppies took position and awaited an attack whilst in the south at the same time MacKenzie's force advanced on Gibeon and Botha did final preparations for his planned advance on Karibib scheduled to start the next day. The position at Trekkoppies was not ideal for an extended defence since the Union lacked artillery support and no extensive defensive positions were prepared. The Union's stance may have led to an underestimation of the risk of a German counterattack on the line of Trekkoppies.

The Germans executed a coordinated attack on the Union position at Trekkoppies with infantry and artillery.[12] Just before 06:00 the Germans accidentally blew up the northern side of the railway instead of the intended southern side which meant that the Union could still get reinforcements up from Arandis.[13] The German forces took position to the north of the South African camp where some rocky outcrops offered them protection.[14] The Germans started the battle with an artillery bombardment North West of the railway line[15], at 07:30 to which the South Africans had no response due to the unavailability of guns. The Germans also ordered an infantry attack from the north and west.[16]

The bombardment lasted three hours and was followed by an infantry attack from the North and West, which met stiff resistance from the Union's infantry made up of the 2nd Transvaal Scottish, 1st Rhodesian Regiment and the 2nd Kimberley Regiment.[17] The armoured cars provided combat support with their mounted machine guns and despite the German attempts they could not break the South African defensive line. The German objective was to penetrate the trench line and occupy the ridge from where they could enfilade the South African position.[18] The armoured cars commanded by Whittal moved north to the flank of the German forces where they opened fire.[19] The high rate of machinegun fire from the armoured cars prevented

11   Trew, *Botha Treks*, p. 122.
12   Nasson, *Springboks on the Somme*, p. 74; Paterson, 'First Allied Victory', p. 6.
13   L'ange, *Urgent Imperial Service*, p. 238; Anon., *Official History*, 44; Whittal, *With Botha and Smuts*, p. 35.
14   Trew, *Botha Treks*, p. 122.
15   DOD Archives, SD, Box 252, 17138, Historical Record of the Campaign in German South West Africa, 4 November 1919.
16   Collyer, *The Campaign in German South West Africa, 1914–1915*, 94; Anon., *Official History*, p. 44; Whittal, *With Botha and Smuts*, p. 36.
17   DOD Archives, SD, Box 252, 17138, Historical Record of the Campaign in German South West Africa, 4 November 1919.
18   L'ange, *Urgent Imperial Service*, p. 238; Whittal, *With Botha and Smuts*, p. 36.
19   Trew, *Botha Treks*, p. 122.

the Germans from taking the ridge.[20] The armoured cars cooperated well with the infantry but the ground was not suitable for extensive motorised movement.[21]

In an attempt at executing a counter-attack, the Imperial Light Horse regiment was ordered to envelop the Germans position however German rifle fire checked the attempt and triggered an intensified artillery bombardment. The German infantry pressed forward again with a direct attack on the trenches but South African infantry fire supported by armoured car machine gun fire repulsed the German forces and eventually forced a complete retreat.[22] The Union soldiers briefly attempted a counterattack which was immediately checked by the German artillery.[23] By 10:30 on 26 April the attack had subsided and the Germans retreated.[24]

The German attack at Trekkoppies was an attempt to impede South Africa's rapid advance.[25] The Union casualties from the battle were three officers and six other ranks dead and thirty two wounded. The German casualties were two officers and five other ranks killed, fourteen wounded and thirty two captured.[26]

The Advance on Windhoek

The defence of Trekkoppies took place while Botha planned his advance on Windhoek, the capital of German South West Africa. The Union obtained an intelligence report that confirmed the presence of a concentrated German force in the north of the colony in and around Karibib.[27] Karibib was an intermediate objective en route to Windhoek.[28] The advance on Karibib was also intended to stop the northern and southern German forces from amalgamating.[29] Botha planned a cross country advance to capture Karibib and Windhoek requiring wagons and mules for the transportation of equipment and stores.

The Union forces were in dire need of logistics to complete the campaign: Botha only had sufficient stores to supply his commandos for five days on the advance. Smuts states that the most difficult question regarding the campaign was the transport

---

20 Whittal, *With Botha and Smuts*, p. 36.
21 Anon., *Official History*, p. 44.
22 Whittal, *With Botha and Smuts*, p. 37.
23 L'ange, *Urgent Imperial Service*, p. 239.
24 Anon., *Official History*, p. 44.
25 E. Dane, *British Campaigns in Africa and the Pacific 1914-1918* (London: Hodder & Stoughton, 1919), p. 58. Trew, *Botha Treks*, p. 121.
26 DOD Archives, SD, Box 252, 17138, Historical Record of the Campaign in German South West Africa, 4 November 1919; Collyer, *The Campaign in German South West Africa, 1914–1915*, p. 94; Paterson, 'First Allied Victory', p. 6.
27 Collyer, *The Campaign in German South West Africa*, 1914–1915, p. 95.
28 Anon., *Official History*, p. 29; DOD Archives, SD, Box 252, 17138, Historical Record of the Campaign in German South West Africa, 4 November 1919.
29 Trew, *Botha Treks*, p. 121; DOD Archives, SD, Box 252, 17138, Historical Record of the Campaign in German South West Africa, 4 November 1919.

question. By 25 March, the ministry had searched the entire country for wagons and drivers. Smuts claims that he required 3,000 drivers and that the 'Cape Boys' were reluctant to serve and as a result Blacks from other parts were being recruited.[30] The role of People of Colour in the driving of the transport system of the Union Defence Force was thus a very important part of the success of the campaign. Interesting that the wagons and oxen were a strategic concern but not the required Black, Coloured and Indian drivers – this exemplified the racial dynamics of the period.

Botha appealed to parliament to make funds available for mules and wagons and his request was duly approved in April 1915 when parliament agreed to fund the provision of 300 wagons and mules for the advance on Windhoek.[31]

The supplies were transported by wagon, of which each one was initially powered by 11 mules, a number that was later increased to 12 mules on Botha's recommendation, because of the sandy terrain in German South West Africa.[32] In order to advance with supplies, the required daily rations equalled 34,000 kilograms and another 18,000 kilograms of kit per brigade. The regimental transport element of a brigade comprised 24 wagons and the Brigade train had another 22 wagons. These waggons were inadequate to carry the kit and sufficient rations for the troops during the advance.[33] The logistical support of the mounted units was thereby increased from 59 ammunition wagons, 110 wagons and 51 water carts on 1 March 1915, to 86 ammunition wagons, 376 wagons and 165 water carts on 12 April 1915 (refer to Graph 8.1).[34] Walker notes in his diary that in April 1915 the transport officer was sending out 737,088kg of supplies per week to the forward position at Riet.[35]

Botha made use of Brits and Myburgh to take charge of the two groupings that he deployed to take Karibib and Windhoek.[36] Despite the best efforts of the Union Defence Force, the German forces managed to unite and retreat north-eastwards. Karibib was taken with little incident and Botha accepted its formal surrender on 6 May 1915. The official surrender of Windhoek was received by Botha on 12 May 1915 achieving the strategic objective of capturing its wireless station which the Germans had dissembled on their own initiative.[37]

30 Correspondence between Smuts and Hull, W.K. Hancock and J. van der Poel (eds), *Selections from the Smuts Papers, Volume III* (London: Cambridge University Press, 1966), p. 262.
31 L'ange, *Urgent Imperial Service*, p. 244.
32 Correspondence between Botha and Smuts, Hancock and Van der Poel (eds), *Selections from the Smuts Papers*, p. 249.
33 Correspondence between Smuts and Hull, Hancock and Van der Poel (eds), *Selections from the Smuts Papers*, 262.
34 DOD Archives, AG 1914–1921, Box 182, Mounted Strengths, Field state, 12 April 1915.
35 H.F.B. Walker, *A Doctor's Diary in Damaraland* (London: Edward Arnold, 1917), p. 56.
36 L'ange, *Urgent Imperial Service*, p. 244;
37 Nasson, *Springboks on the Somme*, p. 74; Anon., *Official History*, p. 40; J. Meintjes, *General Louis Botha* (London: Cassell & Co., 1970), p. 264; Whittal, *With Botha and Smuts in Africa*, p. 62; Paterson, 'First Allied Victory', p. 6; DOD Archives, SD, Box 252, 17138, Historical Record of the Campaign in German South West Africa, 4 November 1919.

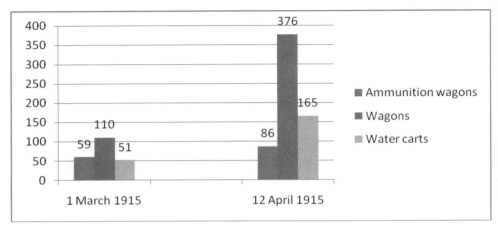

Graph 8.1: Increase in logistical support for the Union Defence Force[38]

Plate 8.1: Botha's motorcade entering Windhoek[39]

38   DOD Archives, AG 1914–1921, Box 182, Mounted Strengths, Field state, 12 April 1915.
39   DOD Archives.

Plate 8.2: Botha and his staff in Windhoek[40]

The Rehoboth Basters, a mixed race population grouping with historic roots from the Northern Cape, mounted their own brief rebellion, which diverted a German battalion. Botha had met with the Baster commander Captain Van Wyk on 1 April where he had offered military assistance to the Union forces. Refusing Van Wyk's offer, Botha was of the opinion that it was a White man's war. [41]

The irony possibly did not escape Van Wyk who must have seen Black, Coloured and Indian drivers, labourers and guides. The Basters eventually went into rebellion and provided limited assistance to the Union forces, in disarming some German reservists, mounting an ambush and fighting a defensive battle at Sam Kubis. Pinned down by the Germans, the Basters were saved by the advance of the Southern Army.[42]

Upon being saved by the South African forces, the Basters went on a theft and murder rampage.[43] Botha wanted the situation to be returned to normal as soon as possible and deployed Colonel H. Mentz to address the Rehoboth uprising. After Mentz met with the Rehoboth Council and guaranteed their safety the Basters

40   DOD Archives.
41   G.J.J. Oosthuizen, 'The Military Role of the Rehoboth Basters during the South African Invasion of German South West Africa, 1914-1915', *Scientia Militaria*, 28, 1 , 1998, p. 98.
42   Ibid., pp. 105-107.
43   Ibid., p. 108.

returned to their homes and a further commission of inquiry was promised to address the causes of the conflict.[44]

The Germans retreated from Windhoek to Tsumeb which was also the location of their last remaining wireless station. Botha then built up forces and logistics for six weeks from mid-May until mid-June in preparation for the final advance.[45]

Between 5 and 14 May 1915 the South African forces were seriously hampered by a lack of rations and supplies.[46] Resupply necessitated the reconstruction of the railway which was completely rebuilt from Swakopmund to Karibib by 14 May 1915.[47] Botha was intensely frustrated by the initial pace of the railway construction and by March, only 42 kilometres of railway line had been constructed for the northerly line. The type of railway gauge had to be changed and thus the entire operation was slowed down. Botha ended up personally inspecting the working sites and demanding that 3.2 kilometres of railway be constructed per day, as the earthworks were already constructed on the previous rail (2 foot line was replaced by 3.6 foot), the Union engineers had to only lay sleepers and the railway line.[48] In the construction of the railway, Coloureds and Blacks provided much of the labour[49], which facilitated the Union's advance to Windhoek.

The watering of the forces from the various wells along the Swakop Riverbed as well as at Riet, Trekkoppies and other key locations were essential for the positioning and deployment of the Union's forces.[50] Botha refused to embark on the final offensive until the railway and supply situation was completely resolved.[51] The date of the final advance was dependent on the time required by the engineers to rebuild the railway.[52] On the completion of the railway line, the management and organisation of the railway system required urgent attention and Botha and Collyer restructured it under command and control of a military railway staff system under the supreme command of Colonel Skinner who was promoted to Brigadier General and General Officer Commanding Lines of Communication.[53]

44   DOD Archives, SD, Box 252, 17138, Reports of Force Commanders in German South West Africa, Despatch number 4 by General Botha covering the period 15 May to 18 July 1915; Oosthuizen, 'Rehoboth', p. 108.

45   Anon., *Official History*, p. 32.

46   Paterson, 'First Allied Victory', p. 6.

47   DOD Archives, SD, Box 252, 17138, Historical Record of the Campaign in German South West Africa, 4 November 1919; L'ange, *Urgent Imperial Service*, p. 147.

48   Botha to Smuts, Hancock and Van der Poel (eds), *Selections from the Smuts Papers*, p. 255.

49   SANA, Smuts Papers, Box 112, Major General Thompson: Report on a visit to German South West Africa, 20-27 March 1915.

50   Botha to Smuts, Hancock and Van der Poel (eds), *Selections from the Smuts Papers*, p. 255.

51   DOD Archives, SD, Box 252, 17138, Reports of Force Commanders in German South West Africa, Despatch number 4 by General Botha covering the period 15 May to 18 July 1915; Collyer, *The Campaign in German South West Africa, 1914–1915*, p. 114.

52   Whittal, *With Botha and Smuts in Africa*, p. 86.

53   DOD Archives, SD, Box 252, 17138, Telegram, Botha to Defence Headquarters, May

The final advance

In June 1915 the government provided an additional 432 wagons to the deploying forces.[54] The Northern Army managed to acquire 20,000 animals from the Union with two to three days supplies for the final advance.[55] Once the supplies were in place, the plan for the final advance was finalised. At this time, Buxton confirmed to 10 Downing Street, that he had been in correspondence with the Portuguese authorities in Angola and that should the German forces cross the border, they would cooperate fully to neutralise the Hun threat.[56]

The plan for the final envelopment involved Lukin and Beves advancing along the railway with Brits and the 1st Mounted Brigade enveloping Etosha Pan and taking Namutoni. Myburgh, with the 2nd Mounted Brigade was to take Grootfontein and Manie Botha, with the 3rd Mounted Brigade, was instructed to advance parallel to the railway to offer support to both enveloping forces.[57] Map 8.1 shows the final envelopments in German South West Africa.

While planning the final advance, the Union's forces were also re-organised to protect the lines of communication. The left wing of the 3rd Mounted Brigade was deployed to Windhoek for the purpose of protecting Botha's lines of communication during the final advance.[58]

The final offensive against the last German position was made by 5,250 mounted men and 4,750 infantrymen with 32 artillery weapons pitted against approximately 5,000 German soldiers in well defended positions and with superior firepower in terms of artillery and machineguns.[59] Botha wrote to Smuts on 15 June 1915, explaining that the chances of early success on the campaign were dependent on whether the Germans decided to fight or retreat. Botha also explained that reports had arrived stating that the Germans were in well-fortified positions at Kalkveld, but he added that the Germans had previously evacuated well prepared positions without fighting.[60]

  1915.
54   DOD Archives, SD, Box 252, 17138, Reports of Force Commanders in German South West Africa, Despatch number 4 by General Botha covering the period 15 May to 18 July 1915.
55   Nasson, *Springboks on the Somme*, p. 74.
56   DOD Archives, SD, Box 654, Military operations relating to Angola, June 1915.
57   DOD Archives, SD, Box 252, 17138, Reports of Force Commanders in German South West Africa, Despatch number 4 by General Botha covering the period 15 May to 18 July 1915; L'ange, *Urgent Imperial Service*, p. 264.
58   DOD Archives, SD, Box 252, 17138, Reports of Force Commanders in German South West Africa, Despatch number 4 by General Botha covering the period 15 May to 18 July 1915.
59   L'ange, *Urgent Imperial Service*, p. 287.
60   DOD Archives, SD, Box 252, 17138, Reports of Force Commanders in German South West Africa, Despatch number 4 by General Botha covering the period 15 May to 18 July 1915.

The advance started on 18 June 1915.[61] Collyer did well to organise the watering of the columns on the advance. He had the quality and quantity of the water tested on the routes of advance and staggered the Union's advance allowing sections of the advancing columns to be watered piecemeal.[62] The Union forces were relatively well supplied, although for only a short duration, which allowed for the temporary use of their full mobility.[63]

The infantry reached Karibib and the commandos were deployed in a semicircle from Karibib to Windhoek. Lukin's 6th Mounted Brigade was deployed at Usakos; Brits and the 1st Mounted Brigade were deployed at Klein Aus; the 1st Infantry Brigade under Beves was at Erongo (Beves' had 124 People of Colour in his Brigade); Manie Botha was at Hohe with the 5th Mounted Brigade; and Myburgh held positions between Wilhelmstal and Okassise with a wing each of the 2nd and 3rd Mounted Brigades.[64]

Brits and Myburgh's forces were sent to cut off the retreat of the Germans by committing to extensive movements and independent actions. Myburgh went via Waterberg to Tsumeb to block a north-easterly retreat and Brits was sent with his commando to Etosha Pan to the north of Namutoni which prevented a German retreat northwards.[65] Meanwhile Lukin moved forward with the infantry at snail's pace with the Germans systematically retreating.[66]

The headquarters of the Northern Army was at the rear of the convoy and used motorcars to rush between the mounted columns to ensure communication. Brits' idea of a broad turning movement was attractive to Botha because it also allowed for the prisoners at Namutoni[67] to be freed.[68] Brits took Omaruru on 19 June 1915,[69] and the advance then moved from Omaruru to Kalkveld where it was thought that the Germans would put up a defensive battle. The Union central column then advanced

61   Meintjes, *General Louis Botha*, p. 267; Whittal, *With Botha and Smuts in Africa*, p. 95; Paterson gives the date for the start of the advance as 20 June 1915: Paterson, 'First Allied Victory', p. 7.

62   DOD Archives, SD, Box 252, 17138, Reports of Force Commanders in German South West Africa, Despatch number 4 by General Botha covering the period 15 May to 18 July 1915; Trew, *Botha Treks*, p. 154.

63   Collyer, *The Campaign in German South West Africa, 1914–1915*, p. 125.

64   Paterson, 'First Allied Victory', p. 7.

65   DOD Archives, SD, Box 252, 17138, Reports of Force Commanders in German South West Africa, Despatch number 4 by General Botha covering the period 15 May to 18 July 1915.

66   Nasson, *Springboks on the Somme*, p. 75.

67   These prisoners of war include the South Africans captured at the battles of Sandfontein and the engagements at the Riet, Pforte, Jakkalsfontein amongst others.

68   DOD Archives, SD, Box 252, 17138, Reports of Force Commanders in German South West Africa, Despatch number 4 by General Botha covering the period 15 May to 18 July 1915; Collyer, *The Campaign in German South West Africa, 1914–1915*, p. 124.

69   M.E. Ritchie, *With Botha in the Field* (London: Longmans, 1915, p. 55. Whittal gives the date as 20 June: Whittal, *With Botha and Smuts in Africa*, p.. 104.

to Otjiwarongo.[70] Whitall advanced from Etiro to Omaruru by 21 June 1915 and then on to Epako on 22 June 1915, where the German fortified positions were found abandoned.[71]

Lukin was in command of the assault on Kalkveld and the brigade bivouacked in Okosongora and departed on the morning of 24 June 1914.[72] Lukin had 602 People of Colour under his command that provided force support to the operation. Reconnaissance was carried out by the budding Union Aviation Corps on the German position at Kalkveld and Botha proceeded with staged operations.[73] Botha was reportedly impressed by the value of aeroplanes in warfare and mentioned that every support should be given to developing the use of aviation in combat.[74] Manie Botha captured Kalkveld unopposed on 24 June 1915.[75]

While Botha moved up country in pursuit of the Germans, Mackenzie arrived at Rehoboth, from the south and by 25 June many of his sick soldiers had been admitted to the field hospital in Windhoek.[76] The north-south railway between Karibib and Keetmanshoop was made operational and assisted the Union Defence Force with an extra 200 tonnage of supply per day.[77]

Meanwhile, the Germans prepared a string of defensive positions spanning Otavi and Tsumeb. Ritter was deployed at Otavifontein with ten machineguns and three artillery pieces; and Von Kleist was positioned between Otavi and Grootfontein to protect the eastern flank of the German position.[78]

The Germans had a strong defensive line and the terrain was well suited for ambushes with some areas of dense bush and other areas of open plains.[79] The Union's vanguard and flank guard minimised the threat of ambush on the main force.[80] The terrain in the hinterland had changed from the sandy soil found on the coast and

---

70 Trew, *Botha Treks*, p. 188.
71 Whittal, *With Botha and Smuts in Africa*, pp. 114, 121.
72 Ibid., p. 128.
73 DOD Archives, SD, Box 252, 17138, Reports of Force Commanders in German South West Africa, Despatch number 4 by General Botha covering the period 15 May to 18 July 1915.
74 Ritchie, *With Botha in the Field*, p. 56.
75 DOD Archives, SD, Box 252, 17138, Reports of Force Commanders in German South West Africa, Despatch number 4 by General Botha covering the period 15 May to 18 July 1915.
76 Walker, *A Doctor's Diary in Damaraland*, p. 170.
77 DOD Archives, SD, Box 252, 17138, Reports of Force Commanders in German South West Africa, Despatch number 4 by General Botha covering the period 15 May to 18 July 1915.
78 L'ange, *Urgent Imperial Service*, p. 288.
79 DOD Archives, SD, Box 252, 17138, Reports of Force Commanders in German South West Africa, Despatch number 4 by General Botha covering the period 15 May to 18 July 1915.
80 Trew, *Botha Treks*, p. 153.

Namib Desert to a low bushveld type of terrain which the South African soldiers found more familiar.[81]

During the final envelopments, Botha understood the probability that he would lose contact with Myburgh.[82] The Union forces advanced over an extensive front of 95 kilometres,[83] and even though the enveloping forces were deployed with field wireless sets they did not work effectively.[84] Myburgh deployed from Wilhelmstal in a wide envelopment to take Grootfontein. Botha allowed Myburgh to use his own initiative, trusting his instincts, as he understood that a rapid and sustained pursuit of the enemy was required. Furthermore, Myburgh understood the plan and the intent of his commander-and-chief.[85] Myburgh deployed with 730 People of Colour in his detachment.

Botha advanced with the main force and ordered a halt to the advance at Omarassa. Botha wanted to consolidate his forces to ensure an effective march on Otavi which was 64 kilometres from Omarassa.[86] Whittal deployed with his armoured cars to Okanjande and then on to Otjiwarongo approximately 48 kilometres from Kalkveld.[87] The Union's advance reached Otjiwarongo on 26 June 1915.[88] Lukin and Myburgh, with their infantry and mounted brigades respectively, deployed to Omarassa from Otjiwarongo on 27 June 1915.[89]

The Union Defence Force reviewed an intelligence report which unequivocally confirmed the German presence in the north in and around Otavi and Otavifontein. In response Botha and the Union forces rode throughout the night of 30 June so as to engage the German force.[90] On 1 July 1915 the main force of the Union's advance managed to secure Otavi.

At the same time Brits was en route to Namutoni whereas Myburgh was heading towards the north of Grootfontein.[91] An anecdote about the advance pertains to Botha who advised Brits to take an ambulance with him but Brits refused, arguing 'if

81 Ritchie, *With Botha in the Field*, p. 56.
82 DOD Archives, SD, Box 252, 17138, Reports of Force Commanders in German South West Africa, Despatch number 4 by General Botha covering the period 15 May to 18 July 1915; Collyer, *The Campaign in German South West Africa, 1914–1915*, p. 133.
83 Trew, *Botha Treks*, p. 153.
84 DOD Archives, SD, Box 252, 17138, Historical Record of the Campaign in German South West Africa, 4 November 1919.
85 DOD Archives, SD, Box 252, 17138, Reports of Force Commanders in German South West Africa, Despatch number 4 by General Botha covering the period 15 May to 18 July 1915; L'ange, *Urgent Imperial Service*, p. 290.
86 L'ange, *Urgent Imperial Service*, p. 291; Whittal, *With Botha and Smuts in Africa*, p. 147.
87 Whittal, *With Botha and Smuts in Africa*, p. 146.
88 Ritchie, *With Botha in the Field*, p. 57.
89 Ibid., p. 146.
90 DOD Archives, SD, Box 252, 17138, Reports of Force Commanders in German South West Africa, Despatch number 4 by General Botha covering the period 15 May to 18 July 1915; Collyer, *The Campaign in German South West Africa, 1914–1915*, p. 137.
91 Anon., *Official History*, p. 34.

I take an ambulance the men will see it and imagine themselves sick and soon it will be full'.[92] Each brigade was organised to be self-sufficient by having an ambulance with medical personnel and was divided into a left and right wing which in turn corresponded with the two wings of the mounted brigade.[93] Despite the fundamental need for medical assistance while on operation, Botha complained that the medical services struggled to keep up with the pace of the commandos.[94]

Franke ordered Ritter to hold out at Otavifontein for at least a week to allow for the preparation of the defences at Tsumeb. The Union forces swooped upon the German defences at Otavifontein on 1 July 1915[95] and the Germans retreated from Osib to the Elefantenberg with the Union Defence Force in pursuit. Putting up a brief fight in their retreat the German force retreated towards the Otaviberg and Elefantenberg Mountains.[96]

Manie Botha advanced towards the German position at Otavifontein while Lukin was deployed to the eastern flank of the Elefantenberg range.[97] Lieutenant Colonel S.W. Pijper was ordered to attack the western flank of the German position.[98] The Germans had 3,372 soldiers with 36 artillery pieces and 22 machineguns at Otavifontein which was not effectively brought to bear on the Union's 5th and 6th Mounted Brigades.[99] Ritter withdrew following the Union's artillery bombardment, however the South African horses were in no state for a rapid pursuit having marched throughout the night to arrive at Otavifontein and give battle. The Germans executed a fighting withdrawal to Grootfontein.[100]

Manie Botha pushed forward through bushy and rugged terrain forcing the German commander to withdraw. He ensured surprise by rushing the German position.[101] Manie Botha had 479 People of Colour serving under his command. They helped

92   Trew, *Botha Treks*, p. 159.
93   Walker, *A Doctor's Diary in Damaraland*, p. 4.
94   DOD Archives, SD, Box 252, 17138, Reports of Force Commanders in German South West Africa, Despatch number 4 by General Botha covering the period 15 May to 18 July 1915.
95   L'ange, *Urgent Imperial Service*, p. 292; Anon., *Official History*, p. 40.
96   Collyer, *The Campaign in German South West Africa, 1914–1915*, p. 138.
97   DOD Archives, SD, Box 252, 17138, Reports of Force Commanders in German South West Africa, Despatch number 4 by General Botha covering the period 15 May to 18 July 1915; Ritchie, *With Botha in the Field*, p. 59.
98   DOD Archives, SD, Box 252, 17138, Reports of Force Commanders in German South West Africa, Despatch number 4 by General Botha covering the period 15 May to 18 July 1915; L'ange, *Urgent Imperial Service*, p. 295.
99   Collyer, *The Campaign in German South West Africa, 1914–1915*, p. 141. Botha gives the strength of the Germans as 900 with 6 artillery pieces: DOD Archives, SD, Box 252, 17138, Reports of Force Commanders in German South West Africa, Despatch no. 4 by Botha, for period 15 May to 18 July 1915. Collyer may have been referring to a larger force that the Germans could have concentrated using internal lines.
100 L'ange, *Urgent Imperial Service*, p. 296.
101 Anon., *Official History*, p. 46.

to support the offensive forces. The German chief-of-staff claimed that should they have had the luxury of an extra hour to prepare they would have destroyed the Union forces.[102] The validity of this claim is dubious at best. The casualties for the engagement at Otavifontein were ten Germans killed, 25 wounded and 41 taken prisoner,[103] while seven South Africans were wounded and four killed.[104]

While the Germans retreated to Grootfontein, the South African infantry advanced on foot towards Otavifontein. They covered more than 480 kilometres of which the last 128 kilometres took only four days. This was a very significant feat and Franke, on hearing about this mass movement of infantrymen, commented that they must have been moved by train.[105] The distance was in fact not covered by train but by forced march. It is difficult to understand the hardship and suffering of the men who were required to undertake extremely demanding forced marches through German South West Africa. Table 8.1 shows some of the best times for forced marches during the campaign.

A poem by Johnstone about the German South West African campaign gives some perspective on the hardship experienced on the campaign:

"Have you just sweated in the sand,
Sweated till your eyebrows crawled,
And in despair stood up for shade.
Then lain and sprawled.

Half mad with thirst, half mad with heat.
Till you could neither stand nor sit.
Till desert, sky, and air became
One blazing pit."[106]

---

102 Collyer, *The Campaign in German South West Africa, 1914-1915*, p. 140; Anon., *Official History*, p. 47.
103 Whittal, *With Botha and Smuts in Africa*, p. 147.
104 DOD Archives, SD, Box 252, 17138, Reports of Force Commanders in German South West Africa, Despatch number 4 by General Botha covering the period 15 May to 18 July 1915.
105 L'ange, *Urgent Imperial Service*, p. 298; Whittal, *With Botha and Smuts in Africa*, p. 149.
106 M.G. Johnstone, *The Avengers and other Poems from South Africa*, (London: Erskine Macdonald, 1918), p. 26.

Best Forced Marches					
		From	To	distance (Km)	time (hours)
Northern Army	Left wing 2nd Mounted Brigade	Husab	Jakkalswater (and back)	122	22
	5th Mounted Brigade	Okaputa	Kilo 500	70	18
	6th Mounted Brigade	Omarassa	Elefantsnek	58	15
	3rd and 5th Mounted Brigades	Riet	Otjimbingue	112	37
Central Force	7th, 8th and 9th Mounted Brigades	Berseba	Gibeon	112	72
Southern Force	Van Deventer's Column	Neu Khais	Kabus	193	144

Table 8.1: Best forced marches[107]

The force under Brits advanced on Outjo and proceeded to Namutoni towards the end of June 1915, while Myburgh was heading for Grootfontein. The wide envelopments were designed to cut off the German retreat and encircle the German position.[108] The Germans had at this stage moved to Khorab where the final stand took place.[109] Map 8.1 indicates the final advance and the positions of the South African and German forces.

Myburgh departed on 18 June and moved via Okasisse and Wilhelmstahl, arriving at the Waterberg plateau on 26 June 1915. Then on 29 June 1915, Myburgh advanced to Otajewita, then on to Omboamgomde and then to Esere, which he reached on

107 DOD Archives, SD, Box 252, 17138 IO, General Botha's Despatch (GOC MC GSW Campaign) 9 July to 28 October 1920, Historical Record of the Campaign in German South West Africa, 4 November 1919.
108 DOD Archives, SD, Box 252, 17138, Reports of Force Commanders in German South West Africa, Despatch number 4 by General Botha covering the period 15 May to 18 July 1915.
109 Anon., *Official History*, p. 46.

2 July 1915. During this extensive march there were times when the troops and horses were without water for up to two days.[110]

Franke had issued a written order (which was found at Otavifontein) which unequivocally stated that the time had come for the Germans to give battle. The German commander made the point that the defensive strategy followed thus far meant that the German fighting force was still intact; it was now required put up a stout defence at the correct time and place.[111]

Franke understood the seriousness of the position of the German forces. Von Kleist had protected the German eastern flank observed and reported the commando's swift movement in the direction of Grootfontein and Franke knew that a South African detachment was also advancing from the west. With knowledge of the broad South African envelopment, he realised only too well that the German position was dire. However, despite the gravity of the situation, Dr T. Seitz, the governor of German South West Africa, was demanding a tactical victory – despite Franke's opinion that if it came to a battle the Germans would be annihilated.[112]

While the South African envelopment was being executed the Germans sought a meeting with Botha to discuss terms of surrender. An armistice was arranged but Botha specifically excluded the movements of Brits and Myburgh.[113] The South African forces received intelligence that the Germans were entrenched at Gaub and the right wing of the 3rd Brigade was tasked to envelop the enemy's rear to the west and the 2nd Brigade to the enemy's rear towards the east.[114] Myburgh defeated the German force at Gaub on 2 July 1915 and then moved to Tsumeb.[115]

On the advance to Tsumeb, the Union Defence Force encountered a German force numbering approximately 500 on 4 July 1915. The *Schutztruppe* was subsequently forced to withdraw, with the South Africans taking 80 prisoners.[116]

Myburgh advanced on Tsumeb and after a misunderstanding about the armistice between Myburgh's force and the German commander at Tsumeb, an exchange of artillery fire ensued. The South African force subsequently entered into negotiations

110 Whittal, *With Botha and Smuts in Africa*, pp. 150, 151.
111 DOD Archives, SD, Box 252, 17138, Reports of Force Commanders in German South West Africa, Translation of an appeal by Lieutenant Colonel Franke, the commander-in-chief of the Protectorate, 28 June 1915; Collyer, *The Campaign in German South West Africa, 1914–1915*, p. 143.
112 L'ange, *Urgent Imperial Service*, p. 299.
113 DOD Archives, SD, Box 252, 17138, Reports of Force Commanders in German South West Africa, Despatch number 4 by General Botha covering the period 15 May to 18 July 1915.
114 Whittal, *With Botha and Smuts in Africa*, p. 151.
115 Trew, *Botha Treks*, p. 159; Ritchie states that Gaub was taken during the extended march: Ritchie, *With Botha in the Field*, p. 59; Whittal states that Gaub was taken unopposed: Whittal, *With Botha and Smuts in Africa*, p. 151.
116 Whittal, *With Botha and Smuts in Africa*, p. 152.

Plate 8.3: Botha negotiating with German Officials[117]

with the Germans at Tsumeb.[118] The negotiations resulted in the Germans surrendering the town on 6 July 1915.[119] Franke claimed that Botha had deceived them by deploying his forces during the armistice but Botha responded that he had only agreed to an armistice for the local forces in direct contact and not for the forces that were busy with enveloping movements.[120] At Tsumeb the South Africans found stores of weapons and ammunition; apparently they were intended to be given to the Afrikaner rebels during the uprising of 1914.[121]

117 Western Cape Archives.
118 Collyer, *The Campaign in German South West Africa, 1914–1915*, pp. 149, 150.
119 Anon., *Official History*, p. 40. Whittal says that the South African forces were ready to attack Tsumeb on 5 July and the town subsequently surrendered: Whittal, *With Botha and Smuts in Africa*, p. 152.
120 DOD Archives, SD, Box 252, Correspondence between General Botha and Lieutenant Colonel Franke on the subject of a breach of armistice by Union troops at Tsumeb, 6 July 1915.
121 Farwell, *The Great War in Africa 1914–1918*, p. 100; Buxton, *General Botha*, p. 116. Whittal indicates that besides the stores they also found 5 000 bottles of rum: Whittal, *With Botha and Smuts in Africa*, p. 152.

The Germans at Namutoni surrendered to Brits on 8 July.[122] In order to achieve this victory Brits had to undertake some extensive and arduous trekking. He departed from Karibib on 18 June when Myburgh left Okasisse, and then moved to Etanaho, Omatjenne and Otijasu where his troops eventually found potable water. Brits's force took Ombika on 3 July and Okakuejo on 4 July; the next day, on 5 July, Rietfontein was captured. Brits's brigade covered 563 kilometres in 13 days, after which Namutoni surrendered.[123] Brits had 512 People of Colour in his force grouping. Botha had virtually no communication with Brits and Myburgh until the envelopments were completed on 5 July 1915.[124] Motorcar and dispatch riders were used to communicate between the various sections, as the wireless field sets were unserviceable.[125]

The final Union envelopments effectively outmanoeuvred the Germans (refer to Map 8.1).[126] Ritchie states that the Germans 'were surrounded before they knew it. So neat and swift was the commander-in-chief's plan that the German commander was incredulous – until his scouts kept coming in and telling him what the real state of affairs was'.[127]

The Germans found themselves facing Botha and the infantry at Otavifontein. Meanwhile Myburgh and Brits had cut off their retreat. On 9 July 1915, following negotiations and discussions between Botha and Seitz the Germans accepted the conditions of unconditional surrender as put forward by Botha.[128] The German forces that surrendered at Khorab included approximately 4,000 troops and 30 artillery pieces.[129] Seitz sent an official letter to the Union Defence Force to confirm the German surrender; Botha received this at 02:00 on 9 July.[130]

The German South West African campaign was the first campaign of the First World War to be successfully concluded by a dominion of the British Empire. It was also the first armistice of the Great War.[131] The casualties for the whole campaign are demonstrated in Table 8.2.

122 Meintjes, *General Louis Botha*, p. 269.
123 Whittal, *With Botha and Smuts in Africa*, p. 153.
124 DOD Archives, SD, Box 252, 17138, Reports of Force Commanders in German South West Africa, Despatch number 4 by General Botha covering the period 15 May to 18 July 1915.
125 DOD Archives, SD, Box 252, 17138 IO, General Botha's Despatch (GOC MC GSW Campaign) 9 July to 28 October 1920, Historical Record of the Campaign in German South West Africa, 4 November 1919.
126 DOD Archives, SD, Box 252, 17138, Reports of Force Commanders in German South West Africa, Despatch number 4 by General Botha covering the period 15 May to 18 July 1915.
127 Ritchie, *With Botha in the Field*, p. 60.
128 Meintjes, *General Louis Botha*, p. 262; Trew, *Botha Treks*, p. 175.
129 Trew, *Botha Treks*, p. 169.
130 DOD Archives, SD, Box 252, 17138, Reports of Force Commanders in German South West Africa, Despatch number 4 by General Botha covering the period 15 May to 18 July 1915.
131 Nasson, *Springboks on the Somme*, pp. 76, 77.

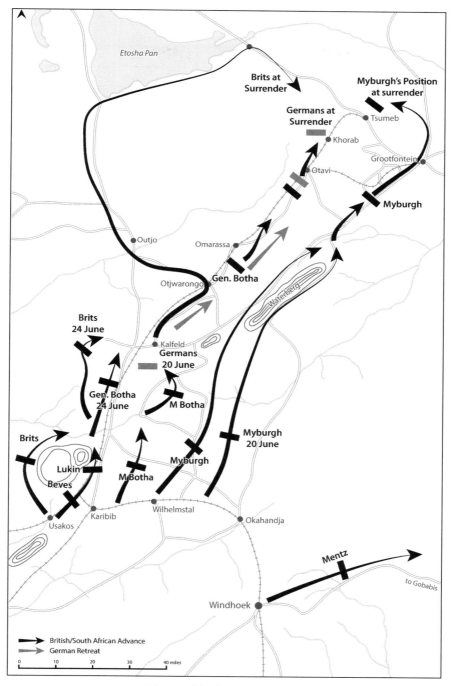

Map 8.1: The final envelopment

	German South West Africa	Afrikaner Rebellion	Totals
Died in action	114	132	246
Died of other causes		181	181
Wounded	318	242	560

Table 8.2: Casualties in the German South West African campaign and the Afrikaner Rebellion.[132] Further research is required on Black, Coloured and Indian casualties.

Analysis of the final envelopment of the German forces with regard to manoeuvre warfare theory

The reasons for defeat and victory are complex and they are by their nature inextricably intertwined. In order to determine the reasons for victory it is also equally important to understand the causes of defeat of a given military force (in this case the German military).

Gooch and Cohen have created a taxonomy for defeat in which the first step is to determine the cause of the military failure or defeat. This step is followed by determining the critical tasks which led to the defeat, and the third step is to undertake a layered analysis of the organisational aspects which led to the failure.[133]

The reason why the Germans suffered defeat was not that they were outnumbered. They were defeated because they did not fight a defensive battle at Khorab. The German force surrendered with almost their entire fighting force intact.

The Germans surrendered with 4,740 soldiers, 37 artillery pieces and 22 machineguns. In addition, they still had substantial amounts of ammunition that had been stockpiled.[134] The German and Union forces did not engage in a sustained pitched battle on the tactical level at the end of the campaign.

Furthermore, the German forces did not complete several critical tasks during the final envelopments. With hindsight they should have engaged in battle at Kalkveld and at Otavifontein. Instead the German position at Kalkveld was simply vacated by the German forces; no battle was offered.

---

132 DOD Archives, Officer Commanding Records, Box 92, OR 139, Statistics re casualties Rebellion, German South West Africa, East and Central Africa and Europe, Casualties sustained by the Union forces in the Rebellion and the German South West African campaign.

133 E.A. Cohen and J. Gooch, *Military Misfortunes: The Anatomy of Failure in War* (New York: The Free Press, 1990), p. 46.

134 H. Strachan, *The First World War, Vol 1: To Arms* (Oxford University Press, Oxford, 2001), p. 568.

Botha maintains that the German forces at Kalkveld withdrew because they feared that they would be surrounded by the Union Defence Force. He posits that the terrain and the circumstances did not allow for an encirclement of the German position at Kalkveld.[135]

The position at Otavifontein was critical to the advance of the Union Defence Force as it contained an important water source. The German force at Otavifontein was of good strength yet they offered virtually no resistance and retreated. Botha argues that if the Union Defence Force had been unable to capture Otavifontein then the Union forces would have been compelled to retreat and regroup.[136]

Franke had opted for a defensive strategy; he conserved his forces to give battle at the critical time and place.[137] The letter written by Franke to his forces conveyed the impression that a colossal clash between the German and Union forces was imminent. Botha states that despite the aggressive tone of Franke's letter and the fact that the comparably larger German force (in comparison to any of the individual advancing South African forces) was virtually intact at the end of the campaign, it was evident that the German morale was badly shaken.[138] Strachan reiterates this point, when he writes that the German retreat from Otavifontein was a clear indication that their morale had collapsed.[139]

According to their theory, Gooch and Handel explain that once the critical failures have been analysed they should be compared to the different levels of organisation. The German failure to give battle at the required times at Otavifontein and Kalkveld was the result of the shaken morale of the German subordinate commanders. Added to this, the German force had no previous experience of engaging in this type of campaign.

The Union force's mobility was something novel and the Germans found themselves retreating on a continuous basis. The German military was unfamiliar with facing a rapid, highly mobile enemy which targeted its logistical and communication lines. During the campaign, the Germans became accustomed to trading space for time and retreating became a rehearsed operational procedure. The constant withdrawal of the German forces resulted in the forces becoming increasingly disconnected with

135 DOD Archives, SD, Box 252, 17138, Reports of Force Commanders in German South West Africa, Despatch number 4 by General Botha covering the period 15 May to 18 July 1915.
136 DOD Archives, SD, Box 252, 17138, Reports of Force Commanders in German South West Africa, Despatch number 4 by General Botha covering the period 15 May to 18 July 1915.
137 DOD Archives, SD, Box 252, 17138, Reports of Force Commanders in German South West Africa, Translation of an appeal by Lieutenant Colonel Franke, the commander-in-chief of the Protectorate, 28 June 1915.
138 DOD Archives, SD, Box 252, 17138, Reports of Force Commanders in German South West Africa, Despatch number 4 by General Botha covering the period 15 May to 18 July 1915.
139 Strachan, *The First World War,* p. 568.

the prospect of an actual pitched defensive battle. The leadership skills of Franke and his subordinate commanders must be questioned in this regard. Furthermore it should be understood that the German force was more acquainted, familiar and comfortable with offensive warfare as opposed to a defensive campaign.[140] Von Kleist and Ritter were perhaps overwhelmed by the magnitude of their commands and their responsibilities in the final phase of the campaign.

The Germans appear to have accepted defeat long before the final surrender. The repetitive tendency of German sections and detachments to retreat may have become an organisational norm which led to the final surrender. Furthermore it is postulated that Franke was dislocated, his morale shattered and his inability to face the Union force reflected the performance of his soldiers. When compared to the feats of Von Heydebreck who masterminded the Sandfontein attack, the efforts of Franke seem inadequate and bordering on incompetent. Franke's counterpart in German East Africa, Lettow-Vorbeck, perhaps in a different strategic and operational context and in different terrain put up a much more determined resistance.

German strategic conceptions of manoeuvre purported that a smaller force could defeat a larger one using aggressive envelopments. Lettow-Vorbeck executed conventional and guerrilla type operations against the British force gaining international acclaim for remaining uncaptured at the signing of the Armistice.[141]

In terms of the formula, total military power equals quantity multiplied by material quality multiplied by non-material quality,[142] the 'quantity' or numerical strength of the Union forces was considerably larger than that of the German forces. The quality of the equipment (the materiel) available to the German and Union forces was approximately equal. As the campaign progressed the Union Defence Force controlled the railway which allowed for the logistical provisioning of the Union forces and the Union Defence Force had aeroplanes deployed for aerial reconnaissance (this tilted the scale of materiel towards the Union Defence Force). Furthermore, the British Navy had control of the seas and allowed for the uninterrupted provision of the Union forces. The non-material 'quality', which refers to issues such as morale, motivation, offensive spirit and leadership, was superior within the rank and file of the Union Defence Force than it was in the German force.

The numbers shows that the Union forces were stronger than the German forces in number, materiel quality and non-material quality. On the point of numerical superiority the Union did not have overwhelmingly stronger numbers than the Germans during the final envelopments. Botha claims that knowing where the enemy

140 The German victories at the Battle of Sandfontein, the Battle of Naulila (against the Portuguese military) and the Herero and Namaqua campaigns (massacres/genocide) are examples of previous German military 'victories' which comprised offensive operations.

141 F. Jon Nesselhuf, 'General Paul Von Lettow-Vorbeck's East African Campaign: Maneuver Warfare on the Serengeti', MA thesis, University of North Texas, 2012, p. 2

142 Handel, *War Strategy and Intelligence*, pp. 95, 96.

forces were located made it feasible to advance with only the required number of troops and no more.[143]

During the last phase of the campaign and the final envelopments by the Union Defence Force, the Germans were on interior lines. The German force held the central position and was able to concentrate superior forces on each of the separate Union detachments which were deployed in a forward position.[144] Hence the numerical superiority of the Union's forces was not the most decisive factor when the final envelopments were in progress.

What was significant about the South African campaign in German South West Africa was its brevity. Handel maintains that qualitative factors are usually the most decisive factors in the outcome of a short war.[145] In this case the offensive spirit, leadership and morale of the Union Defence Force were crucial in the success of the campaign. This should be considered against German's lack of combat cohesion, despite having a homogenous well equipped force, and Franke's inadequate leadership.

According to Handel, quantitative superiority normally becomes important in extended campaigns.[146] The brevity of the German South West African campaign is thus testament to the strength of the qualitative factors of the Union Defence Force. The importance of numerical superiority is in no way undermined, but the reason for the South African victory and the German defeat was not a direct result of numerical strength. If the Germans had repulsed the Union forces in the final envelopments, the campaign would have become protracted. In that case the superior numbers of the Union Defence Force may well have influenced the outcome of the campaign in the longer term. The superior forces allowed for the protection of the Lines of Communication which facilitated the provisioning of troops - as Thompson said, 'the blockhouses eats up the infantry'.[147] The logistical supply enabled the offensive forces which ultimately won the campaign.

In his official correspondence with the Kaiser, Seitz claims that the German defeat was caused by the superior numbers of the Union Defence Force which had encircled them at Khorab by taking the German positions at Namutoni and Tsumeb. Seitz maintains that every attempt to break through the Union encirclement proved futile.[148] This book argues that the Germans had the option to give battle before the final surrender.

143 DOD Archives, SD, Box 252, 17138, Reports of Force Commanders in German South West Africa, Despatch number 4 by General Botha covering the period 15 May to 18 July 1915.
144 Ibid.
145 M.I. Handel, *Masters of War* (London: Frank Cass, 1992, p 96.
146 Ibid., p. 96.
147 SANA, Smuts Papers, Box 112, Major General Thompson: Report on a visit to German South West Africa, 20-27 March 1915.
148 DOD Archives, SD, Box 886, Letter, Dr Seitz to the Kaiser, 4 August 1915.

Botha gives the reason for the Union victory as the effect of surprise on the German force due to the speed of the enveloping attacks on the German positions at Tsumeb and Namutoni.[149] The collapse of morale in the German ranks was central to their defeat. The numerical superiority of the Union was an important factor but to present it as the only cause of victory can be regarded as an oversimplification of the complex phenomenon of military failure and defeat.

This book links the short duration of the campaign to the qualitative factors evident in the Union Defence Force; these are in turn analysed in terms of manoeuvre warfare theory. The final envelopments resulted in the dislocation of the physical and psychological dimensions of the German commanders. The low morale and lack of offensive spirit and cohesion of the German force led to their surrender without suffering substantial physical harm. The surrender of a military force without physical resistance indicates that they were compelled to do so by psychological pressure and the perceived threat of death or destruction. The next chapter addresses the use of aviation in the campaign.

---

149 DOD Archives, WW1 GSWA, Box 23a, Citations, German South West Africa, Northern Army, Commander of the 1st Mounted Brigade Special Appointments, 17 February 1918.

9

Airpower in the German South West African Campaign

During the Great War, aircraft was primarily used for reconnaissance and artillery spotting. The Union of South Africa's First World War campaign in German South West Africa allowed for South Africa's first employment of military aeroplanes in conventional warfare. The creation and employment of the South African Aviation Corps (SAAC) UDF provided ground forces with a substantial force multiplier in terms of forward reconnaissance. The aerial reconnaissance allowed Botha and his subordinate commanders to better understand the tactical picture and further facilitated the battle concept.

This chapter discusses the role and impact of aerial operations in the German South West African campaign. As explained in the previous chapters the campaign in German South West Africa was characterised by sweeping envelopments which were executed by the Union's commandos. During the latter part of the campaign aeroplanes provided the UDF with intelligence in terms of the location and concentration of German forces, which assisted in their final encirclement.

The industrial revolutions of the 19th and early 20th centuries ushered in a new era of technological innovation that revolutionised the way war was fought. The early 20th century brought forward scientific breakthroughs which saw warfare take to the skies. In August 1914 the First World War commenced and ground operations were focussed on massing superior forces at critical points in attempts to invade or defend the respective territories. The European powers were soon locked in a war of attrition on the Western Front where manoeuvre space was exhausted and the defensive position became favoured over the offensive which assumed the majority risk.[1] The Great War became static as mobile operations soon turned out to be impractical

---

1   D. E. Showalter, "Manoeuvre Warfare: The Eastern and Western Fronts", in H. Strachan, (ed.), *The Oxford Illustrated History of the First World War* (Oxford University Press, Oxford, 1998), p. 46.

with the preponderance of trenches and defensive obstacles on the Western Front.[2] Extending over 600 kilometres from the North Sea to the Franco-Swiss border, the Western Front saw extensive operations and high intensity attrition battles. During the stalemate on the Western Front, military aviation became the only option to conduct mobile reconnaissance and artillery spotting.[3] Furthermore military aviation also demonstrated the potential for aerial bombardment.[4]

The First World War took on a different character and shape in the varying operational theatres and whilst the Western Front was reduced to a mass stalemate, the colonial conflicts of the Great War were largely executed over large and open spaces. The use of aircraft in the German South West African campaign assisted the ground operations in providing up to date reconnaissance. During the First World War aerial reconnaissance was used to facilitate the operational planning process and the commander's decision making cycle.[5]

The historiography of the German South West African campaign provides limited focus on the element of air operations. Despite the growing body of literature, there are limited sources which provide in-depth analysis on the juxtaposition between ground and air operations in the German South West African campaign.[6] This chapter aims to address the lack of focus on air operations during the campaign through a ground-breaking study on the use of aerial reconnaissance and rudimentary bombing missions in support of ground operations in 1915.

The development of the SAAC, which was established on 19 January 1915,[7] was slower in comparison to that of the European powers which developed at a rapid pace. During 1915, military aviation, facilitated by new technological innovation quickly developed the fighter plane and pilot.[8] The narrative of airpower throughout

---

2   D.T. Zabecki, *The German 1918 Offensives: A Case Study in the Operational Level of War* (Routledge, New York, 2006), p. 46.

3   A. Whitmarsh, 'British Army Manoeuvres and the Development of Military Airpower 1910 -   1913', *War in History*, 14, 3, 2007, p. 325.

4   J.H. Morrow, 'The War in the Air', Chapter in Strachan (ed.), *Oxford Illustrated History*, p. 268; C. Blount, 'Modern Airpower and the 1916 Arab Revolt: What can the modern Airman do to counter Lawrence of Arabia', *Air and Space Power Journal*, 23, 3, 2009, p. 21.

5   J. Steckfuss, *Eyes all over the Sky: Aerial Reconnaissance in the First World War* (Oxford: Casemate, 2016), p. 2.

6   W.A. Raleigh and H.A. Jones, *The War in the Air: Being the Story of the Part Played in the Great of the Royal Air Force* (Oxford: Carendon Press, 1922); S. Monick, 'The Third Man: Willy Trück and the German Air Effort in South West Africa in World War I', *Military History Journal*, 5, 3, 1981; J.O.E.O. Mahncke, 'Aircraft Operations in the German Colonies 1911–1916: The Fliegertruppe of the Imperial German Army, *Military History Journal*, 12, 2, 2001; K.R. Van Der Spuy, *Chasing the Wind* (Cape Town: Books of Africa, 1966); A. Garcia, 'Airpower in the Union of South Africa's First World War campaign in German South West Africa', *Historia*, 62, 2, 2017.

7   The South African Air Force was established on 1 February 1920.

8   Morrow, "The War in the Air", Chapter in Strachan (ed.), *Oxford Illustrated History*, p. 269.

history involves the central tenet of technological development and progress.[9] The total mobilisation of the Great War resulted in a stalemate where numbers and mass was the main focus and appeared to be the only solution. The application of airpower by the UDF during the campaign in German South West Africa was on a much lower and limited level when compared to that of the European theatre of operations mirroring the intensity of the conflict. Airpower in the German South West African campaign was introduced as a means of aerial reconnaissance which facilitated the offensive manoeuvres executed by the UDF which ultimately led to the surrender of the German forces. This chapter commences with a brief discussion on the context and background of airpower in South Africa, followed by an explanation of the overlap of ground and air operations in the German South West African campaign.

Airpower, the Great War and the Union of South Africa

Initial interest in aviation began with air balloons which were first used by the British Royal Engineers in the 1860s. The Royal Flying Corps (where the first South African pilots were trained) replaced the Air Battalion on 11 April 1912 shortly after the Royal Naval Air Service broke away from the Royal Flying Corps in July 1914. The development of aeroplanes resulted in their operational use in the 1911-12 Italo-Turkish War and in the 1912-13 Balkan War. The British Army manoeuvres and training exercises from 1912 onwards included the use of aircraft and it was determined that the effective use of aeroplanes would become instrumental to achieving victory.[10] Leo Amery[11] explained the importance of aerial reconnaissance for static armies one year before the First World War commenced.[12]

At the start of the First World War, there was a substantial focus on the development of the aeroplane as a weapon of war. The initial use of the aircraft during the Great War was for the purpose of reconnaissance in direct support of the ground forces. This later evolved into strategic reconnaissance. The reconnaissance planes were accompanied by combat planes which provided them with protection. This in turn led to the creation of further combat planes which were designed to destroy the reconnaissance protector planes resulting in the progression of aerial combat.[13] Despite the development of

---

9   S.H. Lukasik, 'Insurgent Airpower in Historical Perspective: An Introduction and Prospectus of Research', *The Historian*, 74, 2, 2012, p. 225.
10   Whitmarsh, 'British Army Manoeuvres', p. 327.
11   Leo Amery was a war correspondent during the South African War who later edited the Times History of the South African War.
12   K.P. Epstein, 'Imperial Airs: Leo Amery, Airpower and Airpower, 1873-1945', *The Journal of Imperial and Commonwealth History*, 38, 4, 2010, p. 575.
13   J.A. Hennessy, 'Men and Planes of World War 1 and History of Lafayette Escadrille', *Air Power History*, 61, 2, 2014, p. 21.

one-on-one and formation aerial combat, the use of large numbers of air patrols struggled to prevent the deployment and success of air reconnaissance flights.[14]

The Union's pilots in German South West Africa were not required to function as fighter pilots as German aircraft in the colony were out of commission by the time the SAAC was deployed. The development of the Union's airpower in German South West Africa was on a much more limited scale when compared to the European theatre and the main purpose of the SAAC remained reconnaissance which directly assisted the ground forces.[15]

The author, politician and former intelligence officer, Amery, was of the opinion that aeroplanes would be of far greater value in those theatres of operations where there were not high concentrations of troops and where extended expanses of terrain and limited communications were combined with highly mobile operations.[16] German South West Africa made for an interesting case study to test Amery's hypothesis as the campaign proved to be one of manoeuvre and vast distances.

One of the functions of airpower is to provide current information to the commander from throughout the operational area. The ability to locate the enemy then allows the commander to 'fix' the enemy thereby limiting their freedom of action and mobility. The domination of the skies and the ability to locate the enemy in turn facilitates complete situational awareness for the commander.[17]

While locating the opposing force was central to tactical considerations, the pace of the campaign was greatly influenced by logistical consideration and the availability of water resources.[18] The campaign was characterised by extensive and rapid manoeuvres which were followed by operational pauses which were used to regroup.[19] Furthermore, the great expanses of German South West Africa were overcome through the use of aerial reconnaissance which became a force multiplier.

The South African Aviation Corps

Interest in flying for military purposes and the creation of the SAAC was facilitated by Beyers who as Commandant General of the Active Citizen Force was sent by Smuts to Britain in 1912 to observe the military manoeuvres and the use of aeroplanes in army operations. On his return Beyers highly recommended the use aeroplanes in

14   A.D. Harvey, 'Air Warfare in Perspective', *Air Power History*, 60, 3, 2013, p. 9.
15   S. Monick, 'The Third Man', p. 1; Mahncke, 'Aircraft operations in the German Colonies', p. 2; H.F. Trew, *Botha Treks* (London: Blackie & Son, 1936), p. 152; G. L'ange, *Urgent Imperial Service* (Rivonia: Ashanti, 1991), p. 118.
16   Epstein, 'Imperial Airs', pp. 578, 579.
17   Blount, 'Modern Airpower and the 1916 Arab Revolt', p. 53.
18   E. Kleynhans, 'A Critical Analysis of the Impact of Water on the South African Campaign in German South West Africa, 1914 1915', *Historia*, 61, 2, 2016, p. 50.
19   See, A. Garcia, 'A Manoeuvre Warfare Analysis of South Africa's 1914-1915 German South West African Campaign', *Scientia Militaria*. 45, 1, 2017.

warfare especially for the purpose of reconnaissance. The 1912 Defence Act created an Aviation Corps under the Active Citizen Force. Smuts was one of the visionaries[20] who foresaw the remarkable potential of the aeroplane,[21] and put in a considerable effort to expedite the process of deploying the SAAC to the theatre of operations in German South West Africa.[22]

The first South African pilots were initially trained in South Africa at the Paterson Aviation Syndicate School in 1913, located at Alexanderfontein (which was later purchased by the UDF) followed by a course at Tempe School and training at the Royal Flying Corps.[23] The initial course at Alexanderfontein trained ten candidate pilots as per the Memorandum of Agreement signed between Smuts and Cecil Compton Paterson.[24]

The South African High Commissioner negotiated for the acquisition of new aeroplanes in October 1914.[25] While the finalisation of negotiations took place, Major General Henderson the Officer Commanding Royal Flying Corps ordered the formation of the SAAC in November 1914 to assist with the German South West Africa campaign. Several types of planes were analysed to determine the ideal aircraft for the climate in German South West Africa, ultimately deciding on the Henri Farman F-27 after which several tests were done in France.[26] The South African pilots who were serving in other theatres during the Great War were recalled to form the SAAC (accompanied by some British officers and soldiers). These pilots included Captain (later Major) Gerard Wallace who became the commander of the Aviation Corps, Lieutenants Clisdal and Carey-Thomas who were observers[27] and Lieutenants

20 In 1917 Smuts had become a member of the British War Cabinet promoted the Air Force as a separate wing, removed from the Army. Leo Amery suggested to Smuts that the Air Force should have a separate and independent staff. Smuts and Amery had become friends during the South African War: Epstein, 'Imperial Airs', p. 577.

21 T. Dedering, 'Air Power in South Africa, 1914-1939', *Journal of Southern African Studies*, 31, 3, 2015; Hennessy, 'Men and Planes of World War 1', p. 16.

22 L'ange, *Urgent Imperial Service*, pp. 268, 269.

23 Mahncke, 'Aircraft operations in the German colonies', pp. 1, 2; DOD Archives, World War 1 War Diaries (hereafter WW1 WD), Box 2, Air/1/1247/204/7/4, Historical record of No 26 (SA) Squadron and South African Aviation Corps and Historical record of the South Africa unit of the Royal Flying Corps; L'ange, *Urgent Imperial Service*, p. 269.

24 See, D.P. Tidy, 'They Mounted up as Eagles: A brief tribute to the South African Air Force', *The Military History Journal*, 5, 6, 1982.

25 L'ange, *Urgent Imperial Service*, p. 273.

26 DOD Archives, WW1 WD, Box 1, Air 1/1247/204/7/1, Report by Major Wallace on the campaign in German South West Africa, 1915, 21 July 1916; L'ange, *Urgent Imperial Service*, p. 269.

27 DOD Archives, WW1 WD, Box 1, Air 1/1247/204/7/1 Vol 3, Aviation report on German South West Africa April 1915 – 1916, War Diary.

Kenneth van der Spuy, Gordon Creed, Basil Turner, Cripps, Marthinus Williams and Edwin Emmet who were military pilots.[28]

During early 1915 Turner and Emmet were sent to the Union of South Africa and German South West Africa respectively. Turner was assigned the task of recruiting further members for the embryonic Aviation Corps and Emmet was responsible for finding a suitable aerodrome in Swakopmund in German South West Africa.[29] In terms of supporting staff, 34 mechanics were transferred from the Royal Naval Air Service to the Union of South Africa.[30] The preliminary staff were supplemented by additional pilots and supporting personnel such as observers and logistical administrators. Strength returns indicate that there were eight People of Colour attached to the SAAC during the final advance.[31]

The SAAC initially comprised four Henri Farmans F-27 and two Blériot Experimental model 2C (B.E.2c) planes. The remaining staff and four of the six aeroplanes (two B.E.2cs and two Henri Farman F-27) arrived by ship in Walvis Bay on 30 April 1915 and the aircraft were disembarked on 1 May 1915. Two of the Henri Farmans were considerably damaged as a result of the sea voyage. The first test flight was taken by Van Der Spuy in one of the B.E.2c planes on 4 May[32] after which the other B.E.2c was tested on 5 May and both aircraft were declared combat ready by 7 May 1915.[33] The first planned task for the newly formed aviation corps was to support operations against Karibib, however the UDF captured Karibib before the SAAC could conduct any reconnaissance missions.

28   DOD Archives, WW1 WD, Box 1, Air 1/1247/204/7/1, Report by Major Wallace on the campaign in German South West Africa, 1915, 21 July 1916.
29   DOD Archives, WW1 WD, Box 1, Air 1/1247/204/7/1, Report by Major Wallace on the campaign in German South West Africa, 1915, 21 July 1916; L'ange, *Urgent Imperial Service*, p. 269.
30   DOD Archives, WW1 WD, Box 2, Air/1/1247/204/7/4, Historical record of No 26 (SA) Squadron and South African Aviation Corps and Historical record of the South Africa unit of the Royal Flying Corps; DOD Archives, WW1 WD, Box 1, Air 1/1247/204/7/1, Report by Major Wallace on the campaign in German South West Africa, 1915, 21 July 1916.
31   DOD Archives, SD, Box 252, Strength of Units during the Final Advance in German South West Africa, July 1915.
32   DOD Archives, WW1 WD, Box 1, Air 1/1247/204/7/1 Vol 3, Aviation report on German South West Africa April 1915 – 1916, War Diary.
33   DOD Archives, WW1 WD, Box 1, Air 1/1247/204/7/1, Report by Major Wallace on the campaign in German South West Africa, 1915, 21 July 1916. Mahncke gives the first reconnaissance flight on 6 May 1915: Mahncke, 'Aircraft operations in the German colonies', p. 3. However, this flight may have indeed been a test flight.

Ground Operations in German South West Africa and the Deployment of the SAAC

The Northern Army advanced from Lüderitzbucht in an easterly direction but was constrained by the availability of logistics, water and transport.[34] The intermediate objective of the northern invasion was Karibib, a strategic rail link,[35] which was captured on 6 May with Windhoek taken unopposed on 12 May 1915.[36] Following the capture of Windhoek the Northern Army took a month and a half operational pause to accumulate the required materiel and logistics required to execute the final advance.[37] Toward the end of May 1915 the SAAC was deployed to the front lines for the first time to conduct aerial reconnaissance in support of the final advance.[38] The deployment of aircraft in the area of operations was eagerly anticipated.[39]

The first task of the Aviation Corps after assembling their planes was to ensure that there were aerodromes along the axis of advance which would allow the planes to land at the required UDF operating bases. There were already existing aerodromes at Karub and Karibib and the SAAC made minor modifications to these structures to accommodate their aircraft after which technical and logistical supplies for the aircraft were sent up on 7 May 1915.[40] The logistical and transport arrangements for the Aviation Corps were not ideal for the conditions in German South West Africa, and these support systems were placed under considerable strain in getting the

34 L'ange, *Urgent Imperial Service*, p. 244; Anon., *Union of South Africa and the Great War, 1914–1918, Official History* (Pretoria: Government Printer, 1924), p. 32; W. Whittal, *With Botha and Smuts in Africa* (Cassel, London, 1917), p. 137; J.J. Collyer, *The Campaign in German South West Africa, 1914–1915* (Pretoria: Government Printer, 1937), p. 23. Kleynhans, 'A Critical Analysis', pp. 41, 42.

35 W.A. Dorning, 'A Concise History of the South African Defence Force 1912–1987', *Militaria, South African Journal for Military Studies*, 17, 2, 1987, p. 4.

36 B. Nasson, *Springboks on the Somme* (Johannesburg: Penguin, 2007), p. 74; Anon., *Official History*, p. 40; J. Meintjes, *General Louis Botha* (Cassel, London, 1970), p. 264; Whittal, *With Botha and Smuts*, p. 62; H. Paterson, 'First Allied Victory: The South African Campaign in German South-West Africa, 1914–1915', *Military History Journal*, 13, 2, 2004, p. 6.

37 Strachan, *The First World War*, p. 565; Anon., *Official History*, p. 32.

38 TNA, ADM 123/144, War Records 1914-1918, General Letters and Proceedings, Walvis Bay, May 1915; DOD Archives, WW1 WD, Box 1, Air 1/1247/204/7/1 Vol 2, Aviation report on German South West Africa April 1915 – 1916, Report of Transport Officer; DOD Archives, WW1 WD, Box 1, Air 1/1247/204/7/1 Vol 10, Aviation report on German South West Africa April 1915 – 1916, Diary Number 2 kept by Lieutenant Carey-Thomas; DOD Archives, WW1 WD, Box 1, Air 1/1247/204/7/1, Report by Major Wallace on the campaign in German South West Africa, 1915, 21 July 1916.

39 SANA, Smuts Papers, Box 112, Major General Thompson: Report on a visit to German South West Africa, 20-27 March 1915.

40 DOD Archives, WW1 WD, Box 1, Air 1/1247/204/7/1, Report by Major Wallace on the campaign in German South West Africa, 1915, 21 July 1916.

required spares, which were often lacking, from the maintenance base in Walvis Bay to the front lines.[41]

On 9 May 1915 Turner and Cripps each flew a B.E.2c each to Karub. On 11 May, while moving his aircraft up to the front, Turner crashed his plane at Karub. Van Der Spuy conducted the first flight with a Henri Farman on 13 May and after experiencing some minor complications the aircraft was returned to the workshop for technical adjustments.[42] Supplies and personnel were sent up from Walvis Bay to Karub and Karibib on 12 May with 11 cars and one trailer to support aviation operations at the front.[43]

The Union headquarters ordered a reconnaissance flight of Omaruru on 23 May 1915 as the final advance was being planned.[44] Van Der Spuy was sent up from Walvis Bay with a Henri Farman on 25 May 1915 and he landed in Karub on the same day proceeding to Karibib on 26 May.[45] The first reconnaissance flight in support of operations was attempted on 27 May but was abandoned due to excessive wind speeds which were considered to be a risk to the aircraft.[46] The reconnaissance flight was carried out the following morning and indicated approximately 20 German soldiers in and around Omaruru with the remainder of the German forces having evacuated the town.[47]

On the German side, aircraft were also used for reconnaissance and for rudimentary aerial bombardment.[48] The German forces had two military pilots, Lieutenant Von Scheele and 2nd Lieutenant Fiedler as well as Willie Truck who was a factory test pilot,[49] who was sent to Karibib by the *Aviatik Automobil und Flugapparatefabrik* aircraft factory in Germany.[50] On 27 May Von Scheele crashed his plane and there

41   DOD Archives, WW1 WD, Box 1, Air 1/1247/204/7/1 Vol 2, Aviation report on German South West Africa April 1915 – 1916, Report of Transport Officer.
42   DOD Archives, WW1 WD, Box 1, Air 1/1247/204/7/1 Vol 2, Aviation report on German South West Africa April 1915 – 1916, Report of Transport Officer.
43   DOD Archives, WW1 WD, Box 1, Air 1/1247/204/7/1 Vol 10, Aviation report on German South West Africa April 1915 – 1916, Diary Number 2 kept by Lieutenant Carey-Thomas.
44   DOD Archives, SD, Box 252, 17138, Reports of Force Commanders in German South West Africa, Despatch number 4 by General Botha covering the period 15 May to 18 July 1915.
45   DOD Archives, WW1 WD, Box 1, Air 1/1247/204/7/1, Report by Major Wallace on the campaign in German South West Africa, 1915, 21 July 1916; DOD Archives, WW1 WD, Box 1, Air 1/1247/204/7/1 Vol 3, Aviation report on German South West Africa April 1915 – 1916, War Diary.
46   DOD Archives, WW1 WD, Box 1, Air 1/1247/204/7/1 Vol 10, Aviation report on German South West Africa April 1915 – 1916, Diary Number 2 kept by Lieutenant Carey-Thomas; DOD Archives, WW1 WD, Box 1, Air 1/1247/204/7/1, Report by Major Wallace on the campaign in German South West Africa, 1915, 21 July 1916.
47   DOD Archives, WW1 WD, Box 1, Air 1/1247/204/7/1, Report by Major Wallace on the campaign in German South West Africa, 1915, 21 July 1916.
48   L'ange, *Urgent Imperial Service*, p. 118.
49   Mahncke, 'Aircraft operations in the German colonies', p. 1.
50   Monick, 'The Third Man', p. 1.

was no record of German flights after this date.[51] While German aviation in German South West Africa came to an end, South African aviation was still in its nascent stage.

Early June 1915 was a time of considerable exploration for the SAAC which tested new and improvised equipment. On 4 and 5 June the aviation support technicians worked on improvised bomb dropping fittings which were installed on the aeroplanes.[52] On 7 June the bomb dropping fittings were tested, dropping petrol bombs from 500 feet however the test was not successful.[53] It is interesting to note that the American military initially opposed the idea of aerial bombing insisting on reconnaissance as the primary function of the aeroplane.[54] The aeroplanes used at the start of the Great War had open cockpits and could reach a maximum altitude of 12,000 feet. The development of aeronautical technology during the First World War greatly improved the limits of aircraft and the surge of development generated planes which could travel up to 130 miles per hour and could reach altitudes of up to 20,000 feet.[55] On 6 June the Henri Farman plane was flown to 12,500 feet which was a record by South African standards.[56] Considering these feats, the SAAC did well in reaching 12,500 feet with the aeroplanes which they had available.

Two more Henri Farmans arrived in Walvis Bay on 7 June and Wallace ordered them to be assembled and sent up to the front for the UDF's final advance. While the planes were being brought up from Walvis Bay, Van Der Spuy conducted a second reconnaissance of Omaruru on 10 June and confirmed the same information as the first reconnaissance. At the same time, two 16 pound bombs were dropped on the position at Omaruru. Although they had limited impact, the newly innovated bomb fittings were reported to be in good working order.[57]

The Final Advance

Botha had managed to accumulate sufficient stores by mid-June to carry the campaign to completion. The final operations involved a central advance and an extensive double

51   L'ange, *Urgent Imperial Service*, pp. 268, 269.
52   DOD Archives, WW1 WD, Box 1, Air 1/1247/204/7/1 Vol 10, Aviation report on German South West Africa April 1915 – 1916, Diary Number 2 kept by Lieutenant Carey-Thomas.
53   DOD Archives, WW1 WD, Box 1, Air 1/1247/204/7/1 Vol 10, Aviation report on German South West Africa April 1915 – 1916, Diary Number 2 kept by Lieutenant Carey-Thomas.
54   Hennessy, 'Men and Planes of World War 1', p. 21.
55   D.R. Baucom, 'Wakes of War: Contrails and the Rise of Air Power 1918 – 1945 Part 1 – Early Sightings and Preliminary Explanations, 1918-1938', *Air Power History*, 54, 2, 2007, p. 18.
56   DOD Archives, WW1 WD, Box 1, Air 1/1247/204/7/1 Vol 3, Aviation report on German South West Africa April 1915 – 1916, War Diary.
57   DOD Archives, WW1 WD, Box 1, Air 1/1247/204/7/1, Report by Major Wallace on the campaign in German South West Africa, 1915, 21 July 1916; DOD Archives, WW1 WD, Box 1, Air 1/1247/204/7/1 Vol 10, Aviation report on German South West Africa April 1915 – 1916, Diary Number 2 kept by Lieutenant Carey-Thomas.

envelopment which aimed to cut off and encircle the German forces. The central column was comprised of largely infantry formations commanded by Brigadiers Lukin and Beves. The pincer movements were executed by Brits and Myburgh who commanded the 1st Mounted and 2nd Mounted Brigades respectively. Brits and the 1st Mounted Brigade took a wide enveloping route in capturing Etosha Pan and Namutoni. Myburgh's forces captured Grootfontein and Tsumeb in a wide envelopment.[58]

The UDF advanced in the face of the retreating German forces with the immediate objectives of capturing Omaruru and Kalkveld. The concept of 'find, fix and destroy' was complicated by the mobile retreat of the German forces. The aerial reconnaissance facilitated the 'find' function of the UDF's ground operations however the chances of battle were negated by the German decisions to avoid combat. Botha was aware of the dilemma and raised it with Smuts in formal correspondence, in June 1915. He doubted whether the Germans at Kalkveld would offer battle as they had previously abandoned well prepared defensive positions in favour of retreat.[59] Botha added that he was unable to stop the Germans from retreating because of the geography of German South West Africa, however if they decided to fight it would be likely that a decisive result would be achieved.[60]

Wallace and an aviation team advanced to Omaruru with Brits' 1st Mounted Brigade and arrived on 18 June 1915. They proceeded to finalise the preparation of the aerodrome at Omaruru which the Germans had started constructing (for their own aircraft). Hinchelwood and Creed arrived at Karibib on 18 June after taking a two-hour flight from Walvis Bay.[61] The construction of aerodromes along the axis of advance allowed for the projection of airpower throughout the operational theatre. The supporting elements of the Aviation Corps had 22 cars (in total) which were used to transport personnel and spares between the required points on the axis of advance and the lines of communication.[62]

While the SAAC moved forward on the lines of communication, Brits and Myburgh's forces commenced their extensive pincer envelopments to the northwest

58 DOD Archives, SD, Box 252, 17138, Reports of Force Commanders in German South West Africa, Despatch number 4 by General Botha covering the period 15 May to 18 July 1915; L'ange, *Urgent Imperial Service,* p. 264.
59 DOD Archives, SD, Box 252, 17138, Reports of Force Commanders in German South West Africa, Despatch number 4 by General Botha covering the period 15 May to 18 July 1915.
60 TNA, CAB 45/112, The Campaign in German South West Africa 1914-1918, Narrative of Events, 21 June 1915.
61 DOD Archives, WW1 WD, Box 1, Air 1/1247/204/7/1 Vol 10, Aviation report on German South West Africa April 1915 – 1916, Diary Number 2 kept by Lieutenant Carey-Thomas; DOD Archives, WW1 WD, Box 1, Air 1/1247/204/7/1 Vol 3, Aviation report on German South West Africa April 1915 – 1916, War Diary; DOD Archives, WW1 WD, Box 1, Air 1/1247/204/7/1, Report by Major Wallace on the campaign in German South West Africa, 1915, 21 July 1916.
62 DOD Archives, WW1 WD, Box 1, Air 1/1247/204/7/1 Vol 2, Aviation report on German South West Africa April 1915 – 1916, Report of Transport Officer.

and northeast respectively. The double envelopment was designed to cut off the German retreat.[63] The 1st Mounted Brigade captured Omaruru on 19 June 1915.[64] Creed flew up from Karibib to Omaruru on 19 June joining Wallace and his team. Three Henri Farman planes were deployed at the front and 30 men under Turner and Emmet remained at Walvis Bay.[65] Cripps crashed his plane on landing at Karibib on 20 June[66] and it was returned by train to the aviation workshop in Walvis Bay.[67]

Five reconnaissance flights were conducted over Kalkveld and Waterberg from Karibib and Omaruru.[68] Two of these detailed 500 German troops present on 21 June, deployed in a semicircle at Kalkveld[69] and on 22 June a reconnaissance flight reported 150 German troops present in the same position.[70] Two more reconnaissance flights on 23 June were taken over Waterberg and Kalkveld where no German troops were found.[71] Botha has noted that the German forces' strength at Kalkveld was known prior to the advance which fortified the UDF's confidence.[72]

A further reconnaissance was done by Van Der Spuy and Wallace on the morning of 24 June: the date for the UDF advance on Kalkveld, with the aim of determining possible locations for aerial bombardments.[73] During the aerial reconnaissance

63   DOD Archives, SD, Box 252, 17138, Reports of Force Commanders in German South West Africa, Despatch number 4 by General Botha covering the period 15 May to 18 July 1915.
64   M.E. Ritchie, *With Botha in the Field* (London: Longmans, 1915), p. 55.
65   DOD Archives, WW1 WD, Box 1, Air 1/1247/204/7/1, Report by Major Wallace on the campaign in German South West Africa, 1915, 21 July 1916.
66   DOD Archives, WW1 WD, Box 1, Air 1/1247/204/7/1 Vol 3, Aviation report on German South West Africa April 1915 – 1916, War Diary; DOD Archives, WW1 WD, Box 1, Air 1/1247/204/7/1 Vol 10, Aviation report on German South West Africa April 1915 – 1916, Diary Number 2 kept by Lieutenant Carey-Thomas.
67   DOD Archives, WW1 WD, Box 1, Air 1/1247/204/7/1, Report by Major Wallace on the campaign in German South West Africa, 1915, 21 July 1916.
68   DOD Archives, WW1 WD, Box 1, Air 1/1247/204/7/1, Report by Major Wallace on the campaign in German South West Africa, 1915, 21 July 1916.
69   DOD Archives, SD, Box 252, 17138, Reports of Force Commanders in German South West Africa, Despatch number 4 by General Botha covering the period 15 May to 18 July 1915; DOD Archives, WW1 WD, Box 1, Air 1/1247/204/7/1 Vol 3, Aviation report on German South West Africa April 1915 – 1916, War Diary.
70   DOD Archives, WW1 WD, Box 1, Air 1/1247/204/7/1, Report by Major Wallace on the campaign in German South West Africa, 1915, 21 July 1916; DOD Archives, WW1 WD, Box 1, Air 1/1247/204/7/1 Vol 3, Aviation report on German South West Africa April 1915 – 1916, War Diary.
71   DOD Archives, WW1 WD, Box 1, Air 1/1247/204/7/1 Vol 3, Aviation report on German South West Africa April 1915 – 1916, War Diary.
72   DOD Archives, SD, Box 252, 17138, Reports of Force Commanders in German South West Africa, Despatch number 4 by General Botha covering the period 15 May to 18 July 1915.
73   DOD Archives, WW1 WD, Box 1, Air 1/1247/204/7/1, Report by Major Wallace on the campaign in German South West Africa, 1915, 21 July 1916; DOD Archives, WW1 WD, Box 1, Air 1/1247/204/7/1 Vol 3, Aviation report on German South West Africa April 1915 – 1916, War Diary.

the German forces were spotted 56 kilometres northeast of Kalkveld.[74] Wallace's reconnaissance flight observed Manie Botha's forces deploying in a 'V' formation but no German forces in their defensive positions were spotted.[75] Manie Botha's 3rd Mounted Brigade took Kalkveld unopposed on 24 June.[76] The Germans allegedly retreated as a result of the threat from Botha's flanking movements.[77] Wallace proceeded to Kalkveld by road where he inspected the aerodrome there and ordered the aeroplanes up from Omaruru.[78]

On his arrival at Kalkveld on 25 June 1915, Van Der Spuy crashed his aeroplane but survived with minor injuries.[79] The aircraft was repaired once spare parts were brought up from Walvis Bay.[80] Wallace moved to Otjitasu accompanying the Union's advance where he found a suitable aerodrome and by 28 June two Henri Farmans were sent to the forward base from where further reconnaissance flights were landed on the German's final defensive positions.[81]

The extension of the lines of communication, resulting from the UDF's advance, placed a strain on the entire Union force, including the SAAC as the aeroplane spares and logistics took a considerable time to get to the front. In the course of the advance an aerodrome was found at Brakpan and was used as a launching base for reconnaissance flights towards Otavi. On 29 June Hinshelwood and Creed each carried out reconnaissance flights towards Otavi during which both pilots came under fire from German troops but despite the German attack, both pilots successfully dropped their eight bomb payload on the German position, hitting trains and troops.[82]

74   DOD Archives, WW1 WD, Box 1, Air 1/1247/204/7/1 Vol 3, Aviation report on German South West Africa April 1915 – 1916, War Diary.
75   DOD Archives, WW1 WD, Box 1, Air 1/1247/204/7/1, Report by Major Wallace on the campaign in German South West Africa, 1915, 21 July 1916.
76   DOD Archives, SD, Box 252, 17138, Reports of Force Commanders in German South West Africa, Despatch number 4 by General Botha covering the period 15 May to 18 July 1915.
77   TNA, CAB 45/112, The Campaign in German South West Africa 1914-1918, Narrative of Events, 24 June 1915.
78   DOD Archives, WW1 WD, Box 1, Air 1/1247/204/7/1, Report by Major Wallace on the campaign in German South West Africa, 1915, 21 July 1916.
79   Van Der Spuy, Chasing the Wind, 81.
80   DOD Archives, WW1 WD, Box 1, Air 1/1247/204/7/1 Vol 3, Aviation report on German South West Africa April 1915 – 1916, War Diary; DOD Archives, WW1 WD, Box 1, Air 1/1247/204/7/1 Vol 10, Aviation report on German South West Africa April 1915 – 1916, Diary Number 2 kept by Lieutenant Carey-Thomas.
81   DOD Archives, WW1 WD, Box 1, Air 1/1247/204/7/1, Report by Major Wallace on the campaign in German South West Africa, 1915, 21 July 1916.
82   TNA, CAB 45/112, The Campaign in German South West Africa 1914-1918, Narrative of Events, 1 July 1915; DOD Archives, WW1 WD, Box 1, Air 1/1247/204/7/1 Vol 3, Aviation report on German South West Africa April 1915 – 1916, War Diary; DOD Archives, WW1 WD, Box 1, Air 1/1247/204/7/1, Report by Major Wallace on the campaign in German South West Africa, 1915, 21 July 1916; DOD Archives, WW1 WD, Box 1, Air 1/1247/204/7/1 Vol 10, Aviation report on German South West Africa April 1915 – 1916, Diary Number 2 kept by Lieutenant Carey-Thomas; DOD Archives, SD, Box 252, 17138,

The German forces were on the back foot and prepared defensive positions on the Otavi – Tsumeb line. The German officers Ritter and Von Kleist were in charge of delaying the UDF. Ritter and his force were deployed at Otavifontein and Von Kleist was deployed between Otavi and Grootfontein.[83]

On 30 June a reconnaissance flight was sent out to Otavi which dropped its payload on the German position. A subsequent flight was sent out to determine the location of Myburgh's forces that had lost contact with Botha.[84] The intelligence report provided no concrete information on the location of the 2nd Mounted Brigade but unequivocally confirmed the presence of German forces in and around Otavi and Otavifontein. Following the receipt of this report Botha and the Union forces departed for Otavi and Otavifontein on the night of 30 June.[85] Manie Botha led the attack on the German position at Otavifontein[86] and following a brief engagement the Germans forces withdrew to Grootfontein.[87]

The 1st and 2nd Mounted Brigades advanced on Namutoni and Grootfontein respectively. The pincer envelopments were aimed at cutting off the retreat of the German forces.[88] The main German force withdrew to Khorab in the northeast where the final surrender took place.[89] On 1 July Creed conducted a reconnaissance and aerial bombardment of the German forces at Khorab. An aerial reconnaissance on 5 July located German forces in and around Tsumeb. The reconnaissance flight doubled up as an aerial bombing mission where the aircraft deployed its payload.[90] The

     Reports of Force Commanders in German South West Africa, Despatch number 4 by General Botha covering the period 15 May to 18 July 1915.
83   L'ange, *Urgent Imperial Service*, p. 288.
84   DOD Archives, SD, Box 252, 17138, Reports of Force Commanders in German South West Africa, Despatch number 4 by General Botha covering the period 15 May to 18 July 1915; DOD Archives, WW1 WD, Box 1, Air 1/1247/204/7/1 Vol 3, Aviation report on German South West Africa April 1915 – 1916, War Diary.
85   DOD Archives, SD, Box 252, 17138, Reports of Force Commanders in German South West Africa, Despatch number 4 by General Botha covering the period 15 May to 18 July 1915; Collyer, *The Campaign in German South West Africa, 1914-1915*, p. 137; L'ange, *Urgent Imperial Service*, p 291; Whittal, *With Botha and Smuts in Africa*, p. 147.
86   DOD Archives, SD, Box 252, 17138, Reports of Force Commanders in German South West Africa, Despatch number 4 by General Botha covering the period 15 May to 18 July 1915; Ritchie, *With Botha in the Field*, p. 59.
87   TNA, CAB 45/112, The Campaign in German South West Africa 1914-1918, Narrative of Events, 3 July 1915; L'ange, *Urgent Imperial Service*, p. 296.
88   DOD Archives, SD, Box 252, 17138, Reports of Force Commanders in German South West Africa, Despatch number 4 by General Botha covering the period 15 May to 18 July 1915.
89   Anon., *Official History*, p. 46.
90   DOD Archives, WW1 WD, Box 1, Air 1/1247/204/7/1, Report by Major Wallace on the campaign in German South West Africa, 1915, 21 July 1916; DOD Archives, WW1 WD, Box 1, Air 1/1247/204/7/1 Vol 10, Aviation report on German South West Africa April 1915 – 1916, Diary 2 kept by Lieutenant Carey-Thomas.

reconnaissance aimed to facilitate ground operations by confirming the final location of German forces.

The 2nd Mounted Brigade advanced on Tsumeb in early July after which they took the town unopposed on 6 July 1915.[91] Brits and the 1st Mounted Brigade captured Namutoni on 8 July where the German forces surrendered.[92] The UDF effectively outmanoeuvred and encircled the German forces in German South West Africa forcing their capitulation which was submitted to Botha at 02:00 on 9 July 1915.[93]

Analysis and conclusion

The use of aeroplanes allowed the UDF commanders to better understand the intelligence picture and further facilitated the deployment of the Union's forces (refer to table 9.1). The knowledge of the location of the German forces expedited the timely execution of the operational plan and the battle concept. For example there were two reconnaissance flights taken over Omaruru prior to the UDF's advance which confirmed the German withdrawal from their defensive positions and allowed the Union forces to advance with confidence and speed, and capture it on 19 June 1915. Referring to the reconnaissance function of the aircraft Botha commented to Lieutenant Kenneth van der Spuy stating that he was a good pilot but an excellent *verkyker* (pair of binoculars). Botha went on to claim that the knowledge of enemy positions enabled him to move and place his troops accordingly.[94] The combination of air reconnaissance with the high mobility of the mounted forces in German South West Africa proved to be effective in the later stages of the campaign. The air reconnaissance allowed the UDF to know where the German forces were deployed and the commando's[95] mobility allowed for surprise to be achieved.[96]

After Omaruru the next position on the UDF's advance was Kalkveld and five reconnaissance flights determined the presence of German forces there from 21 to 23 June 1915, allowing the UDF to take Kalkveld unopposed on 24 June. Following the capture of Kalkveld the Aviation Corps reconnoitred Otavi and confirmed the presence of German forces on 29 and 30 June 1915. The UDF then advanced on

---

91   TNA, CAB 45/112, The Campaign in German South West Africa 1914-1918, Narrative of Events, 8 July 1915; Anon., *Official History*, p 40. Whittal says that the South African forces were ready to attack Tsumeb on 5 July and the town subsequently surrendered: Whittal, *With Botha and Smuts in Africa*, p. 152.

92   Meintjes, *General Louis Botha*, p. 269.

93   DOD Archives, SD, Box 252, 17138, Reports of Force Commanders in German South West Africa, Despatch number 4 by General Botha covering the period 15 May to 18 July 1915; Meintjes, *General Louis Botha*, p. 262; Trew, *Botha Treks*, p. 175.

94   L'ange, *Urgent Imperial Service*, p. 267.

95   Commandos were Afrikaner irregular military units in South Africa. They were characterised as having good tactical initiative, marksmanship and equestrian skills despite being undisciplined.

96   Nasson, *Springboks on the Somme*, pp. 63–65.

Otavi during the night of 30 June arriving on 1 July 1915, after engaging elements of the German force who in turn made a fighting withdrawal. The final positions of Khorab and Tsumeb were aerially reconnoitred on 1 and 5 July respectively before the German forces were completely and effectively enveloped and forced to surrender on 9 July 1915.[97]

Aerial Reconnaissance and Bombing Operations					
Area reconnoitred	Date	Number of operational flights	Reconnaissance flights	Reconnaissance and bombing flights	Outcome in terms of ground action
Omaruru	28-May-15	1	1	0	Intelligence picture amended.
Omaruru	10-Jun-15	1	0	1	Omaruru was taken by 19 June 1915
Kalkveld	21-Jun-15	2	2	0	Intelligence picture amended.
Kalkveld	22-Jun-15	1	1	0	Intelligence picture amended.
Kalkveld	23-Jun-15	2	2	0	Intelligence picture amended.
Kalkveld	24-Jun-15	2	2	0	Determine locations for aerial bombardment.
Otavi	29-Jun-15	2	0	2	Confirmed the presence of German forces. Intelligence picture amended.
Otavi	30-Jun-15	1	0	1	Advance on Otavi on 30 June 1915.
Khorab	01-Jul-15	1	0	1	Intelligence picture amended.
Tsumeb	05-Jul-15	1	0	1	Intelligence picture amended.
Total		14	8	6	

Table 9.1: Aerial reconnaissance and bombing operations in German South West Africa [98]

97   TNA, CAB 45/112, The Campaign in German South West Africa 1914-1918, Narrative of Events, 9 July 1915.
98   DOD Archives, WW1 WD, Box 1, Air 1/1247/204/7/1 Vol 10, Aviation report on German

Aerial operations in the German South West Africa campaign comprised 14 flights in direct support of ground operations (refer to table 9.1 and graph 9.1). The flights provided the UDF command with reconnaissance which assisted in their decision making process in terms of where and when to deploy. Botha confirmed that this intelligence allowed the UDF to deploy with the minimum required number of troops.[99]

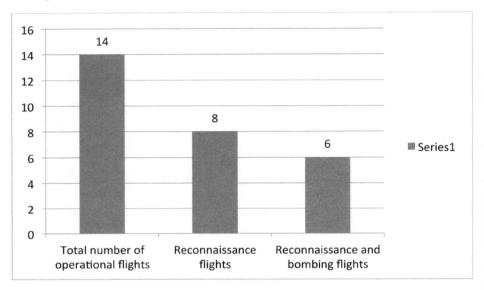

Graph 9.1: Aerial reconnaissance and bombing operations in German South West Africa[100]

Botha gives credit to his subordinate commanders in the execution of their sweeping envelopments of the German forces and describes the reason for the rapid victory as the impact of surprise on the German forces.[101] The final advance commenced on 18

South West Africa April 1915 – 1916, Diary Number 2 kept by Lieutenant Carey-Thomas; DOD Archives, WW1 WD, Box 1, Air 1/1247/204/7/1 Vol 3, Aviation report on German South West Africa April 1915 – 1916, War Diary; DOD Archives, WW1 WD, Box 1, Air 1/1247/204/7/1, Report by Major Wallace on the campaign in German South West Africa, 1915, 21 July 1916.

99   DOD Archives, SD, Box 252, 17138, Reports of Force Commanders in German South West Africa, Despatch number 4 by General Botha covering the period 15 May to 18 July 1915.

100   DOD Archives, WW1 WD, Box 1, Air 1/1247/204/7/1 Vol 10, Aviation report on German South West Africa April 1915 – 1916, Diary Number 2 kept by Lieutenant Carey-Thomas; DOD Archives, WW1 WD, Box 1, Air 1/1247/204/7/1 Vol 3, Aviation report on German South West Africa April 1915 – 1916, War Diary; DOD Archives, WW1 WD, Box 1, Air 1/1247/204/7/1, Report by Major Wallace on the campaign in German South West Africa, 1915, 21 July 1916.

101   DOD Archives, World War 1 German South West Africa (hereafter WW1 GSWA), Box 23a, Citations, German South West Africa, Northern Army, Commander of the 1st

June after which Omaruru was taken on 19 June, followed by Kalkveld on 24 June and Otavi on 1 July 1915. As these German positions were captured by the UDF, the Aviation Corps advanced in unison with the ground forces and prepared aerodromes at the forward bases which allowed for the forward projection of airpower throughout the area of operations (refer to graph 9.2). The number of aerial reconnaissance flights increased in line with the requirements of the UDF's advance.

Van Der Spuy states that according to Botha and Collyer, the use of aircraft had assisted in shortening the campaign considerably.[102] Botha was reportedly impressed by the value of aircraft in warfare and believed that further aviation research and development was of great importance.[103] Following the culmination of the German South West African campaign the SAAC went on to become 26 Squadron of the Royal Air Force and served in the German East African campaign and on the Western Front. Van Der Spuy served with distinction in both World Wars and retired with the rank of Major General.

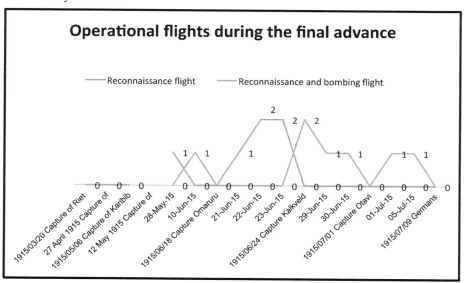

Graph 9.2: Operational flights during the final advance[104]

Mounted Brigade Special Appointments, 17 February 1918.
102 Van Der Spuy, *Chasing the Wind*, p. 82; L'ange, *Urgent Imperial Service*, p. 273.
103 Ritchie, *With Botha in the Field*, p. 56.
104 DOD Archives, WW1 WD, Box 1, Air 1/1247/204/7/1 Vol 10, Aviation report on German South West Africa April 1915 – 1916, Diary Number 2 kept by Lieutenant Carey-Thomas; DOD ArchiveWW1 WD, Box 1, Air 1/1247/204/7/1 Vol 3, Aviation report on German South West Africa April `1915–1916, War Diary; DOD Archives, WW1 WD, Box 1, Air 1/1247/204/7/1, Report by Major Wallace on the campaign in German South West Africa, 1915, 21 July 1916.

10

Analysis of the German South West African Campaign

A central theme to this book addresses the issue of whether the German South West African campaign was won by numerical superiority or whether it was the application of manoeuvre warfare theory that compelled the Germans to surrender. This final chapter addresses this point and provides an analysis of the military theory presented in Chapter 2.

Decisive points and the German centre of gravity

In order to successfully invade German South West Africa, Botha, Smuts, the ministry of defence and the Union Defence Force staff had to determine whether Windhoek, as the capital of the colony, or the headquarters of the *Schutztruppe* was the centre of gravity of the German force. The German field force was believed to be the centre of gravity as opposed to a mere geographical location such as the capital city – Windhoek. This became evident when Windhoek was taken and the German force merely retreated with as much of their equipment and stores as possible. This was similar to the experience of the Afrikaners in the Anglo-Boer War, where the Boers evacuated their capital cities, Bloemfontein and Pretoria in the face of Lord Roberts' advance. In the case of the German South West African campaign, the centre of gravity was the *Schutztruppe* headquarters. In military theory headquarters is often regarded as a centre of gravity.[1] The *Schutztruppe* headquarters moved from Windhoek to Khorab as the South African forces advanced systematically throughout the colony.

In order to reach the centre of gravity the Union applied its military logistical system, making use of external lines of communication to advance on the German headquarters. The logistical question which involved the movement and supply of the fighting forces over vast distances without infrastructure was a key consideration in

---

1   South African Army College, *Operational Concepts: Staff Officer's Operational Manual, Part VII* (Pretoria: 1 Military Printing Regiment, 1996), p. 7/11-8.

the campaign. The logistical supply of the forward forces required a balance between advance and operational pause.

Decisive points are defined as positions in time and space which can threaten the centre of gravity; where lines of operations join decisive points and centres of gravity.[2] The Union Defence Force advanced on Riet, Karibib, Windhoek and Tsumeb, which were decisive points on the line of operations to the German centre of gravity which was the headquarters of the *Schutztruppe*.

In terms of the line of operations in the north of German South West Africa, Karibib was a decisive point and an intermediate objective on route to capture Windhoek.[3] The advance on Karibib involved the 1st, 2nd, 3rd and 5th Mounted Brigades who advanced on Otjimbingwe and Okahandja while the 4th Infantry Brigade advanced at a slower pace on Kubas and Karibib.[4] The Infantry Brigade formed the ordinary force and the extraordinary force was made up of the Mounted Brigades.

The capture of the central railway junction at Windhoek and Karibib neutralised the German use of the railway and with that, their ability to concentrate forces on the Union Defence Force within the broader German South West Africa.[5] Furthermore, the Union's capture of Karibib meant that the Germans no longer had many options in terms of gaining the initiative.[6]

Following the capture of Karibib, the occupation of Windhoek was a mere formality. Collyer describes Windhoek as a decisive point because its capture resulted in the withdrawal of the German forces to the north.[7] Windhoek was not the German centre of gravity but was rather a limited objective of the advance. Collyer was of the opinion that the value of Windhoek in terms of its impact on the Germans was purely sentimental.[8] The northern lines of operations led the Union Defence Force to take Riet, Karibib, and Windhoek as decisive points en route to the *Schutztruppe* headquarters.

The logistical supply of the Union Defence Force was the greatest limiting factor for the enveloping and outmanoeuvring of the final German position. In order to promote mobility and prevent logistical overburden, Botha only kept the mobile forces and infantry units required to execute the final envelopment.

2   B.T. Solberg, 'Maneuver Warfare: Consequences for Tactics and Organisation of the Norwegian Infantry' (MMAS thesis, United States Army Command and Staff College, Kansas, 2000), p. 27.

3   G. L'ange, *Urgent Imperial Service* (Rivonia: Ashanti, 1991), p. 252.

4   Anon., *Union of South Africa and the Great War, 1914-1918, Official History* (Pretoria: Government Printer, 1924), p. 32.

5   J.J. Collyer, *The Campaign in German South West Africa, 1914–1915* (Government Printer, Pretoria, 1937), p. 50.

6   L'ange, *Urgent Imperial Service*, p. 252.

7   Collyer, *The Campaign in German South West Africa, 1914–1915*, p. 51; J. Meintjes, *General Louis Botha* (London: Cassell & Co., 1970), p. 257.

8   Collyer, *The Campaign in German South West Africa, 1914–1915*, p. 50.

Operational pauses versus culmination

Military theory holds that in order to secure victory a given force should maintain the initiative and exploit the lines of communication of the opposing force. In doing so the exploiting force, the attacker, risks reaching culmination.[9] Respectively, there is a state of culmination for the attacker and the defender and thus the supply of the advancing and retreating force is key to tactical and strategic success.

For the attacker, culmination is reached when the combat power used to engage and pursue the enemy runs out. The culmination point for the defender is reached when the defender can no longer defend and counterattack successfully.[10] In military terms the state of culmination should be avoided at all costs. The rapid advances of the South African forces required various operational pauses in order to prevent culmination.

Clausewitz posits that the loss of morale is one of the critical factors in losing the tactical initiative and reaching the culminating point where the spirit of the mass is broken.[11] This point was reached by the German force in that their fighting spirit was broken. In contrast the South African forces avoided culmination by waiting for supplies and preparing for their final advance on the German forces. It should be noted that during an operational pause a given military force is naturally on the defensive and Tzu advises that while a defensive stance allows for security against defeat, victory can only be achieved on the offensive.[12]

The campaign in German South West Africa was characterised by swift advances followed by operational pauses which were used to consolidate the territory gained. The Northern Army paused from 20 March until the end of April 1915 so as to convey the necessary supplies to the front. The Union Defence Force was in the field for 133 days of which only 24 days were spent on the move.[13] The 24 days when the forces were executing operational movements were offset by 109 days of operational pause.

In this regard the People of Colour provided a critical task in the provision of supply and combat support. Their efforts enabled and facilitated manoeuvre warfare. As we discover, write and emphasise new histories, it must be acknowledged that the work done by Black, Coloured and Indian South Africans in the German South West African theatre and at home had a strategic impact on the campaign. During the final advance which led to the surrender of the German forces, there were 3,032 People of Colour in the field.

---

9   Solberg, 'Maneuver Warfare', p. 31.
10 South African Army College, *Operational Concepts*, p. 7/12-2.
11 C. von Clausewitz, tr., J.J. Graham, *On War*, http://www.gutenberg.org/files/1946/1946-h/1946-h.htm, ebook, Accessed 23 January 2012, p. 109.
12 S. Tzu, tr. Sadler, A.L., *The Art of War* (Tokyo: Tuttle, 2009), p. 7.
13 J.J. Collyer, *The Campaign in German South West Africa, 1914–1915* (Pretoria: Government Printer, 1937), p. 158.

Ordinary and extraordinary forces

Leonhard argues that 'operational planners must determine how to use the available combat power to achieve the goals of a campaign'.[14] In German South West Africa Botha did this by making efficient use of the South African commandos and mounted infantry with their high mobility while using the regular infantry to take and hold ground.

The extraordinary and ordinary forces as mentioned by Tzu allude respectively to a highly mobile force used to execute envelopments; and an ordinary force used to take and hold ground.[15] The Union forces had both the ordinary and extraordinary components as mentioned by Tzu but these components had their own South African uniqueness. The extraordinary forces, the commandos and mounted infantry, and ordinary force, the infantry which holds ground and forms the hinge which supports the mobile forces which in turn creates leverage.[16] The infantry provided the hinge on which the commandos swung.[17]

Collyer was of the opinion that the campaign was strategic because it comprised wide enveloping movements that were designed to defeat the German force.[18] Botha understood the importance of mobility and surprise as the most important consideration on the tactical and strategic level.[19] His emphasis on mobility was vividly demonstrated by the Union force strength return in December 1914, which included some 33,308 mounted soldiers which allowed the force to cover vast distances.[20] Collyer held the view that the campaign was strategic because it comprised wide enveloping movements that were designed to defeat the German force.[21] In formal correspondence Botha attributed the German surrender to the surprise which was achieved by the rapid final envelopments.[22] This corresponds with Tzu's view that rapidity is the quintessence of war; it should be applied to take advantage of the enemy's lack of preparation and achieved by taking unexpected routes.[23]

14   R. Leonhard, *The Art of Maneuver* (New York: Ballantine, 1994), p. 10.
15   Solberg, 'Maneuver Warfare', p. 32.
16   R.E. Simpkin, *Race to the Swift* (London: Brassey's Defence Publishers,1986), p. 96.
17   G. L'ange, *Urgent Imperial Service* (Rivonia: Ashanti, 1991), p. 142.
18   Ibid., p.156.
19   Collyer, *The Campaign in German South West Africa, 1914–1915*, p. 173.
20   DOD Archives, AG 1914–1921, Box 150, Summarised states of forces and garrisons, Mounted Brigade field state, 22 December 1914.
21   L'ange, *Urgent Imperial Service*, p. 156.
22   DOD Archives, WW1 GSWA, Box 23a, Citations German South West Africa, Northern Army, Commander of the 1st Mounted Brigade Special Appointments, 17 February 1918; DOD Archives, SD, Box 252, 17138, Reports of Force Commanders in German South West Africa, Despatch number 4 by General Botha covering the period 15 May to 18 July 1915.
23   Tzu, tr. Sadler, *The Art of War*, p. 27.

For the most part, the commandos formed the extraordinary component of the Union Defence Force. In his book on the campaign, Collyer states that without an understanding of the special characteristics of the commandos, it is difficult to understand the significance of their contribution to the German South West African campaign.[24] The commandos were independent in thought and resistant to any formal means of control. The members of commandos were astute and relied on their tactical sense and their rifles as a means of protection.[25] Together, the Boer, his horse and his rifle had become part of South African military history and this was passed down from father to son as part of the Afrikaner tradition. The result was a combatant who could deliver accurate and economical fire and could cross almost any kind of terrain.[26]

The horses used by the commandos were trained to gallop while the riders fired from the saddle and to stand while their riders dismounted to fire.[27] The commandos had their own doctrine which had evolved from their history and experience of war. Broadly, speaking doctrine combines ideology, national culture, technology and the grouping's formative experiences.[28]

The commandos traditionally relied on the horse and rifle in defence and for hunting and the burghers were accustomed to using cover and delivering accurate fire.[29] They acted by instinct more than by command. Their tactics were normally discussed the night before an advance or attack in a democratic fashion once the scouting information was received.[30]

Commandos would assume a formation according to the terrain and the tactical situation. If they were fired upon they would take cover as if they had been ordered to do so. There were no orders needed for a night march because commando members instinctively saddled up and set off following the lead of others. Furthermore the hardy lifestyle that the commandos could endure was an asset that ensured their

24 Collyer, *The Campaign in German South West Africa, 1914–1915*, 9; For the latest study relating to Union Defence Force doctrine see, D Katz 'A clash of military doctrine: Brigadier-General Wilfrid Malleson and the South Africans at Salaita Hill, February 1916', *Historia*. 62/1.2017.

25 Collyer, *The Campaign in German South West Africa, 1914–1915*, p. 11.

26 Anon., *Official History*, 38; DOD Archives, SD, Box 252, 17138, Historical Record of the Campaign in German South West Africa, 4 November 1919; L'ange, *Urgent Imperial Service*, p. 193.

27 Collyer, *The Campaign in German South West Africa, 1914–1915*, p. 12.

28 J. Gooch, 'The Use of History in the Development of Contemporary Doctrine', Conference paper at a conference sponsored by the director of development and doctrine at Larkhill, 1996, p. 6.

29 DOD Archives, SD, Box 252, 17138, Historical Record of the Campaign in German South West Africa, 4 November 1919; L'ange, *Urgent Imperial Service*, p. 193.

30 Anon., *Official History*, p. 38; DOD Archives, SD, Box 252, 17138, Historical Record of the Campaign in German South West Africa, 4 November 1919.

mobility.[31] In the words of Sun Tzu, 'manoeuvring with a flying column is faster than with the entire army, however the flying column must sacrifice baggage and stores'.[32]

The commandos deployed with a minimum of supplies. They used the same tactics that they used against the British in the Anglo-Boer War,[33] although with superior numbers in the German South West African campaign.[34] During the irregular phase of the Anglo-Boer War the commandos had no communication lines; they simply moved over extended distances without any formal re-supply arrangements.[35] The irregular style of the commandos sometimes clashed with the more conventional British military system of the Union Defence Force. The methods employed by the commandos led to some amount of confusion and frustration during the German South West African campaign. At times Collyer was frustrated by the commando scouts and their commandants who were reluctant to give feedback and information. The members of commandos did not always recognise that they were part of a combined fighting force.[36]

Bezuidenhout's actions at Riet are a case in point. Leading the envelopment at Riet he was ordered to move through a gap in the mountain range. However, the gap shown on the map was a topographical error – it did not exist and Bezuidenhout was forced to turn back. On his return he failed to inform Botha or Collyer that he was unable to envelop the German position. This example indicates how the formal channels of reporting and command were difficult to align with the unorthodox approach of the commandos.[37]

The Germans were amazed by the commando's methods of advance and attack. They 'marched on the cannon thunder' – a reference to the fact that when the advance scouts drew fire from the German rear-guard actions, the firing would attract other commando scouts who would promptly join the action.[38] Furthermore, the commandos expected their commanders to lead from the front which boosted morale.[39]

Line of least expectation and resistance

The German South West African campaign illustrated some of the essential psychological aspects necessary to execute manoeuvre warfare. The movement of the

31   DOD Archives, SD, Box 252, 17138, Historical Record of the Campaign in German South West Africa, 4 November 1919; L'ange, *Urgent Imperial Service*, p. 194.
32   Tzu, tr. Sadler, *The Art of War*, p. 14.
33   Collyer, *The Campaign in German South West Africa, 1914–1915*, p. 169.
34   L'ange, *Urgent Imperial Service*, p. 5.
35   Collyer, *The Campaign in German South West Africa, 1914–1915*, p. 18; DOD Archives, SD, Box 252, 17138, Historical Record of the Campaign in German South West Africa, 4 November 1919.
36   L'ange, *Urgent Imperial Service*, p. 196.
37   Ibid., p. 191.
38   H.F. Trew, *Botha Treks* (London: Blackie & Son, 1936), p. 126.
39   L'ange, *Urgent Imperial Service*, p. 201.

South African forces communicated enough of a threat to the German force to sap their morale and sap their will to fight.

Two important maxims of military strategy are that an advance or attack should be along the line of least resistance; and the line of least expectation. These refer to the physical and psychological aspects of warfare. The line of least resistance typically refers to geographical and tactical considerations, while the line of least expectation is linked to surprise.

In terms of the line of least resistance, German South West Africa had natural obstacles such as the desert (and by implication the lack of water supplies) which were barriers to the movement of the Union's forces. Rayner and O'Shaughnessy explain that 'the Germans said that the 80 mile (128 kilometre) stretch of Namib Desert separating Lüderitzbucht from the inland and its comparatively fertile plateau which begins at Aus ... plus their own valuable assistance, would bring about our annihilation'.[40]

The *Official History* states that the Germans believed their position to have been secure because of the natural advantages of the terrain and the lack of water available to the advancing South African force.[41] However, Jomini cautions that remoteness will not necessarily protect a country from invasion.[42] This was the case in the German South West African campaign, where the Germans believed that the terrain to be impassable from all sides.[43] Given that the Germans perceived the terrain as impassable, the rapid advance of the Union forces might well have surprised the enemy.

On the line of least expectation, moral surprise refers to a situation where the enemy is unaware of the advance and pending attack. Material surprise differs in that the enemy is aware of the advance but are unable to effectively respond.[44] In both cases, the element of surprise could result in the dislocation of the mind of the commander. Psychological dislocation occurs as a result of physical dislocation due to supply lines being cut or threatened, or when a force is compelled to change front.[45]

The final envelopments in the German South West African campaign surprised and overwhelmed the German force. German staff officers underestimated the mobility of the Union Defence Force.[46] As Du Picq puts it, the 'surprised adversary does not defend himself, [but instead] he tries to flee'.[47] An army that is surprised cannot make

40   W.W. O'Shaughnessy and W.S. Rayner, *How Botha and Smuts Conquered German South West* (London: Simpkin, 1916), p. 55.
41   Anon., *Official History*, p. 3.
42   A. du Picq, trs., J.N. Greenly and R.C. Cotton, *Battle Studies*, http://www.gutenberg.org/files-h.htm, ebook (Accessed 23 Janaury 2012), p. 100.
43   L'ange, *Urgent Imperial Service*, p. 5.
44   Simpkin, *Race to the Swift*, p. 182.
45   B.H. Liddell Hart, *Strategy of the Indirect Approach* (London: Faber & Faber, 1941), p. 327.
46   Collyer, *The Campaign in German South West Africa, 1914–1915*, p. 18.
47   Du Picq, trs. Greenly and Cotton, *Battle Studies*, p. 34.

effective use of its resources.[48] The German force surrendered with its entire fighting force virtually intact.

Surprise was dependent on the mobility of the South African forces,[49] which was in turn dependent on its logistical support. The provision of transport and supplies was essential to ensure the mobility of the commandos, which in turn ensured surprise. On this point, it is once again important to recognise the work done by Black, Coloured and Indian South Africans, who provided the required labour to move the Union's war machine.

In terms of the line of least resistance and expectation, Liddell Hart maintains that a dispersed advance can have a single objective, a number of successive objectives or alternatively, it could have simultaneous objectives.[50] The dispersed advance in German South West Africa took on successive objectives, applying pressure on the German force from the north, south and the southeast of the colony. The advances and envelopments from the divergent axes attacked the physical and psychological dimensions of the German force. The envelopments of the Union Defence Force were applied on the tactical and operational levels of war in order to achieve strategic objectives.

The many forced marches and extensive sweeping envelopments forced the Germans to retreat because their logistical and communication lines were constantly threatened. As explained by Jomini, such manoeuvre and outflanking movements can be used to dislodge the enemy or turn its position.[51] An attack on the opposing force's lines of communication has a huge psychological impact in that it creates a feeling of no control.[52]

Decentralised forces

Fuller claims that a manoeuvre force requires a general who has exceptional initiative and a minimal command staff.[53] The German South West African campaign mirrored this stipulation in the methods used by Botha and Smuts; they insisted on doing their own reconnaissance and applying the principles of decentralised command. Botha and Smuts's experience in war was based on their command in the Anglo-Boer War. Having studied the activities of the British Army in the South African War Botha understood the strengths and weaknesses of conventional and guerrilla operations and also the pros and cons of the English and Afrikaans elements of his force.

48   Von Clausewitz, tr. Graham, *On War*, p. 65.
49   Collyer, *The Campaign in German South West Africa, 1914–1915*, p. 51.
50   Liddell Hart, *Strategy of the Indirect Approach*, p. 201.
51   A.H. Jomini, tr., G.H. Mendell and W.P. Craighill, *The Art of War* (Rockville: Art Manor, 2007), p. 148.
52   Solberg, 'Maneuver Warfare', p. 29.
53   Solberg, 'Maneuver Warfare', p. 58.

Plate 10.1: Botha and his staff in German South West Africa

A decentralised command system allows subordinate commanders control over the means of achieving the required objectives within the framework of the commander's intent. Only a decentralised military force allows for a fast OODA cycle.[54] This is exemplified by Botha's deployment of his forces with the knowledge that he would not have communications with them.[55] The *Official History* specifically links decentralisation to the commando system and states that, 'manoeuvre control would have been impossible if it was not for the commando influence'.[56]

Some theorists maintain that the command decision has to take place at the lowest tactical level for manoeuvre theory to be effective.[57] The commander's intent forms the

---

54   W.S. Lind, *Manoeuvre Warfare Handbook* (London: Westview Press, 1985), p. 6.
55   Anon., *Official History*, p. 30.
56   Anon., *Official History*, 38; DOD Archives, SD, Box 252, 17138, Historical Record of the Campaign in German South West Africa, 4 November 1919.
57   A. Esterhuyse, 'The Theories of Attrition versus Manoeuvre and the Levels of War', *Strategic Review for Southern Africa*, 23, 2 (2001), p. 93.

decision making framework for subordinate commanders whether on the operational or tactical level.[58] Botha trusted the leadership and initiative of Myburgh and Brits to execute the final envelopments which led to the surrender of the German forces.[59] The decentralised approach affords subordinate commanders the opportunity to use their initiative but the overall commander must allow room for mistakes.[60]

Whittal is of the opinion that 'the chances that were taken by Botha's forces were harrowing for any officer not trained in the guerrilla school of war. For example Manie Botha and Myburgh marched over 160 kilometres through waterless country to cut the German railway'.[61] This is an example of decentralised command and what the *Official History* describes as 'manoeuvre control'. In order to practice decentralised command, there must be a sense of trust and loyalty between the commanders and the rest of the force. Manoeuvre forces achieve maximum efficiency when they are decentralised and they should employ a 'command by influence' system where the commanders are highly trusted and respected and also have a great hold over their subordinates.[62] Botha certainly fulfilled the requirement of 'command by influence', and was described as, 'a charismatic leader with a directness and a personal magnetism that inspires men'.[63]

Furthermore the command by influence system filtered down to the lower levels of command. The commando scouts were often named after their leader, for example Bezuidenhout's Scouts,[64] and the recruitment of commandants was often based on their strength of personality and influence.[65] The selection of suitable subordinate commanders is essential when the overall commander applies decentralised command. The influence of personality, trust and loyalty is deeper and more complex than command based on rank or appointment. As such all of the South African senior officers were veterans of the Anglo-Boer War and were personally selected by Botha.[66]

The final envelopment of the German positions involved both ordinary and extraordinary forces. The extraordinary force comprised the Mounted Brigades under the command of Brits and Myburgh; the ordinary force was made up of the 6th and 1st Infantry Brigades under Lukin and Beves respectively.

58   South African Army College, *Operational Concepts*, p. 7/1-2.
59   DOD Archives, SD, Box 252, 17138, Reports of Force Commanders in German South West Africa, Despatch number 4 by General Botha covering the period 15 May to 18 July 1915.
60   Lind, *Manoeuvre Warfare Handbook*, p. 14.
61   W. Whittal, *With Botha and Smuts in Africa* (Cassel, London, 1917), p. 66.
62   Solberg, 'Maneuver Warfare', pp. 50–52.
63   Whittal, *With Botha and Smuts in Africa*, p. 25.
64   Collyer, *The Campaign in German South West Africa, 1914–1915*, p. 72.
65   Collyer, *The Campaign in German South West Africa, 1914–1915*, p. 57; DOD Archives, AG 1914–1921, Box 8, G10/307/9199 Rebellion, Letter from Defence Headquarters to Military Districts, 3 November 1914.
66   L'ange, *Urgent Imperial Service*, p. 242.

The final surrender was a close cut decision when analysed with the advantage of hindsight. The mass of the Union's forces were at Otavifontein with limited rations. The lines of communication were overextended and the South Africans were counting on forcing the Germans to surrender. The decision not to give battle but rather to surrender is largely based on the leadership and the state of mind of the commander.

The German force was still physically able to give battle; however the manoeuvres of the Union Defence Force had dislocated Franke and his subordinate commanders and psychologically weakened the German force. The Germans thus chose not to give battle as a result of their low morale and weakened psychological state. Franke's shaking hands were an indication of his weakened psychological state, perhaps worsened by substance abuse, which Botha witnesses at their meeting.

A quick decision in war, operations and or battle indicates a slow decision making process by the defeated army.[67] The decisive outcome was thus evidence of a slow decision making cycle by the German forces. They were dislocated on the operational level and their physical and psychological spheres were compromised by being surrounded and cut off. A feeling of helplessness ensues when a force is outmanoeuvred; when the psychological dimension is broken and the force loses its will to fight.[68] The Germans surrendered in their final position without firing a single shot. The German force was pre-empted on the tactical level which was a likely result of dislocation on the operational level.

Botha commented to Buxton that the final result might well have been more difficult to achieve had the Germans put up more of a fight in their final position. Their defensive position was very strong and it had artillery and machine gun support.[69] Because they did not have the will to engage in a defensive battle, the Germans opted for a quick decision and immediate German surrender.

Numerical superiority versus manoeuvre warfare

South Africa's divergent lines of advance into German South West Africa using external lines of operations required a reasonably large force on the four divergent axes, with a considerable logistical demand. The divergent lines of advance had a paralysing effect on the German force. So much so that it is probably safe to presume that if the Union Defence Force had deployed a smaller force on each axis of advance it would still have gained a similar result.

The South African force that enveloped the German force's final position comprised less than 5,000 soldiers. These soldiers were divided into three force groupings. The German force was numerically equal to the Union force that participated in the final envelopments. Furthermore the German force held the central position and could

---

67   Von Clausewitz, tr. Graham, *On War*, p. 113.
68   South African Army College, *Operational Concepts*, pp. 7/5-4, 7/5-5.
69   S.C. Buxton, *General Botha* (London: Hazel, Watson & Viney, 1924), p. 117.

have concentrated superior forces on any of the separate advancing Union forces. The Union's force deployments was proportional to the geographic space occupied. Across a larger space the Union required more troops and in a more limited area, they required less troops. The central idea around the deployment of the Union's forces was to deploy them as required to bring the Germans to a decision.

The numerical superiority of the Union Defence Force facilitated the taking and holding of ground. The lines of communication were secured by the infantry. The large number of commandos allowed the Union forces to pursue different lines of advance while ensuring mobility and rapidity. Although the importance of numbers cannot be underestimated, the decisive factor in the operational and strategic success points towards manoeuvre theory and Botha's innate understanding of its attributes. In support of this analysis, Donn Starry, former United States general and contributor to the Air Land Battle doctrine,[70] states that within reasonable limits it does not matter if the enemy is outnumbered.[71] Leonhard expands on the issue of numerical superiority by stating, 'the commander who pre-empts the enemy may be numerically stronger or weaker than his foe and his weapons may be better or worse ... if the commander's decisive approach to the conflict is overwhelmingly superior'.[72]

This decisive approach involves the intention and the mind-set of the commander and the way the forces are used. In the case of the campaign pre-emption was applied which is the threat of force communicated by the use of mobile forces so as to induce the enemy to surrender or prevent the enemy's intended action.[73] The analysis of the final envelopments in Chapter 8 determined that the reason for the defeat of the German forces was that they did not put up defensive battles at the required time and place. Instead of taking a stand, the German forces chose to retreat on various occasions – which was indicative of low morale and poor combat cohesion.

The numerical superiority of the Union Defence Force did not result in the final surrender of the German forces. Protracted campaigns that are usually won by numerical superiority and greater materiel. In the event that the German forces had repulsed the Union Defence Force by means of a stout and spirited defensive battle at Khorab, then over time one could reasonably assume that the numerical superiority of the Union Defence Force would eventually have been crucial to achieve victory. The essential difference between these two scenarios is the time taken to achieve the military victory.

Clausewitz explains that 'if a detachment is sent away to cut off the retreat of a fleeing enemy, and the enemy surrenders in consequence without further resistance, it is through the combat which is offered to him by this detachment sent after him

70 AirLand Battle doctrine is a United States war fighting doctrine that is comprised of rapid ground operations integrated with Air support.
71 Simpkin, *Race to the Swift*, p. x.
72 Leonhard, *The Art of Maneuver*, p. 63.
73 Simpkin, *Race to the Swift*, p. 141.

that he is brought to his decision'.[74] Applying this to the German South West African campaign, the final envelopments of the German positions resulted in the defeat of the German forces. Tzu maintains that 'the victorious strategist seeks battle after the victory[75] has been won'.[76] Thus, after the final German position was surrounded, the Union forces could have won by the surrender of the Germans, which ensured a rapid result or by siege in which case there would have been a delay in concluding operations. Should the Germans have offered battle, the campaign would no doubt have been prolonged. The Union logistics would have had to be brought up systematically and the increased numerical superiority of the Union forces would have been brought to bear.

The final positioning of forces made the situation untenable for the Germans and their surrender was inevitable. Manoeuvre theory holds that mobility is more important that firepower, but that certain elements of the opposing force will have to be destroyed; and following that the eventual positioning of forces will induce defeat with the threat of annihilation.[77] This positioning of forces fulfils the psychological and physical requirements of dislocation of the enemy. Sun Tzu states that when you surround a foe – an outlet should be left free.[78] This does not have to be physical but can be the option of surrender.

74   Von Clausewitz, tr. Graham, *On War*, p. 79.
75   Tzu refers to victory in the operational or strategic sense, in that by positioning one's forces in such a way that offering battle would result in the forgone conclusion of victory.
76   Tzu, tr. Sadler, *The Art of War*, p. 8.
77   Solberg, 'Maneuver Warfare', p. 132.
78   Tzu, tr. Sadler, *The Art of War*, p. 16.

Epilogue

Louis Botha was the prime minister of the Union of South Africa as well as the commander-in-chief of the Union's expeditionary force in German South West Africa. Botha met all the classical requirements of a great commander, including decisiveness, ingenuity, power of personality and charisma, which enabled him to motivate his troops. In terms of the operational strategy applied in the German South West African campaign, he displayed an understanding of the complexities of the campaign which included logistical considerations and the limitations and capabilities of the commandos, the mounted infantry and the regular infantry.

Trew is of the opinion that Botha's campaign was that of a genius in the art of war. He goes on to question whether future historians will rate him as one of the great commanders of the past.[1] Collyer argues that there are not many strategists who had Botha's tactical ability and strategic insight.[2] Reflecting on Botha's military background, Whittall claims that 'his elastic military training allowed for the accomplishment of the campaign'.[3]

Botha, although a man of his time, had a distinct vision in terms of military strategy. Speed and surprise were key aspects to the campaign and were inextricably intertwined with the German defeat. His war experience and insight into military operations made him the ideal commander for the campaign in German South West Africa considering the forces he had at his disposal. Botha employed a strategy in German South West Africa that was congruent with those executed by the great captains of war throughout history. The decisive campaign led by Botha was the first successful campaign of the First World War to be concluded by a dominion of the British Empire. The campaign induced the surrender of the German forces without extensive loss of life or materiel.

Despite Botha's abilities and that of the other commanders and staff, there were many other factors that contributed to the defeat of the Germans, such as their inability to put up a strong defence at critical times due to the collapse of their morale. The

---

1   H.F. Trew, *Botha Treks* (London: Blackie & Son, 1936) p. vi.
2   J.J. Collyer, *The Campaign in German South West Africa, 1914–1915* (Pretoria: Government Printer, 1937), p. 168.
3   W. Whittal, *With Botha and Smuts in Africa* (Cassel, London, 1917), p. 4.

German force's reluctance to engage in battle is perhaps also related to organisational aspects such as their lack of defensive campaign experience when faced by a rapidly advancing and determined enemy.

Political consequences

The primary focus of this book was the military theoretical and strategic aspects as it applied to the German South West African campaign. This section gives a brief overview of the political consequences of the campaign. The military efforts which resulted in the campaign victory did not necessarily translate into direct political victory for Botha and Smuts's South African Party. The second Union elections, resulted in a significant loss in support for Botha and the South African Party.

Plate E.1: A victorious Botha addressing a crowd in Cape Town.[4]

The rise of Afrikaner nationalism was a prominent factor which influenced the political landscape. Botha was initially seen as the Afrikaner republican hope in the

4   Department of Defence Archives.

post Anglo-Boer War era, however his policies of conciliation and united White South Africanism eventually led to the loss of substantial Afrikaner votes. The First World War was the trigger for the clash between, cultures, traditions and political agendas.

The pro-British press pressured the Botha government to mobilise an expeditionary force for German East Africa and the Western Front. The payment of the contingent became a bone of contention between opposing political parties. In response and following the success in German South West Africa, Britain offered to finance the deployment of the expeditionary contingent, easing local tensions. Botha balanced local party politics with the requirements of Empire, and halted active campaign recruiting between his return from the campaign in July 1915 and the elections in October 1915.[5] Despite Botha's attempts at balancing various interests the expeditionary force was sent out prior to the elections. This was a mistake and resulted in the loss of much needed votes.[6]

Botha lost the support of approximately 78,000 Afrikaner votes but gained that of approximately 50,000 Unionists in 1914.[7] The 1915 Union elections were heavily contested and represented a significant split in support for Botha and Hertzog. The Union's entry into the Great War was supported by Labour and the Unionists whose members were largely English; and it was only through the help of the Unionists that Botha managed to retain the premiership in 1915. Despite Botha's loss in popularity, one saving grace was that the economy of South Africa diversified and increased by 70 percent in its manufacturing sector - the initial difficulties experienced by the lack of export of raw materials boomeranged into a thriving local trade; which was built on the foundation of two thirds supply of all British gold requirements.[8] The economic boom was facilitated by the geographic distance from the main theatres of the conflict.

The Union's political difficulties were further offset by the temporary annexation of the German colony. This was to last until the end of the First World War, and allowed for the settlement of poor and struggling South African farmers within more fertile parts of German South West Africa.[9] Following the War, German South Africa was placed under South African protection as a Class C mandated territory.[10] Where South Africa can hardly be regarded as the epitome of liberal colonisers, the Union government was certainly less oppressive than the Germans, who attempted

5   A. Samson, Chapter in, T. Paddock, (ed.), *World War I and Propaganda* (Boston: Brill, 2014), p. 128.
6   I. Van Der Waag, *A Military History of Modern South Africa* (Johannesburg: Jonathan Ball Publishers, 2015), p. 322.
7   A. Samson, *Britain, South Africa and the East African Campaign, 1914-1918: The Union Comes of Age* (London: I.B. Tauris, 2006), p. 91.
8   B. Nasson, *World War 1 and the People of South Africa* (Cape Town: Tafelberg, 2014), pp. 163-165.
9   B. Nasson, *Springboks on the Somme* (Johannesburg: Penguin, 2007), p. 82.
10 J. Dugard, *The South West Africa/Namibia Dispute: Documents and Scholarly Writings on the Controversy Between South Africa and the United Nations* (Los Angeles: University of California Press, 1973), p. 79.

to exterminate local populations by genocide. The South African occupation led to investigations and commissions into previous German abuses and further organised humanitarian actions to assist the starving indigenous populations. South Africa's occupation was not all peaceful and also used force in the face of rebellion in German South West Africa.[11]

The German South West African campaign was a springboard for further military operations in Africa, Palestine and the Western Front. By the end of the War, South Africa had dedicated the service of approximately 146,000 White men, 400 White female nurses and 60,000 Black and Coloured[12] auxiliaries and combat servicemen.[13] The loyal support of the SANNC to the Union government, resulted in increased expectations in the post Great War environment. Their deputations and appeals for rights and concessions mostly fell on deaf ears, however it was the start of the growth of a new African consciousness.[14]

Over 3000 People of Colour took part in the final operations in German South West Africa. Many Black, Coloured and Indian soldiers remain unacknowledged for their service. As a final point in this book, I would like to mention the names of some Black and Coloured soliders:

> Cross, July, Trusnell, Jacobus Christian, Alex Soldana and Calcolm died at the Battle of Sandfontein. The following Black and Coloured soldiers were wounded at the Battle of Sandfontein: T.J. Egerton, J.P.V. Ogilvie, Hendrick, Nochonga, Simon Letchaba, Andries Goosen, Joseph Alexander, Andrew Brown, Ruben Dube, Thomas, Du Toit, Linde Gumzana, John, Maartens, John Noongoza, Harry Marashe, Joel Mbalo, Harry Mitchel, Freddy Manifeldt, Philip Ncongola, William Norris, John stableveldt, Umfula Zenzeli, Paul.

At the Battle of Gibeon Coloured soldiers A Jacobs and Percy Weigh were wounded. We salute you. These names are by no means an exhaustive list but they are an indication of the service of People of Colour. Further research is required on this theme. Their sacrifice is no longer invisible.

---

11 Nasson, *Springboks on the Somme*, pp. 84, 85.
12 In South Africa, coloured refers to a mixed race population group.
13 Nasson, *World War 1*, p. 184.
14 A. Grundlingh, *War and Society:Participation and Remembrance, South African Black and Coloured Troops in the First World War, 1914-1918* (Stellenbosch, Sun Press, 2014), pp. 106-112,

Bibliography

Archival Sources

South African Department of Defence Archives
South African National Archives
University of Cape Town Libraries, Archives and Manuscripts
United Kingdom National Archives

Books

Angstrom, J., and Widen, J.J., *Contemporary Military Theory: The Dynamics of War* (New York: Routledge, 2015).
Anon., *The Times History of the War* (London: The Times, 1915).
Anon., *Union of South Africa and the Great War, 1914–1918: Official History* (Pretoria: Government Printer, 1924).
Armstrong, H.C., *Grey Steel, J.C. Smuts: A study in Arrogance* (London: Arthur Barker, 1937).
Baer, E.R., *The Genocidal Gaze: From German Southwest Africa to the Third Reich* (Detroit: Wayne State Press, 2017).
Baylis, J., *et al.*, *Contemporary Strategy* (London: Croom Helm, 1987).
Blue Book, Cd 9146, *Report on the Natives of South West Africa and their Treatment by the Germans*, (London: Government Printer, 1918)
Bottomley, E.J., *Poor White* (Cape Town: Tafelberg, 2012).
Bouch, R.J., *Infantry in South Africa* (Pretoria: Documentation Service SADF, 1977).
British Army, *Operations, British Army Doctrine* (Andover: Army Publications, 2010).
Burgan, M., *Great Empires of the Past: Empire of the Mongols* (New York: Facts on File, 2005).
Buxton, S.C., *General Botha* (London: Hazel, Watson & Viney, 1924).
Carnegie Commission, *The Poor White Problem in South Africa* (Stellenbosch: Pro Ecclesia, 1932).
Campbell, B., *War and Society in Imperial Rome, 31 BC-AD 284* (New York: Routledge, 2002).
Changuion, L., and Steenkamp, B., *Disputed Land, The Historical Development of the South African Land Issue, 1652-2011* (Pretoria: Protea, 2012).
Cohen, E.A., and J. Gooch, J., *Military Misfortunes: The Anatomy of Failure in War* (New York: The Free Press, 1990).
Collyer, J.J., *The Campaign in German South West Africa, 1914–1915* (Pretoria: Government Printer, 1937).
Couzens, T., *The Great Silence* (Johannesburg: Tzuday Times, 2014).
Cruise, A., *Louis Botha's War: The Campaign in German South West Africa 1914-1915* (Johannesburg: Zebra, 2015);
Dane, E., *British Campaigns in Africa and the Pacific 1914–1918* (London: Hodder & Stoughton, 1919).
Davenport, T.R.H., and Saunders, C.C., *South Africa, A Modern History* (New York: St. Martin's Press, 2000).

Difford, I.D., *The Story of the 1st Battalion Cape Corps, 1915-1919*, (Cape Town: Hortons, 1920).

Dollard, J., Miller, N.E., Leonard., W., et al., *Frustration and Agression* (New Haven: Yale University, 1939).

Dugard, J., *The South West Africa/Namibia Dispute: Documents and Scholarly Writings on the Controversy Between South Africa and the United Nations* (Los Angeles: University of California Press, 1973).

Evans, D., *War: A Matter of Principles* (London: MacMillan Press, 1998).

Farwell, B., *The Great War in Africa 1914–1918* (New York: Norton, 1986).

Gal, R., and Mangelsdorff, D.A. eds., *Handbook of Military Psychology* (New York: John Wiley & Sons, 1991).

Gates, S., and Roy, K., *Unconventional Warfare in South Asia: Shadow Warriors and Counterinsurgency* (New York: Routledge, 2016).

Giliomee, H.B., *The Afrikaners, A Biography of a People* (London: Hurst & Co, 2003).

Glad, B. ed., *Psychological Dimensions of War* (London: Sage, 1990).

Gleeson, I., *The Unknown Force: Black, Coloured and Indian Soldiers through the Two World Wars* (Rivonia: Ahanti, 1994).

Goldblatt, I., *History of German South West Africa* (Cape Town: Juta, 1971).

Gray, C.S., *War, Peace and International Relations* (London: Routledge, 2007).

Grundlingh, A., *Participation and Remembrance: South African Black and Coloured Troops in the First World War, 1914 – 1918* (Stellenbosch: Sun Press, 2014).

Grundlingh, A., and Swart, S., *Radelose Rebellie, Dinamika van die 1914 – 1915 Afrikanerrebellie* (Pretoria: Protea Boekhuis, 2009).

Gurr, T.R., *Why Men Rebel* (Princeton: Princeton University Press, 1970).

Gurr, T.R., *Why Men Rebel 40th Anniversary Edition* (New York: Routledge, 2016).

Halpern, P.G., 'The War at Sea', in Strachan, H. ed., *The Oxford Illustrated History of the First World War* (Oxford: Oxford University Press, 1998).

Handel, M.I., *Masters of War* (London: Frank Cass, 1992).

Handel, M.I., *War Strategy and Intelligence* (London: Frank Cass, 1989).

Hancock, W.K., and Van der Poel, J. eds., *Selections from the Smuts Papers, Volume II* (London: Cambridge University Press, 1966).

Hancock, W.K., and Van der Poel, J. eds., *Selections from the Smuts Papers, Volume III* (London: Cambridge University Press, 1966).

Hayden, H.T., Warfighting: *Maneuver Warfare in the U.S. Marine Corps* (London: Greenhill Books, 1997).

Holmes, R., *The Oxford Companion to Military History* (Oxford: Oxford University Press, 2001).

Hooker, R. D., *Manoeuvre Warfare: An Anthology* (New York: Presidio, 1993).

Houghton, D.H., *The South African Economy* (Oxford: Oxford University Press, 1964).

Hoyt, M.L., *Maneuver Warfare and General W.T. Sherman's Atlanta Campaign* (Newport: Naval College, 1997).

Kasarak, P., *A National Force: The Evolution of the Canadian Army 1950-2000* (Toronto: UBC Press, 2013).

Kemp, J.C.G., *Die Pad van die Veroweraar* (Cape Town: Nasionale Pers, 1946).

Johnstone, M.G., *The Avengers and other Poems from South Africa*, (London: Erskine Macdonald, 1918).

Jomini, A.H., tr. Mendell, G.H. and Craighill, W.P., *The Art of War* (Rockville: Arc Manor, 2007).

Jones S., and Müller, A.L., *South African Economy, 1910 – 1990* (New York: St. Martin's Press, 1992).

Killingray, D., 'The War in Africa', in Strachan, H. ed., *The Oxford Illustrated History of the First World War* (Oxford: Oxford University Press, 1998).

King, A., *Combat Solder: Infantry Tactics and Cohesion in the Twentieth and Twenty-First Centuries* (Oxford: Oxford University Press, 2013).

Krüger, D.W., *The Age of the Generals* (Johannesburg: Dagbreek Book Store, 1958).

L'ange, G., *Urgent Imperial Service* (Rivonia: Ashanti, 1991).

Lawrence, T.E., *Seven Pillars of Wisdom* (London: Jonathan Cape, 1935).

Lentin, A., *Jan Smuts* (Johannesburg and Cape Town: Jonathan Ball, 2010).

Leonhard, R., *The Art of Maneuver* (New York: Ballantine, 1994).

Lind, W.S., *Manoeuvre Warfare Handbook* (London: Westview Press, 1985).

Liddell Hart, B.H., *Strategy of the Indirect Approach* (London: Faber & Faber, 1941).

Liddell Hart, B.H., *Strategy* (London: Faber & Faber, 1967).

Malik, J.M., 'The Evolution of Strategic Thought', Chapter in, Snyder, C.A., ed., *Contemporary Security and Strategy* (New York: Routledge, 1999).

Martin, A.C., *The Durban Light Infantry, Volume 1, 1854 to 1934* (Durban: Hayne & Gibson Ltd, 1969).

Meintjes, J., *General Louis Botha* (London: Cassell & Co., 1970).

Musashi, M., tr. T. Cleary, *The Book of Five Rings* (London: Shambala, 2005).

Nasson, B., *Abraham Esau's War: A Black South African War in the Cape, 1899-1902* (Cambridge: Cambridge University Press, 1991).

Nasson, B., *Springboks on the Somme* (Johannesburg: Penguin, 2007).

Nasson, B., *World War 1 and the People of South Africa* (Cape Town: Tafelberg, 2014).

Nasson, B., and Grundlingh A.M., eds, *The War at Home: Women and Families in the Anglo-Boer War* (Cape Town: NB Publishers, 2013)

Naveh, S., *In Pursuit of Military Excellence: The Evolution of Operational Theory* (London: Frank Cass, 1997).

Olsen, J.A., and Gray, C.S. eds., *The Practice of Strategy* (Oxford: Oxford University Press, 2011).

O'Neill, B.E., *Insurgency and Terrorism, Inside Modern Revolutionary Warfare*, (New York: Brasseys, 1990).

Orpen, N., *The History of the Transvaal Horse Artillery 1904–1974* (Johannesburg: Alex White & Co., 1975).

O'Shaughnessy, W.W. and Rayner, W.S., *How Botha and Smuts Conquered German South West* (London: Simpkin, 1916).

Parker, G. ed., *The Illustrated History of Warfare: The Triumph of the West* (Cambridge: Cambridge University Press, 1995).

Pakenham, T., *The Boer War* (London: Abacus, 1979.

Parkhouse, V.B., *Memorializing the Anglo-Boer War of 1899-1902: Militarization of the Landscape: Monuments and Memorials in Britain* (Leistestershire: Matador, 2015).

Pirow, O., *James Barry Munnik Hertzog* (Cape Town: Howard Timmins, 1958).

Reitz, D.E., *Trekking On* (London: Travel Book Club, 1947).

Ritchie, M.E., *With Botha in the Field* (London: Longmans, 1915).

Robinson, P.K.J., *With Botha's Army* (London: Allen & Unwin, 1916).

Ross, R., Mager, A.K., and Nasson, B., eds., *The Cambridge History of South Africa, Volume 2 1885 – 1994* (Cambridge: Cambridge University Press, 2012).

Sampson, P.J., *The Capture of De Wet: The South African Rebellion 1914* (London: Edward Arnold, 1915).

Samson, A., *Britain, South Africa and the East African Campaign, 1914-1918: The Union Comes of Age* (London: I.B. Tauris, 2006).

Sarkin, J., *Germany's Genocide of the Herero: Kaiser Wilhelm II, His General, His Settlers, His Soldiers* (Cape Town: UCT Press, 2010).

Seegers, A., *The Military in the Making of Modern South Africa* (London: Tauris, 1996).

Segal, R. and First, R. eds., *South West Africa, Travesty of Trust: The Expert Papers and Findings of the International Conference on South West Africa* (London: Andre Deutsch, 1967).

Shalit, B., *The Psychology of Conflict and Combat* (New York: Praeger, 1988).

Simpkin, R.E., *Race to the Swift* (London: Brassey's Defence Publishers, 1986).

Silvester, T., and Gewald, J., *Words Cannot Be Found: German Colonial Rule in Namibia: An Annotated Reprint of the 1918 Blue Book* (Boston: Brill, 2003).

Simpkins, B.G., *Rand Light Infantry* (Cape Town: Howard Timmins, 1965).

Stejskal, J., *The Horns of the Beast: The Swakop River Campaign and World War I in South West Africa, 1914-1915* (Solihull: Helion, 2014)

Smuts, J.C., *Jan Christian Smuts* (London: Cassell, 1952).

Smuts, J.C., *War-Time Speeches: A Compilation of Public Utterances in Great Britain* (New York: Doran, 1917).

Solomon, V., ed., *Selections from the Correspondence of Percy Alport Molteno, 1892-1914* (Cape Town: National Book Printers, 1981).

South African Army College, *Operational Concepts: Staff Officer's Operational Manual, Part VII* (Pretoria: 1 Military Printing Regiment, 1996).

Strachan, H., *The First World War, Vol 1: To Arms* (Oxford: Oxford University Press, 2001).

Tzu, S., tr. Sadler, A.L., *The Art of War* (Tokyo: Tuttle, 2009).

Tosh, J. and Lang, S., *The Pursuit of History* (London: Pearson Longman, 2006).

Thompson, L.M., *A History of South Africa* (New Haven: Yale University Press, 1990).

Thompson, L.M. *The Unification of South Africa 1902-1910* (London: Oxford University Press, 1960).

Trew, H. F., *Botha Treks* (London: Blackie & Son, 1936).

Tucker, C.A., *False Prophets: The Myth of Maneuver Warfare and the Inadequacies of FMFM-1 Warfighting* (Fort Leavenworth: US Army Command and General Staff College, 1995).

Tucker, S.C., *The Almanac of American Military History* (Santa Barbara: ABC Clio, 2013).

Van Creveld, M., *The Transformation of War* (New York: The Free Press, 1991).

Van der Waag, I., *The South African Military Yearbook 1997* (Pretoria: Prestige Publications, 1997).

Van Der Waag, I., *A Military History of Modern South Africa* (Johannesburg: Jonathan Ball Publishers, 2015).

Van Der Spuy, K.R., *Chasing the Wind* (Cape Town: Books of Africa, 1966).

Vego, M.N., *Joint Operational Warfare: Theory and Practice* (Newport: Naval War College, 2007).

Venter, V.I., *Coloured: A Profile of Two Million South Africans* (Cape Town: Human & Rouseau, 1974).

Walker, H.F.B., *A Doctor's Diary in Damaraland* (London: Edward Arnold, 1917).

Walker, I., and Smith, H.J., *Relative Deprivation, Specification, Development and Integration* (Cambridge: Cambridge University Press, 2004)

Whiting, M.C., *Imperial Chinese Military History 8000BC-1912AD* (New York: Writers Club Press, 2012).

Whittal, W., *With Botha and Smuts in Africa* (London: Cassell, 1917).

Williams, D., *Springboks, Troepies and Cadres: Stories of the South African Army 1912-2012* (Cape Town: Tafelberg, 2012).

Wilkinson, R., and Pickett, K., *The Spirit Level, Why Equality is Better for Everyone* (London: Penguin, 2010).

Williams, B., *Botha, Smuts and South Africa* (London: Hodder & Stoughton, 1946).

Wilson, M., and Thompson, L.M., *The Oxford History of South Africa* (Oxford: Oxford University Press, 1969).

Zabecki, D.T., *The German 1918 Offensives: A Case Study in the Operational Level of War* (New York: Routledge, 2006).

Chapters in Books

Cedergren, A., 'Doctrine, Expertise and Arms in Combination: A Reflection of the Iraq War', Chapter in, Hallenberg, J., and Karlsson, H., eds., *The Iraq War: European Perspectives on Politics, Strategy and Operations* (New York: Routledge, 2005).

Du Plessis, A., and Hough, M., 'Civil War in South Africa?, Conceptual Framework, Ramifications and Proneness', Chapter in Snow, D.M., *Uncivil Wars* (London: Lynne Rienner, 1996).

Giliomee, H., 'Afrikaner Nationalism, 1902-1948', Chapter in Pretorius, F., *A History of South Africa: From the Distant Past to the Present Day* (Pretoria: Protea, 2014).

Johnston, P., 'The Myth of Manoeuvre Warfare: Attrition in Military History', Chapter in, English, A.D., ed., *The Changing Face of War: Learning from History* (Kingston: McGill-Queen's University Press, 1998);

Keegan, T., 'The Sharecropping Economy, African Class Formation and the 1913 Natives' Land Act in the Highveld Maize Belt', Chapter in Marks, S., and Rathbone R., eds., *Industrialisation and Social Change in South Africa, African Class Formation, Culture and Consciousness 1870-1930* (London: Longman Group, 1982).

McNall, S.G., and Huggins, M., 'Guerilla Warfare, Predisposing and Precipitating Factors', Chapter in Sarkesian, S.C. ed, *Revolutionary Guerilla Warfare* (Chicago: Precedent, 1975).

Morrow, J.H., 'The War in the Air', Chapter in, Strachan, H., ed., *The Oxford Illustrated History of the First World War* (Oxford: Oxford University Press, 1998).

Nasson, B., 'Africans at War', Chapter in, J. Gooch (ed.), The Boer War: Direction, Experience and ImageI (New York: Routledge, 2013).

Rothenberg, G.E., 'Moltke, Schlieffen, and the Doctrine of Strategic Envelopment', Chapter in, Paret, P., ed., *Makers of Modern Strategy: From Machiavelli to the Modern Age* (Princeton: Princeton University Press, 1986).

Samson, A., Chapter in, Paddock, T., ed., World War I and Propaganda (Boston: Brill, 2014).

Showalter, D. E. 'Manoeuvre Warfare: The Eastern and Western Fronts', Chapter in

Strachan, H., ed., *The Oxford Illustrated History of the First World War* (Oxford: Oxford University Press, 1998).

South African National Defence Force, 'The Principles of War', Chapter in, *South African Military History Reader* (Stellenbosch: University of Stellenbosch, 2004).

Wallace, J.J.A., 'Manoeuvre Theory in Operations other than War', Chapter in, Reid, B.H., ed., *Military Power: Land Warfare in Theory and Practice* (New York: Routledge, 2013);

Journal Articles

Angstrom, J., 'Towards a Typology of Internal Armed Conflict, Synthesising a Decade of Conceptual Turmoil', *Civil Wars*, 4,3 (2001).

Baucom, D.R. 'Wakes of War: Contrails and the Rise of Air Power 1918 – 1945 Part 1 – Early Sightings and Preliminary Explanations, 1918-1938', *Air Power History*, 54, 2, (2007).

Blount, C., 'Modern Airpower and the 1916 Arab Revolt: What can the modern Airman do to counter Lawrence of Arabia', *Air and Space Power Journal*, 23, 3, (2009).

Bisset, W.M., 'Unexplored Aspects of South Africa's First World War History', *Scientia Militaria*, 6, 3 (1976).

Berkowitz, L., 'Frustration-Agression, Examination and Reformulation', *Psychological Bulletin*, 106, 1 (1989).

De La Sablonniere, R., and Tougas, F., 'Relative Deprivation and Social Identity in Times of Dramatic Social Change, The Case of Nurses', *Journal of Applied Social Psychology*, 38, 9 (2008).

Dorning, W.A., 'A Concise History of the South African Defence Force 1912–1987', *Militaria, South African Journal for Military Studies*, 17, 2 (1987).

Epstein, K.P., 'Imperial Airs: Leo Amery, Airpower and Airpower, 1873-1945', *The Journal of Imperial and Commonwealth History*, 38, 4, (2010).

Esterhuyse, A., 'The Theories of Attrition versus Manoeuvre and the Levels of War', *Strategic Review for Southern Africa*, 23, 2 (2001).

Garcia, A., 'Airpower in the Union of South Africa's First World War campaign in German South West Africa' *Historia*. 62, 2, 2017.

Garcia, A., 'A Manouevre Warfare Analysis of South Africa's 1914-1915 German South West African Campaign' *Scientia Militaria*. 45, 1, 2017

Geyer, R., 'The Union Defence Force and the 1914 Strike, The Dynamics of the Shadow of the Burgher', *Historia*, 59, 2 (2014).

Gurr, T. R., 'Psychological Factors in Civil Violence', *World Politics*, 20, 2, (1968).

Harvey, A.D., 'Air Warfare in Perspective', *Air Power History*, 60, 3, (2013).

Hennessy, J.A. 'Men and Planes of World War 1 and History of Lafayette Escadrille', *Air Power History*, 61, 2, (2014).

Huntington, S.P., 'The Clash of Civilisations?', *Foreign Affairs*, 72, 3 (1993).

Katz, D., 'A clash of military doctrine: Brigadier-General Wilfrid Malleson and the South Africans at Salaita Hill, February 1916', *Historia*. 62/1.2017.

Kleynhans, E., "A Critical Analysis of the Impact of Water on the South African Campaign in German South West Africa, 1914 1915", *Historia*, 61, 2, 2016;

Lillie, A.C., 'The Origin and Development of the South African Army', *Militaria, South African Journal for Military Studies*, 12, 2 (1982).

Lukasik, S.H., 'Insurgent Airpower in Historical Perspective: An Introduction and Prospectus of Research', *The Historian*, 74, 2, (2012).

Mahncke, J.O.E.O., 'Aircraft Operations in the German Colonies 1911–1916: The Fliegertruppe of the Imperial German Army', *Military History Journal*, 12, 2 (2001).

Miller, N.E., 'The frustration-aggression hypothesis', *Psychological Review*, 48, 4, (1941).

Monick, S., 'The Third Man: Willy Trück and the German Air Effort in South West Africa in World War I', *Military History Journal*, 5, 3 (1981).

Nasson, B., 'Delville Wood and South African Great War Commemoration', *English Historical Review*, 119, 480 (2004).

Nkuna, N., 'Black involvement in the Anglo-Boer War, 1899-1902', *Military History Journal*, 11, 3, 1999.

Oosthuizen, G.J.J., 'The Military Role of the Rehoboth Basters during the South African Invasion of German South West Africa, 1914-1915', *Scientia Militaria*, 28, 1 , 1998.

Paterson, H., 'First Allied Victory: The South African Campaign in German South-West Africa, 1914–1915', *Military History Journal*, 13, 2 (2004).

Pettigrew, T. M., 'Samuel Stouffer and Relative Deprivation', *Social Psychology Quarterly*, 78, 1 (2015).

Saleh, A., 'Relative Deprivation Theory, Nationalism, Ethnicity and Identity Conflicts', *Geopolitics Quarterly*, 8, 4 (2013).

Swart, S., "A Boer and his Gun and his Wife are Three Things Always Together', Republican Masculinity and the 1914 Rebellion', *Journal of Southern African Studies*, 24, 4 (2008).

Swart, S., "Desperate Men' The 1914 Rebellion and the Polities of Poverty', *South African Historical Journal*, 42,1 (2000).

Swart, S., 'The "Five Shilling Rebellion": Rural White Male Anxiety and the 1914 Boer Rebellion', *South African Historical Journal*, 56, 1 (2006).

Van Der Waag, I., 'Boer Generalship and the Politics of Command', *War in History*, 12,15 (2005).

Van der Waag, I., 'Smuts's Generals: Towards a First Portrait of the South African High Command, 1912–1948', *War in History*, 18, 1 (2011).

Van der Waag, I., 'The Battle of Sandfontein, 26 September 1914: South African Military Reform and the German South-West Africa Campaign, 1914–1915', *First World War Studies*, 4, 2 (2013).

Warwick, R.C., 'The Battle of Sandfontein: The Role and Legacy of Major General Sir Henry Timson Lukin', *Scientia Militaria South African Journal of Military Studies*, 34, 2 (2006).

Whitmarsh, A., 'British Army Manoeuvres and the Development of Military Airpower 1910 – 1913', *War in History*, 14, 3 (2007).

Theses

Angerman, W.S., 'Coming Full Circle with Boyd's OODA Loop Ideas: An Analysis of Innovation, Diffusion and Evolution' (MSMIS thesis, United States Air Force Institute of Technology, Dayton, 2004).

Delport, A, "'Boks and Bullets, Coffins and Crutches": An Exploration of the Body, Mind and Places of 'Springbok' South African Soldiers in the First World War', Stellenbosch University, 2015)

Fouche, C., 'Military Strategy and its Use in Competitive Strategy with Reference to the Nelson Mandela Metropole Automotive Industry' (MBA thesis, Nelson Mandela Metropolitan University, Port Elizabeth, 2005).

Garcia, A., 'Manoeuvre Warfare in the South African Campaign in German South West Africa during the First World War', MA thesis, University of South Africa, 2015.

Montanus, P.D., 'The Saratoga Campaign: Maneuver Warfare, the Continental Army, and the Birth of the American Way of War' (MMS thesis, United States Marine Command and Staff College, Quantico, 2001).

Nortier, E.W., 'Major General Sir Henry Timson Lukin (1860–1925): The Making of a South African Hero' (MMil, Military Academy Stellenbosch University, Stellenbosch, 2005).

Solberg, B.T., 'Maneuver Warfare: Consequences for Tactics and Organisation of the Norwegian Infantry' (MMAS thesis, United States Army Command and Staff College, Kansas, 2000).

Springman, J.A., 'The Rapier or the Club: The Relationship between Attrition and Manoeuvre Warfare' (MSS thesis, United States Army War College, Carlisle, 2006).

Ungleich, T.R., 'The Defence of German South West Africa during World War I' (MA thesis, University of Miami, Miami, 1974).

Unpublished Sources

Boyd, J.R., 'Destruction and Creation', Unpublished essay, September 1976.

Bottomley, E.J., 'The South African Rebellion of 1914, The Influence of Industrialisation, Poverty and 'Poor-Whitism'', *African Studies Seminar Paper*, University of Witwatersrand, June 1980.

Fourie, J., 'The South African Poor White Problem in the Early 20th Century, Lessons for Poverty Today', Stellenbosch Economic Working Papers, 14/6. 2007.

Gooch, J., 'The Use of History in the Development of Contemporary Doctrine', Paper presented at a conference sponsored by the Director of Development and Doctrine at Larkhill, Larkhill, 1996.

Morris, A., and Herring, C., 'Theory and Research in Social Movements, A Critical Review', *University of Michigan Center for Research on Social Organisation Working Paper Series*, Number 307, 1984.

Internet Sources

Du Picq, A., tr. J.N. Greenly and R.C. Cotton, *Battle Studies*, available at http://www.gutenberg.org/files/7294/7294-h/7294-h.htm, ebook, Accessed 23 January 2012.

New York Times, Germany Grapples with its African Genocide, https://www.nytimes.com/2016/12/29/world/africa/germany-genocide-namibia-holocaust.html?mcubz=3. Accessed 24 September 2017;

Owen, W.F., 'The Manoeuvre Warfare Fraud', *The Small Wars Journal*, http://webcache.googleusercontent.com/search?q=cache:OOzaJk7LWUwJ:smallwarsjournal.com/blog/journal/docs-temp/95-owen.pdf%3Fq%3Dmag/docs-temp/95-owen.pdf+&cd=3&hl=en&ct=clnk&gl=za.

Tzu, T., tr. L. Giles, *The Art of War*, available at http://www.gutenberg.org/files/132/132.txt, ebook, Accessed 23 January 2012).

Von Clausewitz, C., tr. J.J. Graham, *On War*, available athttp://www.gutenberg.org/files/46-h., ebook, Accessed 23 January 2012.

Index